About CROP

G000097446

CROP, the Comparative Research Progi
from the academic community to the prob
was initiated in 1992, and the CROP Secretariat was officially opened in June
1993 by the Director General of UNESCO, Dr Federico Mayor.

In recent years, poverty alleviation, poverty reduction and the eradication
of poverty have moved up the international agenda, with poverty eradication
now defined as the greatest global challenge facing the world today. In
cooperation with its sponsors, the International Social Science Council
(ISSC) and the University of Bergen (UiB), CROP works in collaboration with
knowledge networks, institutions and scholars to establish independent,
alternative and critical poverty research in order to help shape policies for
long-term poverty prevention and eradication.

The CROP network comprises scholars engaged in poverty-related
research across a variety of academic disciplines. Researchers from more
than a hundred different countries are represented in the network, which is
coordinated by the CROP Secretariat at the University of Bergen, Norway.

The CROP series on International Studies in Poverty Research presents
expert research and essential analyses of different aspects of poverty
worldwide. By promoting a fuller understanding of the nature, extent, depth,
distribution, trends, causes and effects of poverty, this series will contribute
to knowledge concerning the reduction and eradication of poverty at global,
regional, national and local levels.

For more information contact:

CROP Secretariat
PO Box 7800, 5020 Bergen, NORWAY
Phone: +47 55 58 97 44
Email: crop@uib.no
Visiting address: Jekteviksbakken 31
www.crop.org

Series editors

Juliana Martínez Franzoni, associate professor of political science, University
of Costa Rica

Thomas Pogge, Leitner professor of philosophy and international affairs, Yale
University

CROP INTERNATIONAL STUDIES IN POVERTY RESEARCH
Published by Zed Books in association with CROP

David Gordon and Paul Spicker (eds), *The International Glossary on Poverty*, 1999

Francis Wilson, Nazneen Kanji and Einar Braathen (eds), *Poverty Reduction: What Role for the State in Today's Globalized Economy?*, 2001

Willem van Genugten and Camilo Perez-Bustillo (eds), *The Poverty of Rights: Human Rights and the Eradication of Poverty*, 2001

Else Øyen et al. (eds), *Best Practices in Poverty Reduction: An Analytical Framework*, 2002

Lucy Williams, Asbjørn Kjønstad and Peter Robson (eds), *Law and Poverty: The Legal System and Poverty Reduction*, 2003

Elisa P. Reis and Mick Moore (eds), *Elite Perceptions of Poverty and Inequality*, 2005

Robyn Eversole, John-Andrew McNeish and Alberto D. Cimadamore (eds), *Indigenous Peoples and Poverty: An International Perspective*, 2005

Lucy Williams (ed.), *International Poverty Law: An Emerging Discourse*, 2006

Maria Petmesidou and Christos Papatheodorou (eds), *Poverty and Social Deprivation in the Mediterranean*, 2006

Paul Spicker, Sonia Alvarez Leguizamón and David Gordon (eds), *Poverty: An International Glossary*, 2nd edn, 2007

Santosh Mehrotra and Enrique Delamonica, *Eliminating Human Poverty: Macroeconomic and Social Policies for Equitable Growth*, 2007

David Hemson, Kassim Kulindwa, Haakon Lein and Adolfo Mascarenhas (eds), *Poverty and Water: Explorations of the Reciprocal Relationship*, 2008

Ronaldo Munck, Narathius Asingwire, Honor Fagan and Consolata Kabonesa (eds), *Water and Development: Good Governance after Neoliberalism*, 2015

Abraar Karan and Geeta Sodhi (eds), *Protecting the Health of the Poor: Social Movements in the South*, 2015

Forthcoming titles

Alberto D. Cimadamore, Gro Therese Lie, Maurice B. Mittelmark and Fungisai P. Gwanzura Ottemöller (eds), *Development and Sustainability Science: The Challenge of Social Change*, 2016

Einar Braathen, Julian May and Gemma Wright (eds), *Poverty and Inequality in Middle Income Countries: Policy Achievements, Political Obstacles*, 2016

Julio Boltvinik and Susan Archer Mann (eds), *Peasant Poverty and Persistence*, 2016

POVERTY AND THE MILLENNIUM DEVELOPMENT GOALS

A CRITICAL LOOK FORWARD

*edited by Alberto D. Cimadamore, Gabriele Koehler
and Thomas Pogge*

Zed Books
London

Poverty and the Millennium Development Goals: A Critical Look Forward was first published in 2016 by Zed Books Ltd, The Foundry, 17 Oval Way, London SE11 5RR, UK.

www.zedbooks.co.uk

Typeset in Plantin and Kievit by Swales & Willis Ltd, Exeter, Devon
Index: Rohan Bolton
Cover designed by www.kikamiller.com

A catalogue record for this book is available from the British Library.

ISBN 978-1-78360-619-1 hb
ISBN 978-1-78360-618-4 pb
ISBN 978-1-78360-620-7 pdf
ISBN 978-1-78360-621-4 epub
ISBN 978-1-78360-622-1 mobi

Printed and bound by CPI Group (UK) Ltd, Croydon, CR0 4YY

CONTENTS

FIGURES, TABLES AND BOXES

Figures

ACKNOWLEDGEMENTS

This book has its origin in a workshop organized by the CROP Secretariat for its Scientific Committee members and invited guests. The workshop had the title 'The MDGs and poverty reduction in the 21st century: a critical assessment' and took place in Bergen, Norway, in August 2012.

We are pleased that the book is being published at a challenging moment in time, as the international community transits from the Millennium Development Goals (MDGs) to the Sustainable Development Goals (SDGs) and negotiates climate change action.

The editors would like to express sincere thanks to the CROP Secretariat, the contributing authors and all those involved in producing the final result: *Poverty and the Millennium Development Goals: A Critical Look Forward*.

PART ONE

THE GLOBAL POVERTY CHALLENGE

1 | POVERTY AND THE MILLENNIUM DEVELOPMENT GOALS: A CRITICAL LOOK FORWARD

Alberto D. Cimadamore, Gabriele Koehler and Thomas Pogge

Poverty has been at the centre of the debate on development for several decades. A series of UN Decades on development and on the eradication of poverty[1] framed the discourse of the international community. Institutional and material resources have been mobilized at national and international levels since the 1950s, but with modest results. Poverty has remained a structural feature in most societies, accompanied by growing and increasingly visible income and wealth disparities. Despite progressive discourses and policies, high- and middle-income countries witnessed an unprecedented accumulation of wealth, and developing countries saw a skewed concentration of welfare and human development outcomes to the disadvantage of poor and socially excluded communities. National and international systems have worked very well for the elites, while the majority of the world population continues to suffer multiple deprivations, foremost among them extreme poverty and hunger.

It does not take an academic or an expert in social relations to realize that the systemic biases towards income and wealth concentration in the face of persistent – and increasing – poverty render current national and international systems ethically unacceptable and politically unsustainable. This is the conviction and the concern which drive this volume.

The new millennium: from an overarching Declaration to specific goals

In the year 2000, the rousing Millennium Declaration and its timid operationalization, the Millennium Development Goals (MDGs), conveyed the message that concrete and stepped-up action was needed: the economic and social systems were reproducing poverty and exclusions at levels that were not compatible with democratic ideals and the notion of dignity and a decent life for all. These had been promised by the UN and the multilateral system since 1945 (Stokke 2009; Koehler this volume).

There was a noticeable change in the discourse and mobilization of resources during the first fifteen years of this century, and another shift may be on its way (UN SG 2014). A critical assessment of the MDGs is necessary and we could have reached a moment in history conducive to producing the meaningful changes required to fulfil the commitment to eradicating extreme poverty and achieving human development and a better life for all. This volume intends to provide that kind of assessment, combined with a look ahead at the new development agenda, currently cast as the Sustainable Development Goals (SDGs).

The Millennium Declaration signed by leaders of 189 states resulted in one of the most visible and unified global campaigns to address poverty in the history of multilateral development cooperation: the Millennium Development Goals (UN SG 2001). A critical review of the MDGs needs to acknowledge their merits, even if the text of the eight MDGs considerably weakened and watered down the core tenets of the Millennium Declaration. Chapter III of the Millennium Declaration, on development and poverty eradication, for example, had clearly spelt out the commitment of the leaders of the world to 'spare no effort to free our fellow men, women and children from the abject and dehumanizing conditions of extreme poverty' and 'to making the right to development a reality for everyone and to freeing the entire human race from want'. The road out of poverty was more vaguely defined as the aspiration to create an environment – at national and global levels alike – 'conducive to development and to the elimination of poverty'.[2]

Still, the Declaration conveyed a strong commitment at the highest level in world politics. Fifteen years later, its fragility and ineffectiveness are more than evident: we observe an environment that is not especially conducive either to the elimination of poverty, or to fair development for all. On the contrary, hunger and poverty remain an oppressive reality for many people, and we observe growing inequality as well as extreme economic, political, social and environmental inequities. Some analysts argue that the depth of income and wealth inequalities is unprecedented (Piketty 2014), and that the exploitation of nature has already outstripped several planetary boundaries (Steffen et al. 2015).

The time has therefore come to critically highlight the shortcomings of the Millennium Declaration. This is primarily because a 'rosy' picture of MDG success tends to obscure their weaknesses and failures. During recent years, UN top officials have been reaffirming 'that the MDGs have made a profound difference in people's lives' and that 'global poverty has been halved five years ahead of the 2015 timeframe' (UN 2014c: 3; see also UN 2014b and UN 2012: Foreword). Many other examples could be cited of international and national politicians, journalists and development professionals making selective use of statistics to proclaim good news about the worldwide decline in poverty. Moreover, and perhaps more importantly, poverty reduction is causally attributed to the MDGs: 'the MDGs have helped to lift millions of people out of poverty' (UN 2011: 3).

There are always different ways to look at the same social reality. The official discourse of states and the UN system tends to focus on progress and success. This is understandable, since they need to remain credible and have a responsibility to sustain the momentum of the development agenda. Academics and civil society, however, need to push the boundaries of knowledge, and have a responsibility to elucidate and advocate for social justice as a necessary condition for better societies. Their task is to provide a critical view: to assess progress analytically, expose the lack of achievement, provide explanations for both – and offer genuine alternatives.

Critical analysis and monitoring of national and international policy responses to poverty, and the offering of alternatives, are among the core objectives of the Comparative Research Programme on Poverty (CROP). For that reason, CROP convened a workshop on the MDGs in 2012, to discuss – among other things – these and other related UN assessments of poverty eradication initiatives, and the plausibility of crediting the MDGs as a driving force for contemporary poverty reduction.

Three interrelated questions shaped the 2012 CROP workshop, with a view to producing a constructive evaluation of the impact of the MDGs on substantially reducing poverty around the world. These questions were:

- Has poverty really declined in a way consistent with international legal and political commitments?
- What role have the MDGs played in producing meaningful changes?

- What are the main lessons to be learned from the joint analysis of the workshop towards conceptualizing a post-MDG agenda – a new development agenda?

This volume was conceived as a response to these questions from an analytical, academic perspective.

Assessing the impact of the MDGs on global poverty

In order to answer the first two questions, workshop participants considered it absolutely necessary to have a precise measurement of the extent of poverty in the base year. Only then is it possible to track performance over time. However, there was considerable controversy about the accuracy of available poverty statistics and measurement, as well as about the baseline chosen to evaluate this complex social phenomenon.

The following problems emerged (Pogge 2013; CROP 2013):[3]

1 Distortion through use of general-consumption purchasing power parities (PPPs). These give much less weight to food prices than these have in the actual consumption of the poor. Because of this distortion, PPPs drastically overstate the purchasing power of poor households with respect to foodstuffs – by roughly 50 per cent.

2 Excessive sensitivity of the measured poverty trend to the selected level of the international poverty line (IPL). For example, between 1990 and 2011, the number of people with less than $1.25 per day had reportedly fallen by 47.4 per cent, but the number of people below the $3.00 IPL had fallen by only 7.1 per cent (iresearch. worldbank.org/PovcalNet/).

3 Excessive sensitivity to the base year chosen to determine the purchasing power of all currencies relative to one another.

4 Distortions through the use of general consumer price indexes which likewise give less weight to food prices than these have in the consumption of the poor. This leads to an overly rosy trend picture during periods when food prices are rising relative to prices in general.

5 A simple binary measure that classifies households as either poor or non-poor incentivizes policy-makers to prioritize people just below the poverty line.

6 Such a measure also disregards the intra-household distribution and varying course-of-life needs, since the aggregated view masks the

differing implications of poverty for women, children, seniors and people living with disability in the same household.

7 By focusing on income/consumption expenditures alone, the prevalent methodology also reifies poverty and disregards other dimensions of poverty: the amount of labour required to gain the relevant income, environmental challenges, availability of goods and services, issues such as powerlessness, exploitation or fear, time for the care 'economy' and leisure time for women, men and children.

The World Bank is the primary agency contributing data and analysis for progress on Goal 1: 'Eradicate extreme poverty and hunger' and its Target 1A: 'Halve, between 1990 and 2015, the proportion of people whose income is less than $1.25 a day' (UN 2014c: 56).[4] The World Bank's Development Research Group produces its statistics based on data obtained from government statistical offices and World Bank country departments (UN 2003). As a result, the data tend to be biased in the direction of an optimistic trend, because governments and international institutions want to convey a sense of success for the policies they employ or recommend.

In addition to these methodological biases, there are also significant gaps in the data. One of the MDG Reports acknowledges the problem: 'The task of monitoring progress on poverty reduction is beset by a lack of good quality surveys carried out at regular intervals, delays in reporting survey results, and insufficient documentation of country level analytical methods used. It is also hampered by difficulties in accessing the underlying survey micro-data required to compute the poverty estimates.' These gaps remain especially problematic in sub-Saharan Africa, where the data necessary to make comparisons over the full range of MDGs are available in fewer than half the countries (UN 2011: 7). These are central problems for both academic and policy evaluation, and are difficult to solve in the short term.

According to the latest information provided by the World Bank on data and analysis for Goal 1, the number of people living on less than US$1.25 a day (2005 PPP) declined globally from 1.922 billion in 1990 to 1.011 billion in 2011. The proportion of extreme poor (that is, living on below US$1.25 a day, 2005 PPP) as a percentage of the population of the developing countries decreased from 43.35 per cent in 1990 to 16.99 per cent in 2011 (iresearch.worldbank.org/PovcalNet/). As we can easily see, even though the *number* of poor people was not halved, 'the *proportion* of people whose income is less than $1.25 a day' was. Therefore, Target 1A was reached because the World Bank and UN agreed to operationalize the poverty definition in this particular way.

It is quite clear that, according to this measurement, extreme poverty can be reported as reduced. Figure 1.1, based on the World Bank data, also represents this optimistic view.

'Poverty rates have been halved, and about 700 million fewer people lived in conditions of extreme poverty in 2010 than in 1990' (UN 2013). Such 'quick facts' are presented to show that the MDG campaign is moving in the right direction.

The important question is now how this assessment was made. The following figure provides some information.

China reduced the number of extreme poor from 694 million in 1990 to 123 million in 2010 (iresearch.worldbank.org/PovcalNet/). This is the most significant reduction of acute income poverty made by a single country in the history of humankind. If we also consider the region where China is located, we can see that the number of extreme poor fell from 939 million in 1990 to 207 million in 2010 (iresearch. worldbank.org/PovcalNet/).

Accordingly, the number of people categorized as living below the absolute poverty line was reduced by 732 million in the East Asia and

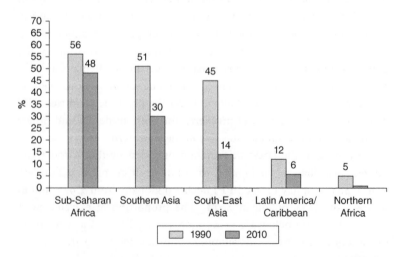

1.1 Proportion of people living on less than $1.25 a day, 1990 and 2010 (percentage) (*source*: United Nations 2013)

Pacific region. This fact accounts for most of the reported *global* success of the MDGs campaign (see also Koehler this volume).

However, Figure 1.2 shows that developing countries in general, and sub-Saharan Africa in particular, are not doing well. In fact, the number of people living in extreme poverty increased noticeably from 287 million in 1990 (baseline) to 416 million in 2011 (iresearch.worldbank. org/PovcalNet/). According to the latest available estimates measuring Goal 1, Target 1A, sub-Saharan Africa will have 403 million people living in extreme poverty when the MDGs are assessed and replaced by a new development agenda in September 2015 (World Bank 2015).

Moreover, the projections are not encouraging. The calculations on poverty and poverty projections from the World Bank PovcalNet database indicate that by 2030 the number of people living in extreme poverty will reach around 335 million (ibid.: Table 1).

This projection reveals three great challenges for the future. First, it signals the need for a methodological shift – to use the absolute number of poor as a measuring rod for progress, instead of the proportion of poor, which was the indicator used to guide evaluations of the MDGs. The

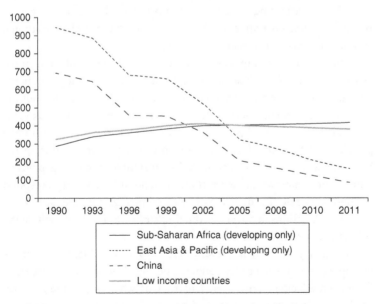

1.2 Number of poor (at less than $1.25 a day, PPP, in millions) in selected countries and regions, 1990–2011 (*source*: World Bank: Poverty and Inequality Data Base, 2015. Date of access: 25 January 2015)

goal set in the new proposal to 'end poverty in all its forms everywhere' (UN 2014a) implies reducing extreme poverty to zero while at the same time dealing with other forms of poverty within the context of the SDGs. Secondly, the consistently high level of extreme poverty in low-income countries, and the number of extreme poor in sub-Saharan Africa, brings into question the strategies implemented or encouraged by the agents of the MDGs process. Thirdly, it points to the need to introduce meaningful policy changes when adopting the SDGs.

What was the causal role of the MDGs?

Over the past decades, the international community and individual countries have been mobilizing towards the common objective of poverty eradication. The official discourse voiced by UN top officials (and uncritically reproduced by many) suggests that the MDGs had in fact a causal effect in reducing poverty globally. This is the implication of statements such as 'the MDGs have made a profound difference in people's lives' (UN 2014c: 3) or 'the MDGs have helped to lift millions of people out of poverty' (UN 2011: 3). Such pronouncements are, at best, ambiguous as they suggest a causal role for an international initiative, disregarding (in analytical and practical terms) the specific role of states and government policies on the one hand, and international systemic issues on the other.

States can be – and in fact often are – part of the problem as much as the solution. Nevertheless, the performance of the state in reducing or eliminating poverty has been crucial in recent history and its efforts need to undergo empirical evaluation (Cimadamore et al. 2005: 16). If we analyse countries' performances, we can easily see which public policies and historical forms of states produced or are producing the best and worst results respectively in substantially reducing poverty. This is something we can learn from. The point here is not to respond to these very relevant questions but to emphasize that any search for causal explanations in poverty reduction strategies needs to include the role of the state from the outset.

Identifying the analytical level where relevant variables are located is as important as having a clear understanding of the type of policies that have been effective. This is particularly true when one of the goals on the international agenda is to 'end poverty in all its forms everywhere' (UN 2014a), which implies reducing extreme poverty to zero while at the same time dealing with other forms of poverty. Extreme poverty cannot be eradicated if states maintain, as they currently do, policy frameworks and development strategies that contribute to the creation and re-creation of massive poverty. As Albert Einstein observed, doing the same thing over and over again and expecting a different result can be considered a form of insanity.[5]

However, this is the case with respect to the neoliberal Washington Consensus, applied in countries where most of the poor are concentrated. As is well known, some of its tenets include a downsizing of the role of the state and an exclusive orientation towards the private sector for economic growth. It also favours systematic reductions in government spending as well as privatization and deregulation of public goods and services such as education, health services or access to drinking water and sanitation. The role of the state in enhancing productivity is ignored.[6]

Many of the countries that displayed slow or no progress on poverty reduction are found to have adopted neoliberal political, institutional and macroeconomic frameworks. This was despite ample evidence showing that structural adjustment and austerity policies have produced poverty everywhere, particularly in the South (Alvarez Leguizamon 2005; Cimadamore and Cattani 2007). Neoliberal policies have been supported by the most powerful nation-states and by influential international organizations.

Ironically, one of these has even carved in stone at its Washington headquarters its institutional mission: 'Our Dream is a World Free of Poverty'. However, as a result of structural adjustment policies (among other policies) the number of poor people remains high, despite the discourses and interventions motivated by the MDGs process.

Meanwhile, countries as historically and economically diverse as Japan, South Korea, China, Brazil and the northern European countries implemented policies of a different type. Regardless of the many political differences among them,[7] these countries acted as 'developmental states' (Chang 2002; Ringen et al. 2011; UNRISD 2010; UNDP 2013). This means that government takes a strong interventionist role, directing private (or public) investment along the lines of a defined industrial policy and using the government budget in an anti-cyclical fashion. Most of these countries adopted large-scale programmes of social protection for income support, and in some cases applied active labour market policies. In other words, they followed Keynesian-type policies instead of the recipes that emerged from the Washington Consensus. Nor did they expressly follow the MDG agenda. The results of these policies were generally positive in terms of absolute poverty reduction (e.g. in China), as Figure 1.2 shows. Such approaches, however, are not found in the 'menu' offered by current mainstream international policy consensus.

Heterodox approaches can be conceived as viable alternatives to orthodoxy. There is a growing recognition of rapidly intensifying income inequities globally, between countries, and nationally, within countries (Milanovic 2011; Fukuda-Parr 2010; Piketty 2014; Jomo this volume) that constitute perhaps the single most important impediment to a successful campaign towards poverty eradication and prevention. The link of persistent acute poverty to inequality is illustrated by the following facts:

- In just seventeen years, the richest 5 per cent of human beings have gained a greater share of global household income (3.49 per cent) than the poorer half had left at the end of this period (2.92 per cent).
- The ratio of average incomes of the richest 5 per cent and the poorest quarter rose from 185:1 to 297:1 in this period (1988–2005).
- Had the poorer half held steady, its 2005 share of global household income would have been 21 per cent higher (3.53 per cent instead of 2.92 per cent).
- Had the poorest quarter held steady, its 2005 share of global household income would have been 49 per cent higher (1.16 per cent instead of 0.78 per cent).
- Had it been allowed to gain the 3.49 per cent of global household income that was in fact gained by the richest 5 per cent, the poorer half would have doubled its share to 7.02 per cent in 2005. Severe poverty could already have been overcome by 2005 (CROP 2013: Table 1, p. 6).[8]

These trends suggest that, at the country level, income redistribution policies need to accompany poverty alleviation or eradication strategies. This has not been the case; neither in neoliberally oriented economies nor in the developmental states. Some of the countries that have shown considerable success in decreasing acute poverty, such as China, have in fact witnessed vastly increased income inequality. Measures to improve primary income distribution, through wage policy, secondary income distribution or progressive tax policy, were not in place. This was one of many reasons for the enormous increase in income and wealth disparities.

The second issue with both neoliberal and Keynesian-oriented policies is their eco-blindness. They are based on a macroeconomic growth model that is resource intensive and not compatible with planetary sustainability. Disregard for sustainability over the past decade has intensified environmental catastrophes such as global warming, climate change and the loss of biodiversity (Klein 2014).

Thirdly, and most crucially, it must be recognized that poverty, as well as its eradication and prevention, is a manifestly political issue. They are all directly related to the use and distribution of existing and future resources, and the location of power in making these decisions (see Rogers and Balázs, and Boltvinik and Damián this volume). Policies that do not analyse the impact of power relations on the creation and re-creation of poverty can have only limited and superficial success.

Faulty policy and eco-blindness are among the factors that have hampered the effectiveness of MDGs at the national level, but the effectiveness of policies to reduce or eradicate poverty – even if well conceived and perfectly delivered at the country level – is highly dependent on the international environment. Political, institutional and macroeconomic frameworks inconsistent with effective measures against poverty have been maintained at the international level despite ample evidence showing that they produce and reproduce poverty (Montes this volume). Therefore, even though the international community has been mobilizing towards the common objective of poverty eradication over the past fifteen years, substantial results at a global level have not been reached. This is particularly visible in regions where severe poverty is concentrated, as shown above (Figures 1.1 and 1.2).

Goal 8 of the MDGs was directed at the international 'partnership', i.e. the conditions of trade, international investment and official development assistance (ODA). ODA flows did indeed increase,[9] and the higher budget allocations of the OECD Development Assistance Countries (DACs) are often associated with the momentum and commitments generated by the MDGs. However, regarding international trade and investment regimes, there was a marked lack of progress, such as in the Doha Round of trade negotiations, or even retrogression, such as in the area of international investment agreements (see Montes this volume and Montes 2015). The MDGs' unsatisfactory performance on poverty reduction must also be attributed to an international economic system that is skewed against the interests of developing countries and the concerns of people living in poverty.[10] The MDG agenda did not alter this.

The SDGs and a look ahead

The MDG approach concentrated on lifting a certain proportion of people out of poverty while retaining a model of development that continues to produce poverty and tolerate massive violations of human, social and economic rights. Unparalleled success in poverty reduction, concentrated primarily in one country – China – allowed prominent members of the international community to declare success at a global level. However, the number of people living in acute poverty remains very high, and, as mentioned above, the World Bank itself is forecasting that the number of extreme poor will be around 700 million persons in 2020, and over 400 million in 2030, 81 per cent of whom will be living in sub-Saharan Africa. Moreover, the number of people who have escaped from poverty is arguably cancelled out by the number of persons who have become impoverished owing to the financial crisis, misguided macroeconomic policies or rising food prices as a result of commodity market speculation.

Available evidence on poverty trends and our policy analyses suggest that continuing with the same set of policies and measures will not suffice to eradicate extreme poverty, or even to achieve a substantial reduction in acute and other forms of poverty by 2030. A critical analysis of the outcome of the MDG agenda, a probing review of the causalities of poverty and the most effective policy approaches to address it, and a more radical vision of eradicating, rather than merely alleviating, poverty would, in our view, be appropriate as inspiration for the post-2015 development agenda. What that new agenda can take from the current MDG discourse, however, is the immense drive and consensus at a normative level for the moral obligation to address poverty.

The Sustainable Development Goals (SDGs) are likely to replace the MDGs if the negotiations during 2015 go smoothly. The SDG proposal, presented in August 2014 by the Open Working Group of the General Assembly on Sustainable Development Goals (OWG) (UN 2014a),[11] assumes that a greener type of growth will benefit the poor and create new incentives and opportunities for sustainable livelihoods for all. Within this framework, the OWG proposal characterizes poverty eradication as 'the greatest global challenge facing the world today and an indispensable requirement for sustainable development'. This definition implicitly acknowledges that poverty is currently causing the death and suffering of millions of human beings, despite the fact that there are enough resources in the world for humanity to be free from poverty and hunger (Ziegler 2014).

Both on the normative and on the conceptual and analytical levels, the SDG agenda necessitates a serious and participatory debate on the definition of poverty and, in particular, extreme poverty. Extreme poverty – the type of poverty targeted to be eradicated – is defined in the OWG draft as income below $1.25 (2005 US currency purchasing power) per person per day. A more comprehensive definition of poverty is needed, sensitive to the multidimensional nature of poverty (Wisor et al. 2014; OPHI n.d.; CROP 2013; Rogers and Balázs this volume). Meanwhile, the extremely low line needs to be revised upwards in order to be consistent with progress towards the goal of ending poverty in all its forms everywhere and ensuring that all people can live in dignity (see Boltvinik and Damián this volume; similarly Paes-Sousa and De Martino Jannuzzi this volume). Child poverty (both income and multidimensional) should be specifically targeted and closely monitored in order to break the vicious circle of intergenerational poverty and its reproduction. Chronic and severe poverty also needs to be prioritized and monitored from the inception of the SDGs process.

With respect to policy, and in order to overcome the errors of the MDGs, the SDG agenda needs to incorporate the analyses and lessons of recent and past history. To some extent it does. The formal SDG proposal recommends macroeconomic policies prioritizing full 'decent' employment and equitable distribution of economic resources, as well as social protection floors. For this to become stringent, Targets 8.3 ('promote development-oriented policies ...'), 8.5 ('achieve full and productive employment for all ...') and 8.6 (substantially reduce youth unemployment), and Target 1.3 on social protection, need to be operationalized following the ILO[12] or other similar models. Macroeconomic policies stimulating employment should be implemented as soon as possible in order to achieve the employment targets of Goal 8. The implementation of 'nationally appropriate social protection systems and measures for all, including floors, and by 2030 achieve substantial coverage of the poor and the vulnerable' (UN 2014a: SDGs Goal 1.3) would represent a substantial improvement if resulting social protection and basic income measures reach the poorest and are sufficiently resourced to move all affected, including hard-to-reach individuals and communities, to at least the national poverty line. These policies and measures are central to poverty reduction and eradication, and need to be amply funded and sustained over time in order to move people out of poverty and make sure that their children are able to escape the intergenerational poverty trap.

A critical look ahead needs to evaluate the multiple relationships between Goal 1 of the SDG proposal and the other goals. Goal 1 is directly and indirectly related to all the goals, but success in the eradication of poverty is especially dependent on immediate and substantial progress towards Goals 2 ('end hunger, achieve food security and improved nutrition …'), 8 (promote sustained inclusive growth, full employment and decent work), 10 ('reduce inequality'), 16 (on inclusive societies with access to justice for all) and 17 ('global partnership for sustainable development'), and their respective targets. Among the goals addressing the international economic system, Target 17.14 ('enhance policy coherence for sustainable development') should be better specified and operationalized. It is crucial to the achievement of Goal 1, particularly in regions where the trend shows that policy and institutional frameworks are dysfunctional, and policies cancel each other out.[13] Target 16.4 ('by 2030 significantly reduce illicit financial … flows') is also particularly relevant, because it is prerequisite to strengthening fiscal capacities in developing countries (see Montes this volume; see also Kar and Spanjers 2014; UN 2014a). This target would need to be reached well before 2030, with the cooperation of all countries that maintain bank secrecy and tolerate tax havens facilitating not only illicit flows, but also tax evasion and abuse.

Monitoring and evaluation need to be radically improved, based on lessons extracted from the MDG era. Poverty indicators have to be monitored within the context of macroeconomic, labour and social policies in order to observe the trend in areas where anti-poverty policies have so far proved ineffective. Universities' involvement in the measuring and monitoring process can increase the level of transparency, accuracy and independence from national governments and international bodies responsible and accountable for reaching the goals.

The SDGs approach represents a fresh and updated version of earlier framings of both poverty reduction and environmental management.

But one thing seems quite clear: without understanding and addressing the systems and paradigms that produce and perpetuate both poverty and unsustainability, even the best-intentioned SDGs are likely to have only superficial effects, and there is the risk that they might achieve nothing more than replicating the shortcomings associated with the MDGs (CROP 2013; see also Koehler this volume).

What is this volume offering its readers?

This book was conceived as a response to the sunny picture, and to help direct the Millennium Declaration and MDGs' promises and commitments towards becoming a reality. The CROP Scientific Committee met in Bergen in 2012 to evaluate the MDGs and stimulate reflection on the post-2015 development agenda. The results and conclusions of those debates are reflected in this book.

The contributions are diverse in their positions. They are shaped by the plurality of the authors' theoretical and political positions, and nuanced by varying degrees of optimism and pessimism. Despite their heterogeneity, however, all the contributions address the three questions posed at the beginning of this chapter, presenting a variety of analytical viewpoints and scientific trajectories.

The concern with poverty is central to all chapters, as is the interest in alternatives and a new vision of development. The contributions converge around a set of three distinct but interrelated themes, and are therefore clustered as follows:

- Part I: The Global Poverty Challenge
- Part II: Devising and Refining Development Goals
- Part III: Policy and Societal Alternatives

Part I of the book concentrates in particular on the notion of poverty, which is flawed at best and misleading at worst. For Jomo, Rogers and Balázs, and Boltvinik and Damián, the definition of poverty is methodologically wrong. At a primary level, this has implications for poverty measurement – as outlined also in this first chapter. Poverty increased in absolute numbers in Africa, and remains a salient structural feature in most societies (Cimadamore, Koehler and Pogge this chapter); it is not correctly measured (Jomo), and it is not an appropriate measure, notably if equity (Jomo) and empowerment (Rogers and Balázs) are factored in. This argument is corroborated by the emphasis on dignity offered by Boltvinik and Damián in Part III of the book.

Jomo argues that rising inequality and poverty in many developing countries have dented the overall achievements in poverty reduction. The MDG 1A incidence of poverty indicator has become the single most important development indicator for the MDGs. The chapter raises concerns about how poverty has been measured for MDG reporting purposes, given methodological and other shortcomings in the poverty estimates. As the original poverty line was defined principally in terms of the cost of securing enough food, comparing the poverty indicator to the MDG 1C hunger or prevalence of undernourishment indicator is revealing. The significant differences between regional and country poverty and hunger trends during the MDG reporting period raised concerns about both indicators. The chapter underscores the 'poverty of the conventional poverty policy discourse'. As poverty is slated to continue to be the most-watched indicator of success in the post-2015 Sustainable Development Goals, the chapter highlights the urgent need to review and reconsider poverty measurement and analysis, as well as policies.

The chapter by Rogers and Balázs valorizes the knowledge of people living in poverty-stricken communities, and compares their observations with hard data findings. The chapter's core observation is that 'the decisions and actions of those with money is a primary cause of inequality, poverty, and impeded development'. Drawing on a major global survey, Rogers and Balázs present qualitative information contributed by people who experience poverty, identifying mechanisms by which the unequal distribution of wealth adds up to generate poverty. Their perceptions tally with evidence from key academic studies, demonstrating the explanatory power of those observations by the poor themselves. The chapter examines the implications of these findings for crafting a set of post-2015 SDGs and connected policies, which would be more effective at reducing poverty and promoting sustainable development.

The misleading concepts and measurement of poverty in turn lead to a problematic formulation of development goals. This is the focus of Section II of the book. Ivanova and Escobar-Pemberthy analyse the trajectory and evolution of global development goals from the International Development Goals of the OECD, through the MDGs to the SDGs, and articulate key implications of this path for the SDG process. They point out that the SDGs have recaptured the 'spirit of integration of economic, social and environmental variables'. The chapter provides an analytical comparison of these three goal sets, illustrating which of the Open Working Group (UN 2014a) proposal's goals and targets relate to economic, social and environmental dimensions and their governance. The chapter argues that decisions regarding the SDGs have two equally important dimensions: the formulation of development goals – as is under way – and their implementation. A meaningful implementation of the SDGs would, however, require translating the proposals at the goals level into operational policy decisions, as well as identifying relevant targets and indicators for an innovative and effective governance and monitoring process.

This aspect is the focus of the chapter by Paes-Sousa and De Martino Jannuzzi. They assess social protection policy in Brazil, starting from the *Fome Zero* (Zero Hunger) strategy launched in 2003. They argue that social transfers succeeded in taking 22 million people out of extreme poverty (less than US$1.25 per day), but that public policy would now need to give more attention to a broader group of income poor and to the newly emerging lower middle class. Brazil – which has been visible in the shaping of the SDGs in connection with the Rio+20 Summit and its follow-up – needs to formulate domestic policy for an 'updated development objective' for the eradication of all forms of poverty, building on the international debate on SDGs.

In his analysis of the conceptualization of goals, Montes shows how the practice of international cooperation systemically disregards the internationally agreed meaning of sustainable development. The MDG approach unduly focused on individual-level social development, discounting the economic and genuinely environmental aspects of sustainable development, which are unattainable without macroeconomic development and structural change. Montes examines the manner in which mechanisms in international trade and finance and premature external 'openness' have hindered development in developing countries. He argues that poverty eradication is an overly narrow objective of development, because it does not recognize that it requires the movement of a significant proportion of the population from traditional, subsistence-sector jobs to productive employment in the formal sector. Moreover, the simplifying poverty eradication approach draws attention away from the international system, whose structure serves mainly 'the economic and political interests of powerful factions in developed countries'. Such systematic analytical and policy neglect of the poorly structured international system has adverse medium- and long-term economic, social and environmental implications. This analysis logically makes the case for a different type of development goal.

At the country and sectoral levels, Campos, Duarte and Soares examine a specific MDG – Goal 2, which aimed to 'ensure that, by 2015, children everywhere, boys and girls alike, will be able to complete a full course of primary schooling'. In Brazil, the goal focused on the expansion of compulsory education for children aged seven to fourteen, with considerable success. However, this made children over fifteen who had not received a primary education at the appropriate age even more vulnerable to social exclusion and poverty. Campos, Duarte and Soares argue that the post-2015 development agenda now needs to address the unintended (negative) consequences of policies, prioritize secondary education, and urgently address the poverty risk of uneducated youth.

Regarding the role the MDGs have played, several of the chapters illustrate how the misconception of poverty in the MDG agenda has had a direct impact on policy. For Rogers and Balázs, ignoring the role of power defeats any poverty eradication strategy. Similarly, Boltvinik and Damián discuss poverty eradication policies from a political economy point of view, arguing that an erroneous analysis cannot even begin to tackle poverty. For Montes, the overvaluation of poverty eradication as a central development goal has led the development community to completely disregard the international system that produces and reproduces poverty, a view shared by Cimadamore, Koehler and Pogge in this chapter.

Part III of the book is hence devoted to alternative policies and visions. Boltvinik and Damián discuss the main forces determining global poverty trends, namely periodic economic crises and the process of automation. They compare Keynesian and neoliberal variants of capitalism, arguing that Keynesian policy approaches mitigate capitalism's tendency to produce poverty, while neoliberalism reinforces it. Against this analytical framework, the chapter examines the relevance of the MDG poverty target. It argues that poverty reduction goals are futile, methodologically and, more importantly, analytically. This is because automation continuously decreases the number of jobs required to produce a potentially increasing number of goods and services.[14] As jobs decrease, the income in the hands of the vast majority of consumers also decreases, making the sale of goods produced impossible. The chapter therefore makes the case for a mechanism that decouples income from paid jobs, in the form of a 'Universal Sufficient and Unconditional Citizens' Income (USUCI)'. This argument is directly relevant for the SDGs discussion, which in Goal 1 contains the recommendation for a universal social protection floor.

Deacon too reviews the discussion within and around the UN with a view to the development agenda after 2015. He makes the case that the continuing global politics of poverty alleviation and eradication need to shift towards 'a new global politics of building social solidarity'. Like Boltvinik and Damián, but from a political rather than an economic angle, this supports the case for a social protection floor initiative. As its ethical underpinning, Deacon highlights the increased attention given to the concept of freedom from poverty as a human right. He also argues for a renewed focus on state-led development, and the need to reconcile the interests of the middle classes with those of the poor in order to create solidarities. This proposal, coming from a social solidarity tradition rather than a direct critique of capitalism, supports Boltvinik and Damián's case for the USUCI.

Koehler reviews the history of development agendas, in order to place the MDGs in the context of development decades pursued by the UN and the international community since the 1960s. She posits that the MDGs were a success in terms of raising the visibility of poverty and social development as global political concerns, but a failure in that the majority of the targets were not met. She argues that the MDGs had conceptual shortcomings, but more importantly lacked an explicit policy design and vision. The main conclusion is that policy is central to a successful development agenda, and it is therefore crucial to reinstate the role of public policy, sidelined in the neoliberal agenda. In short, Koehler emphasizes the role of the state in eradicating poverty and hunger, and argues for it to become part and parcel of the SDGs.

When examining common ground across the chapters and sections of the book, one observes that all the contributions address the lessons of the MDGs for the SDGs. Several contributions track the genesis and evolution of national (Paes-Sousa and De Martino Jannuzzi) or international development agendas (Montes; Koehler), and situate conceptual the progress and shortcomings of the emerging SDGs in that context (Ivanova and Escobar-Pemberthy).

In terms of the evolving social contract, Deacon and Paes-Sousa and De Martino Jannuzzi argue for a broadening of the notion of the poor, to reach also the middle classes, implicitly making the case for a new social contract or what Deacon aptly terms 'social solidarity'. Both chapters see the need to align domestic policy with international policy recommendations in the new development agenda. Campos, Duarte and Soares draw attention to a new group of highly vulnerable people – uneducated youth – who were left out by the MDG effort and now face competition from a younger generation that did benefit. Montes makes that point more strongly, arguing that the development agenda serves particular interests.

Several authors are adamant about the demand for more clearly formulated public policy (Ivanova and Escobar-Pemberthy), and for a return to enlightened, rights-based and democratic state-led development (Deacon, Koehler). With respect to concrete policy recommendations, several of the chapters make a strong case for social protection (Deacon) or a minimum income guarantee (Boltvinik and Damián) – very much anticipating a key proposition of the SDGs.

Concluding summary

This introductory chapter has sought to provide a critical overview of the MDG agenda on extreme poverty. It provides a critique of the MDGs' underlying poverty concept as well as its role in reducing global poverty. It has also aimed to frame the analysis, insights and ideas for a new development agenda contained in the following chapters.

Thus, the volume hopes to offer a diverse and hopefully thought-provoking contribution to poverty discourse and analysis. Perhaps it can modestly help to instigate a fundamental reframing of the notion of poverty and provide pointers towards the type of policies necessary to eradicate all forms of poverty, and to achieve this in a sustainable manner. This is what we would work towards analytically, aspire to ethically, and strive for politically.

Notes

1 www.un.org/en/events/ observances/decades.shtml. See also Jomo, Ivanova and Escobar-Pemberthy, Roberts and Balázs, Montes, and Koehler in this volume, and Koehler 2015.

2 United Nations Millennium Declaration. Resolution 55/2adopted by the General Assembly, www.un.org/ millennium/declaration/ares552e.htm, accessed 23 February 2015.

3 See CROP Brief no. 13, www.crop. org/Publications/BriefsSeries/default. aspx, accessed 24 February 2015.

4 There is an agreed division of labour in terms of which agency monitors which of the MDG targets. See UN (2003).

5 www.news.hypercrit.net/2012/11/13/ einstein-on-misattribution-i-probably-didnt-say-that/.

6 On the centrality of productivity for economic development, and its neglect in the MDG agenda, see Montes this volume and Gore (2013).

7 Developmental states have been criticized for a lack of democracy – from the violation of labour rights and core labour standards, to human rights violations in terms of civil and political rights. There is therefore a movement to define democratic developmental welfare states which combine a human rights base with the aspirations of welfare states, and the role of government for economic development and restructuring. See Mkandawire (2004); Robinson and White (1998); UNRISD (2010); Koehler this volume.

8 See also see Oxfam (2014) in a similar vein.

9 ODA from the OECD Development Assistance Countries increased from US$82 billion in 2000 to US$134 billion in 2013; the EU institutions' flows increased from US$8.5 billion to US$15 billion, not quite doubling over the period. OECD aid statistics, www.compareyourcountry.org/ oda?cr=20001&cr1=oecd&lg=en&page=1, accessed 26 February 2015.

10 Again, China is one of the exceptions. Its progress on poverty reduction has much to do with its transformation into a major exporter of manufactures, which enabled a transition from agricultural to manufacturing employment.

11 See Koehler this volume for the full list of proposed SDGs.

12 For the principle of decent work, the ILO Declaration on Fundamental Principles and Rights at Work can serve as a preliminary orientation. It includes freedom of association and the effective recognition of the right to collective bargaining; the elimination of all forms of forced or compulsory labour; the effective abolition of child labour; and the elimination of discrimination in respect of employment and occupation; www. ilo.org/declaration/thedeclaration/ textdeclaration/lang--en/index.htm.

On the social protection floor, see www.ilo.org/secsoc/areas-of-work/policy-development-and-applied-research/social-protection-floor/lang--en/index.htm and www. socialprotectionfloor-gateway.org/, accessed 26 February 2015.

13 The European Commission (EC 2014), for example, is promising policy coherence for development, to overcome the fact that policies in the areas of trade or energy undermine and contravene development cooperation efforts.

14 On the role of automation and policy responses, see also Roubini (2015).

References

Alvarez Leguizamon, S. (ed.) (2005) *Trabajo y produccion de pobreza en Latinoamerica y el Caribe*, Buenos Aires: CLACSO.

Chang, H. (2002) *Globalization, Economic Development, and the Role of the State*, London: Zed Books.

Cimadamore, A. D. and A. D. Cattani (eds) (2007) *Produção de pobreza e desigualdade na América Latina*, Porto Alegre: Tomo Editorial.

Cimadamore, A. D. et al. (eds) (2005) *The poverty of the State: Reconsidering the role of the state in the struggle against global poverty*, Buenos Aires: CLACSO.

CROP (2013) 'Poverty and the Millennium Development Goals (MDGs): a critical assessment and a look forward', Brief no. 13, January, www.crop. org/viewfile.aspx?id=453, accessed 29 June 2015.

EC (European Commission) (2014) 'A decent life for all: from vision to collective action', Communication from the Commission to the European Parliament, the Council, the European Economic and Social Committee and the Committee of the Regions, COM(2014) 335 final, 2 June 2014, Brussels, ec.europa. eu/europeaid/sites/devco/files/part1-a-decent-life-for-all.pdf, accessed 27 February 2015.

Fukuda-Parr, S. (2010) 'Reducing inequality – the missing mdg: a content review of PRSPs and bilateral donor policy statements', *IDS Bulletin*, 14(1): 26–35.

— (2012) 'Recapturing the narrative of international development', Gender and Development Paper 18, Geneva: UNRISD.

Gore, C. (2013) 'Beyond the romantic violence of the MDGs. Development, aid and human rights', in M. Langford, A. Sumner and A. E. Yamin, *The Millennium Development Goals and Human Rights. Past, Present and Future*, Cambridge: Cambridge University Press, pp. 383–407.

Kar, D. and J. Spanjers (2014) *Illicit Financial Flows from Developing Countries: 2003–2012*, Global Policy Forum, New York, www.globalpolicy. org/component/content/article/216-global-taxes/52722-new-report-illicit-financial-flows-from-developing-countries-2003-2012.html, accessed 26 February 2015.

Klein, N. (2014) *This Changes Everything: Capitalism vs. the Climate*, London: Penguin.

Koehler, G. (2015) 'Seven decades of "development" and now what?', *Journal of International Development*, August.

Milanovic, B. (2011) *The Haves and the Have-Nots: A Brief and Idiosyncratic History of Global Inequality*, New York: Basic Books.

Mkandawire, T. (2004) 'Social policy in a development context: introduction', in T. Mkandawire (ed.), *Social Policy in a Development Context*, Basingstoke: Palgrave Macmillan.

Montes, M. (2015) 'The Third Financing for Development conference. What are the issues?' Mimeo, Geneva: South Centre.

Oxfam (2014) *Even it up – time to end extreme inequality*, policy-practice. oxfam.org.uk/publications/even-it-up-time-to-end-extreme-inequality-333012, accessed 26 June 2015.

OPHI (Oxford Poverty and Human Development Initiative) (n.d.) *Missing Dimensions of Poverty*, Oxford: Oxford Department of International Development, www.ophi.org. uk/research/missing-dimensions/, accessed 26 February 2015.

Piketty, T. (2014) *Capital in the Twenty-First Century*, Boston, MA: Harvard University Press.

Pogge, T. (2013) 'Poverty, hunger and cosmetic progress', in M. Langford, A. Sumner and A. E. Yamin (eds), *The Millennium Development Goals and Human Rights: Past, Present and Future*, Cambridge: Cambridge University Press, pp. 209–31.

Ringen, S. et al. (2011) *The Korean State and Social Policy*, Oxford: Oxford University Press.

Robinson, M. and G. White (1998) *The Democratic Developmental State: Political and institutional Design*, Oxford: Oxford University Press.

Roubini, N. (2014) 'Where will all the workers go?', Project Syndicate,

December, www.policyinnovations.
org/ideas/commentary/data/00317.

Steffen, W. et al. (2015) 'Planetary
boundaries: guiding human
development on a changing
planet', *Science*, 347(6223), www.
stockholmresilience.org/21/research/
research-news/1-15-2015-planetary-
boundaries-2.0---new-and-improved.
html, accessed 29 June 2015.

Stokke, O. (2009) *The UN and
Development: From Aid to
Cooperation*, Bloomington: Indiana
University Press.

UN (United Nations) (2003) *Indicators
for Monitoring the Millennium
Development Goals: Definitions,
Rationale, Concepts and Sources*, New
York: UN.

— (2011) *The Millennium Development
Goals Report 2011*.

— (2012) *The Millennium Development
Goals Report 2012*, www.
un.org/millenniumgoals/pdf/
MDG%20Report%202012.pdf.

— (2013) *The Millennium Development
Goals Report 2013*.

— (2014a) *Introduction to the Proposal
of the Open Working Group for
Sustainable Development Goals*,
sustainabledevelopment.un.org/
focussdgs.html, accessed 17 February
2015.

— (2014b) *Millennium Development Goals:
2014 Progress Chart*, mdgs.un.org/
unsd/mdg/News.aspx?ArticleId=79,
accessed 17 February 2015.

— (2014c) *The Millennium Development
Goals Report 2014*, www.un.org/en/
development/desa/publications/
mdg-report-2014.html, accessed 23
February 2015.

UN SG (2001) *Road Map towards the
Implementation of the United
Nations Millennium Declaration*,
Report of the Secretary-General,
A/56/326, unpan1.un.org/intradoc/
groups/public/documents/UN/
UNPAN004152.pdf.

— (2014) *The Road to Dignity by 2030:
Ending Poverty, Transforming All Lives
and Protecting the Planet*, Synthesis
Report, A/69/700, www.un.org/ga/
search/view_doc.asp?symbol=A/69/
700&referer=/english/&Lang=E.

UNDP (2013) *The Rise of the South: Human
Progress in a Diverse World*, Human
Development Report 2013, New York:
UNDP, hdr.undp.org/en/2013-report.

UNRISD (2010) *Combating Poverty and
Inequality: Structural Change, Social
Policy and Politics*, Geneva: United
Nations, www.unrisd.org.

Wisor, S., S. Bessell, F. Castillo, J.
Crawford, K. Donaghue, J. Hunt, A.
Jaggar, A. Liu and T. Pogge (2014)
*The Individual Deprivation Measure:
A Gender-Sensitive Approach to
Poverty Measurement*, Melbourne:
International Women's Development
Agency, www.iwda.org.au/wp-
content/uploads/2014/10/The-IDM-
Report1.pdf.

World Bank (2015) *Global Monitoring
Report: Poverty Forecasts*, www.
worldbank.org/en/publication/
global-monitoring-report/poverty-
forecasts, accessed 23 February 2015.

Ziegler, J. (2014) *Retourner le fusil! Choisir
son champs*, Paris: Editions Seuil.

2 | THE MDGS AND POVERTY REDUCTION

Jomo Kwame Sundaram[1]

Global poverty trends

World leaders agreed to the Millennium Declaration at the UN Millennium Summit in September 2000. This was later reformulated as eight Millennium Development Goals (MDGs) and approved by UN member states. The first MDG seeks to halve the proportion of people in the developing countries living on less than one (1985 PPP [purchasing power parity] dollar) a day between 1990 and 2015.

There has been some success in reducing global poverty rates in the past three decades. According to recent estimates of the World Bank (World Bank 2013), the proportion of people in the developing countries living on less than 1.25 (2005 PPP dollars) per day has decreased from 52 per cent in 1981 to 21 per cent in 2010. Curiously, this represents one percentage point less than half the poverty rate of 43 per cent that prevailed at the time when the MDGs were adopted. Thus, one can celebrate the achievement of the target of halving global poverty five years ahead of 2015!

However, the extent of the achievement in absolute terms is more modest as the number of people living in extreme poverty has declined by about 700 million in three decades. According to the World Bank, the number of extreme poor in the developing world declined from 1,962 million in 1981 to 1,011 million in 2011.[2] The 1994 Cairo Conference on Population and Development and the 1995 Copenhagen Social Summit had committed the international community to more ambitious targets, which were significantly revised downwards in the MDGs. For example, halving the number of poor would have been more ambitious than halving the share or percentage of the poor.

The distribution of people living in poverty within and across regions has changed significantly over the last three decades. While 56 per cent of the world's extreme poor lived in East Asia and the Pacific (including China) in 1981, the sub-region was home to 18 per cent of the global poor in 2010. China's share of global poverty declined from 43 per cent in 1981 to 11 per cent in 2010. In contrast, India's share of global poverty rose from 21 per cent to 35 per cent during the same period.[3] This has contributed to the rise in the share of the world's extreme poor in South Asia from 29 per cent in 1981 to 42 per cent in 2010. The share of sub-Saharan Africa in global poverty tripled from 11 per cent to 36 per cent between 1981 and 2010! Thus, sub-Saharan Africa accounts for more than one third of the world's extreme poor compared to one ninth over three decades ago. The changing regional distribution of poverty reflects broad changes in economic performance. More importantly, the rise in the global share of poverty despite rapid growth in these regions underscores the consequence of the concurrent rise in inequality (Oxfam 2014).

To what extent can we really celebrate the achievements in reduction of global poverty? Rising inequality and poverty in many developing countries have dented the overall achievements in poverty reduction. Many analysts have also noted methodological and other shortcomings in the poverty estimates. Thus, one needs to be circumspect before claiming too much success in the global fight against poverty.

Methodological issues in estimating poverty

The main problem in estimating poverty involves the utilization of the poverty line as a meaningful measure of poverty. Considerable evidence suggests that the poverty line seriously misrepresents the actual extent of poverty. For instance, global poverty is said to have been halved

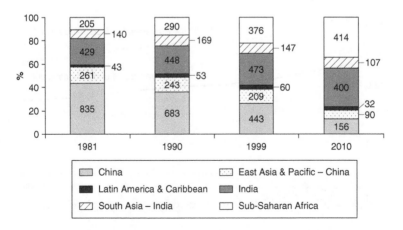

2.1 Number of people living on less than $1.25/day (*source*: World Bank (2013))

from 1990 to 2010, while global hunger has not decreased to the same extent despite the fact that the poverty line is supposed to be principally determined by the money income needed to avoid being hungry.

The poverty line was originally – and controversially – defined with reference to the purchasing power of a 'dollar a day' in 1985 US currency. Before its latest (2008) revision, the World Bank's estimate of poverty for 2004 was under a billion. This was drastically revised upwards by over 40 per cent in 2008 when the 2005 survey data became available and the international poverty line was redefined with reference to the purchasing power of $1.25 a day in 2005 US currency. Such a high margin of adjustment raises serious questions about the accuracy of all poverty estimates, as well as related projections and estimates, and of the utility of making policy using such poverty numbers.

If the poverty line is fixed where the World Bank set it for 2005, at $1.25/day, which is equivalent to $38/month, then the number of poor was 1,923 million in 1990 and 1,128 million in 2010 – equivalent to a 41 per cent reduction over twenty years – hardly enough to halve the number, but enough to halve the proportion of poor people in developing countries, mainly thanks to the massive reduction of poverty in China, where the reported number of extreme poor declined from 689.4 million in 1990 to 122.9 million in 2010.

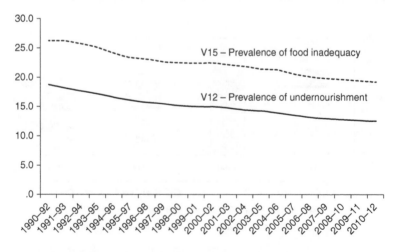

2.2 Prevalence of chronic undernourishment in the world, 1990–2012 (%)

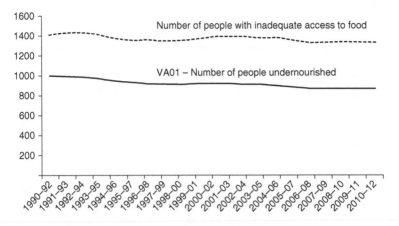

2.3 Number of chronically undernourished in the world, 1990–2012 (millions)

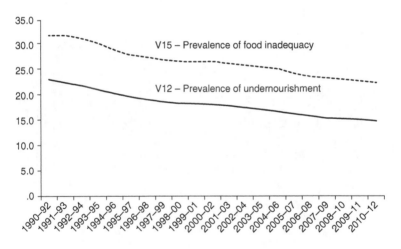

2.4 Prevalence of chronic undernourishment in developing countries, 1990–2012 (%)

Although the World Bank poverty line was originally – and controversially – defined as a 'dollar a day', the line has not been adjusted to the United States inflation rate. As Thomas Pogge[4] has pointed out, much depends on the starting point. If one starts from the original poverty definition of $1/day (in 1985 dollars) used for drafting MDG1,

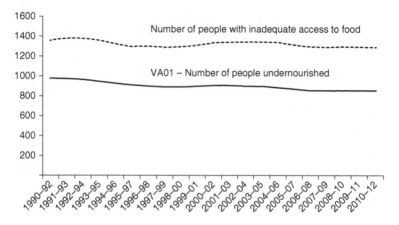

2.5 Number of chronically undernourished in developing countries, 1990–2012 (millions)

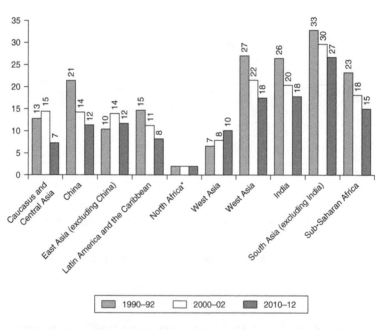

2.6 Prevalence of chronic undernourishment in developing countries by region, 1990–2012 (%)

Note: * Includes data for Sudan, which are not included in the figure for sub-Saharan Africa, following the partition of the country when South Sudan became an independent state in 2011.

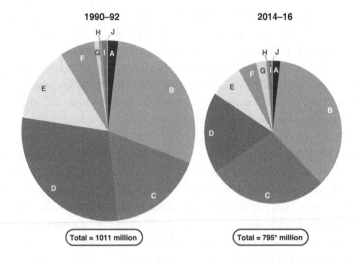

	Number (millions)		Regional share (%)	
	1990–92	2014–16	1990–92	2014–16
Ⓐ Developed regions	20	15	2.0	1.8
Ⓑ Southern Asia	291	281	28.8	35.4
Ⓒ Sub-Saharan Africa	176	220	17.4	27.7
Ⓓ Eastern Asia	295	145	29.2	18.3
Ⓔ South-Eastern Asia	138	61	13.6	7.6
Ⓕ Latin America and the Caribbean	66	34	6.5	4.3
Ⓖ Western Asia	8	19	0.8	2.4
Ⓗ Northern Africa	6	4	0.6	0.5
Ⓘ Caucasus and Central Asia	10	6	0.9	0.7
Ⓙ Oceania	1	1	0.1	0.2
Total	**1011**	**795***	**100**	**100**

2.7 The changing distribution of hunger in the world: numbers and shares of undernourished peoples by region, 1990–92 and 2014–16 (*source*: FAO, IFAD and WFP, 2015. The State of Food Insecurity in the World 2015. Meeting the 2015 international hunger targets: taking stock of uneven progress. Rome, FAO.)

Note: The areas of the pie charts are proportional to the total number of undernourished in each period. Data for 2014–16 refer to provisional estimates. All figures are rounded.

* Includes data for Sudan, which are not included in the figure for sub-Saharan Africa, following the partition of the country when South Sudan became an independent state in 2011.

and then corrects for US inflation in the 1985–2005 period,[5] one gets an equivalent poverty line of $1.815/day (in 2005 dollars), or $55.18/month, which is clearly much higher than the $1.25/day for 2005 used by the World Bank.[6] The number of poor would then be 2,698.42 million in 1990 and 2,146.68 million in 2010 – for a mere 20.5 per cent reduction over twenty years, nowhere near enough to halve the proportion, let alone the number, of poor in developing countries.

Global poverty estimates by the World Bank underscore the methodological problems of its poverty measurement. Sanjay Reddy (2011) shows that the 2008 revision of the Bank's 2005 global poverty estimates, based on a new $1.25 (2005 purchasing power parity or PPP) poverty line, has only reaffirmed their unreliability. Reddy argues that the Bank's poverty line is not only flawed in conception, but also not very useful, if not downright problematic, for policy purposes. As various aspects of the Bank's approach can hardly be justified, much less weight should be given to the Bank's poverty estimates in monitoring progress on the first Millennium Development Goal (MDG) to reduce poverty and hunger rates by half from 1990. He argues that its conceptual and methodological problems require adopting an altogether different method involving international coordination by the key institutions involved.

The single largest item in the basket of goods and services presumed to constitute the poverty line is food. Hence, the poverty line is often popularly understood as the income needed to avoid being hungry. Thus, the divergence between poverty and hunger trends over the period 1990–2010 should be a cause for concern. The graphs showing the two trends for the world – or even for all developing countries – are less different, but the trends for the regions are much more dramatically divergent, as the graphs show. This is not the place to discuss the relative merits and demerits of the poverty and hunger indicators used to monitor progress in achieving the first Millennium Development Goal (MDG1).

The MDG1c hunger indicator has been defined in terms of the 'Prevalence of Undernourishment' (PoU) indicator, understood as chronic hunger defined in relation to the minimum dietary energy (caloric) intake for a minimal normal ('sedentary') activity level corresponding to a physical activity level (PAL) coefficient of 1.55. The PoU has been traditionally estimated by assuming an 'average' or 'regular' distribution of physical activity levels in the population. Such an estimate would constitute a conservative or minimum lower bound for a population not engaged in much physical activity. The lower PoU line thus provides the most conservative estimate of the number of people suffering from chronic undernourishment, while the new 'Prevalence of Food Inadequacy' (PoFI) indicator, based on a minimal PAL of 1.75, is a less conservative, but more plausible, estimate if none of the hungry can afford to have a sedentary lifestyle.

Trends in inequality also have a bearing on poverty trends. Not only are there wider income gaps between rich and poor countries, but within-country income inequalities have also increased in the majority of countries during this period. For example, between the early 1980s and 2005, income inequality rose in fifty-nine of the 114 countries for which data are available, and declined in forty countries (UN 2010).

Poverty challenge

By almost any standards, including the 1994 United Nations Conference on Population and Development, the 1995 Copenhagen Social Summit and the 2000 Millennium Declaration, there has been modest, but insufficient, progress globally in reducing poverty and deprivation over the last three decades. If we leave out the spectacular reduction of poverty in China and other parts of East Asia over this period, the record for the rest of the world looks even more dismal. Wide-ranging deficits in the human condition remain endemic and ubiquitous in most poor countries, but also in some rich countries, especially for certain vulnerable groups.

What is particularly disturbing is that these disappointing outcomes on many crucial dimensions have persisted despite several growth spurts at the global level and even more sustained growth in several large developing countries. This shameful failure has continued despite pious declarations and professed commitments by the global community to the worthy goals of the Millennium Declaration. This situation is likely to deteriorate owing to subdued growth in developing countries, as the global economy remains anaemic following the financial crisis of 2008/09. While global economic recovery is still tepid, it is certain that job recovery and the advancement of decent work conditions lag considerably, with severely adverse consequences for real incomes and living conditions.

The United Nations' *Report on the World Social Situation 2010: Rethinking Poverty* sought to contribute to rethinking poverty and its measurement, as well as policies and programmes to promote poverty reduction. It affirmed the urgent need for a strategic shift away from the market fundamentalist thinking, policies and practices of recent decades towards more sustainable development and equity-oriented policies appropriate to national conditions and circumstances. The report noted that:

- *The number of people living on less than $1.25 a day declined globally from 1.9 billion in 1981 to 1.4 billion in 2005* according to the World Bank. This decline was largely due to rapid growth of employment and incomes in China despite fast-rising inequalities. However, the absolute number of poor people actually went up during this period in many countries in sub-Saharan Africa, Latin America, the Middle East and North Africa, as well as Central Asia.
- *The recent global financial, food and fuel crises, as well as the ongoing implications of climate change, threaten efforts* to reduce extreme poverty, even undermining some gains achieved since the 2000 Millennium Summit. The negative economic and social impacts of these crises threaten the lives of people living in poverty as well as many more living in precarious or vulnerable situations, and call into question the sustainability of past poverty reduction.
- *The experience of poverty is multidimensional,* consistent with the wider definition of poverty adopted by the 1995 World Summit for Social Development. This implies that understanding poverty should include consideration of the causes and consequences of deprivation, social exclusion and lack of participation. With this broader definition, the situation today may be even worse than a monetary income poverty line alone would indicate, as suggested by the Multidimensional Poverty Index.[7]
- *Experience has shown that current conventional policy approaches to poverty eradication are insufficient, if not ineffective, and require serious rethinking by policy-makers.* The obstacles to reducing global poverty remain formidable, numerous and complex, and have been exacerbated by the economic crisis. We need to prioritize sustainable development and structural transformation – involving sustained growth of output, employment and incomes, with inclusive development benefiting people living in poverty.

Why and how has this predicament come about? *Rethinking Poverty*

summarized key flaws in mainstream thinking on poverty measurement, analysis and policy:

- Dominant mainstream perspectives on poverty and deprivation have
  contributed to considerable misunderstanding and poor analysis, in
  turn leading to poor and ineffectual policy prescriptions.
- Neither microeconomic economic liberalization reforms nor
  macroeconomic stabilization programmes have ignited rapid and
  sustained growth, as promised by the conventional wisdom favoured
  by the international financial institutions and most donors. Policies
  since the 1980s have generally failed to address these issues and
  often made things worse as the policy prescriptions slowed growth
  and increased inequality in most countries.
- Policy prescriptions, often imposed on recipient countries through
  aid conditionalities, have further constrained developing countries'
  policy space. Failure to spur growth and loss of revenue due to
  various tax incentives have also reduced developing countries' fiscal
  space. Reduction of policy and fiscal space has greatly reduced
  developing countries' resilience, especially in the face of external
  shocks or natural disasters, with dire consequences for poverty and
  destitution.
- Those economies which have done well over the last three decades,
  in terms of both growth and poverty reduction, have generally
  adopted pragmatic, heterodox economic development policies.
  While invoking market-friendly rhetoric, they have used public
  policies and investments to induce private investments, especially in
  desired economic activities, e.g. those creating many employment
  opportunities, directly or indirectly, as well as those offering
  increasing returns to scale.
- While growth has been necessary for poverty reduction, the creation
  of decent employment opportunities has been crucial for raising
  incomes and poverty reduction (United Nations 2007). Extensive
  social provisioning and protection as well as other redistributive
  policies have been sustained by ensuring growth, thus raising average
  incomes as well as the fiscal basis for greater social spending.
- Social policies have involved increased targeting, ostensibly to
  achieve greater cost-effectiveness. Social policies targeting the poor,
  or the 'poorest of the poor', have often proved to be expensive and
  politically unsustainable, while missing out many of the deserving

poor. Instead, universal social policies have generally proved to be much more effective as well as politically sustainable.

- Special programmes, such as micro-finance, issuing land titles and 'good governance' reforms, have generally not significantly reduced poverty.
- Without significant job creation and sustained per capita income growth, other policies to help the poor will have limited impact. Growth can become more stable with consistently counter-cyclical macroeconomic policies and better capacity to deal with exogenous shocks. Also crucial are measures reducing inequality and accelerating structural change.

Rethinking poverty analysis and policies[8]

The inadequacy of much contemporary thinking about poverty as well as its amelioration seems to parallel the poor understanding of macro-financial stability, which has contributed to the ongoing global financial and economic crisis. Erik Reinert (2011) criticizes the 'terrible simplifications' in economic theory contributing to such poor understanding and analyses of financial crises and persistent poverty. He argues that similar economic reasoning has contributed to these parallel failures.

Reinert focuses attention on what Hyman Minsky termed 'destabilizing stability', referring to long periods of stability leading to greater vulnerability and, eventually, financial crisis. Long periods of economic progress in core countries have led to increasingly abstract and irrelevant economic theories. A similar failure in economic theorizing in the first half of the nineteenth century led to turning points – referred to by him as the '1848 moment' – resulting in more relevant economic theories. He also identifies key variables that need to be reintroduced into economic theory for poor countries to develop the productive structures for sustained economic development to eliminate poverty.

The only sustainable basis for mass poverty reduction involves economic growth, development policy and employment creation. Lance Taylor (2011) argues that without sustained growth in per capita output and significant job creation, policies seeking to directly reduce poverty in a sustainable manner will not succeed. Instead, he proposes growth-promoting policies, and insists that the growth process will also be more stable and sustainable with consistently counter-cyclical macroeconomic policies, especially in dealing with exogenous shocks from abroad.

Macroeconomic prices, such as exchange and interest rates, can be managed to support developmental objectives. Taylor advocates pursuing industrial and trade policies to promote desirable economic activities, especially to encourage increasing returns to scale. Also, measures promoting appropriate developmentally proactive financial development are crucial for development. Particularly for the poorest countries, making more productive use of foreign aid can be crucial owing to the severe resource constraints they face. The overriding policy concern should be to ensure that national economies have sufficient policy space to achieve sustained growth and structural change.

The nature of the growth process, rather than economic growth per se, is critical for poverty reduction as growing inequalities can prevent the benefits of growth from reaching the poor. Jayati Ghosh (2011) reviews recent trends in poverty reduction in China and India, suggesting that appropriate structural change accompanying growth can generate productive non-agricultural employment, thus reducing rural and urban poverty. Meanwhile, fiscal means have to be ensured to finance the provision of basic needs and essential social services. Government mediation of market processes and of global economic integration can be crucial for determining economic and social outcomes.

Recognizing that poverty reduction is influenced by economic growth and income distribution as well as distribution changes, Mushtaq Khan (2011) suggests that governance impacts both economic growth and distribution. The mainstream 'market-enhancing' governance paradigm seeks to enhance market efficiency through 'good governance' reforms, ostensibly to trigger or sustain more rapid economic growth. Structural and fiscal constraints prevent significant improvements in governance capabilities while market failures remain significant and are unlikely to be greatly reduced by governance reforms. Like stabilizing property rights, good rule of law and significantly reducing corruption, achieving good governance goals requires fiscal capacities and state capabilities not available in most developing countries.

More recently, ostensibly 'pro-poor' good governance reforms claim to have enhanced the scale and efficiency of service delivery to the poor. Khan challenges the claim that the good governance approach enhances economic growth more broadly. He argues that neither theory nor evidence strongly supports the claim of significant poverty reduction by advancing the 'good governance' agenda. Instead, he suggests that alternative governance approaches to addressing poverty are more likely to accelerate poverty reduction. Developing countries therefore need to focus on alternative governance capabilities that will better address market failures.

In recent years, those promoting neoliberal reforms to reduce poverty have strongly supported the 'Bottom of the Pyramid' (BoP) approach that presumes that the poor are all 'resilient and creative entrepreneurs and value-conscious consumers'. Aneel Karnani (2011) argues that this romanticized view of the poor has hurt them in at least two ways. First, it has resulted in too little emphasis on legal, regulatory and social mechanisms to protect the poor, who are, by and large, vulnerable to various marketing gimmicks and generally unable to take advantage of economies of scale in consumption. Secondly, it romanticizes and overemphasizes microcredit while under-emphasizing the crucial importance of large modern enterprises that can provide stable and decent employment opportunities for the poor. Besides its touching faith in market miracles, the approach does not acknowledge the critical role and responsibility of the state in poverty reduction.

While micro-finance has enabled some innovative management and entrepreneurial strategies, its overall impact on poverty reduction remains moot. Anis Chowdhury (2011) critically reviews the debate on micro-finance as a poverty reduction tool. Some criticisms – such as of the high interest rates typically charged for microcredit, despite the high rate of implicit subsidization and the social opportunity cost of such subsidies – are already well known.

Micro-finance provides credit for contingencies and for smoothening consumption while borrowers may also benefit from learning-by-doing and from developing greater self-esteem as a consequence. By 'democratizing' the credit market, the micro-finance movement has not only curtailed the power of moneylenders, but also constrained creditors' excesses in dealing with poor borrowers. However, to make any significant dent on poverty, the focus of public policy should be on growth-oriented, equity-enhancing programmes, such as broad-based productive employment creation.

Poor people not only lack current income, but also the economic assets with which to generate incomes. For billions of rural poor and urban squatters, access to land may not be well recognized legally. While legislation may provide more secure land tenure for the poor, and thus reduce poverty, this outcome is hardly assured by simply strengthening property rights or by the rule of law. Policies that have not taken into account the complexities of strengthening property rights have backfired, sometimes even reducing poor people's security of tenure.

Ruth Meinzen-Dick (2011) has reviewed links between property rights and poverty reduction, including the gender distribution of property rights. She highlights the ambiguous nature of property rights, the implications of multiple claims on property, and how this complicates property rights reform. Meinzen-Dick also explores the implications of strengthening property rights for the poor, particularly how understanding legal pluralism can lead to more effective policies and interventions to strengthen poor people's control over assets.

Economic security depends on the ability to cope with shocks, uncertainty and hazards, and to recover from adverse developments. Over the last decade, *conditional* cash transfer programmes have been promoted in many parts of the world, often with reference to the Brazilian and Mexican experiences. However, *universal* cash transfers may be a better way of improving economic security, as conditions are likely to be perceived as instrumental, patronizing and not consistent with a genuine recognition of rights. Meanwhile, rapid globalization, climate change and other sources of economic insecurity increasingly threaten livelihoods.

Guy Standing (2011) reviews evidence of outcomes of various non-cash transfers, such as food aid or vouchers, vis-à-vis various types of cash transfer schemes implemented in developing countries. In contrast to food aid and vouchers, which have distortionary effects on domestic production and consumption patterns, cash transfers promote work and dignity as well as satisfying various principles of social justice, besides being more efficient and cost-effective. He concludes that the experiences with cash transfers strengthen the case for universal unconditional cash transfers as the best way of ensuring basic incomes for all.

Need to rethink poverty policy

Although the current monetary poverty-line approach provides a useful definition of absolute poverty and allows for various types of comparison, it has considerable shortcomings that could be significantly overcome by multidimensional poverty measurement. The ongoing economic crisis has served as a reminder that poverty is not an attribute of a fixed group, but rather a condition that all vulnerable persons risk experiencing. It is essential for people to be well fed, healthy, educated and housed to be more productive and, in turn, to contribute to society. Approaches to poverty reduction should therefore be developmental and holistic, integrating economic and social policies to achieve equitable, welfare-enhancing development outcomes.

RWSS 2010 critically examined the conventional policy framework and poverty programmes in the context of persistent poverty, rising inequality and lacklustre growth in many developing countries. Current approaches are largely based on pro-cyclical macroeconomic policies accompanied by microeconomic interventions targeted at the poor. Most do not emphasize the need for governments to play a truly developmental role, but presume government responsibility for reducing poverty. This would entail an integrated approach to economic and social policies designed to promote employment growth, reduce inequality and promote justice in society.

Poverty, and its reduction, always occur within a macroeconomic context. Countries that adopted stabilization measures and structural adjustment programmes generally lowered average economic growth as well as increased inequality and, often, poverty during the 1980s and 1990s, especially in Africa and Latin America. In general, macroeconomic stabilization measures led to declines in public investment and increased the volatility of economic growth and employment.

The mixed record of poverty reduction calls into question the efficacy of conventional approaches involving economic liberalization and privatization. Reductions in public investment in health, education and other social programmes disproportionately affect people living in poverty. They were also adversely affected by increased output and employment volatility, especially since unskilled workers tend to be the first to lose their jobs, and because job recovery generally lags well behind output recovery (see also UN 2011).

Finally, it is important to acknowledge that targeting the poor, so much favoured by conventional approaches, is not only expensive, but also excludes many who are deserving. Furthermore, many poverty programmes favoured by some donors have not been very effective in actually reducing poverty, although some have undoubtedly served to ameliorate the crushing burden of poverty, especially during times of crisis. For example, microcredit has helped 'smooth' consumption by the poor, but its contribution to poverty reduction has been more modest.

In light of the preceding observations, policies for poverty reduction should therefore include:

- *Macroeconomic policies for the rapid, sustained growth of output, incomes and employment.* Countries should be able to pursue consistently counter-cyclical fiscal and monetary policies to achieve stable growth and to boost employment and incomes to reduce poverty; fiscal and monetary restrictions should not be unnecessarily stringent. Macroeconomic stabilization should not be limited to controlling inflation, trade and fiscal deficits – as has been the case in recent decades. Instead, it should be consistently counter-cyclical, not only to reverse downturns, but also to check against booms generating unsustainable bubbles. Macroeconomic policy can play an important counter-cyclical role, especially if resources are accumulated during boom periods, and then deployed to fund expansionary policies during downturns. Macroeconomic policies can be supportive by accommodating counter-cyclical measures and development activities, especially by supporting measures to promote employment and reduce poverty. Public social expenditures should be safeguarded and even increased – counter-cyclically – during economic downturns.

- *Social policy must consider the determinants of poverty as well as asset and income inequality.* Social policy and spending can be important in breaking the intergenerational transmission of inequality and poverty. Many country experiences show that employment and universal social protection are central to poverty reduction. Expansion of social policies and programmes (e.g. to provide a social protection floor) is usually essential to protecting society's more vulnerable members against livelihood shocks and risks, to enhance the social status and rights of the marginalized, and to protect workers against ill health, unemployment and destitution, in an integrated manner. The current global crises and their social impacts in developed and developing countries further underscore the importance of providing a universal social protection floor, i.e. for the poor as well as the non-poor (UN 2011). While there has been progress in advancing education and health in developing countries over the last decade, serious gaps remain. There are important discrepancies in access between children from rich and poor households, in urban and rural areas, as well as other major determinants of well-being.

Public social expenditures, particularly investments in education and health, are critical for human resource development.

- *Promotion of participation, inclusion and voice of poor* people is crucial to overcoming some of the political and structural determinants of poverty and its perpetuation. The importance of participation for poverty reduction is based on the fundamental premise that people, including those living in poverty, not only have the right to influence decisions that affect their lives, but are also crucial participants in transforming and improving their conditions. It is therefore crucial to remove barriers to participation and to proactively promote the social inclusion and voice of poor people.

The reshaping of the global development discourse over the last decade and a half in terms of the Millennium Development Goals (MDGs) has had profound and far-reaching consequences. The MDG1a incidence of poverty indicator has become the single most important indicator of development for the MDGs. While this chapter has not addressed whether the attention given to this indicator is appropriate, it raises some serious concerns about how poverty has been measured for MDG reporting purposes. As the original poverty line was defined principally in terms of the cost of securing enough food, comparing the poverty indicator to the MDG1c hunger or prevalence of undernourishment indicator is revealing. The significant differences between regional and country poverty and hunger trends during the MDG reporting period must surely raise concerns about both indicators. The chapter has also raised other problems with the MDG-related poverty discourse, underscoring the inadequacy of the conventional poverty policy discourse. As poverty is likely to continue to be the most watched indicator in the post-2015 Sustainable Development Goals, it is important to urgently take this opportunity to review and reconsider poverty measurement, analysis and policies.

Notes

1 I am grateful to Anis Chowdhury for his support and collaboration since 2008, especially in preparing *Poor Poverty* (Jomo and Chowdhury 2011), *RWSS 2010* (United Nations 2010) and *RWSS 2011* (United Nations 2011), which this chapter draws upon, and in helping update some recent poverty data. I am also appreciative of the work of Carlo Cafiero, who was principally responsible for the new hunger estimation methodology in SOFI 2012 (FAO 2012) and contributed to the new graphs included here. Finally, I must thank Thomas Pogge for his improvement of

the discussion on US inflation adjustment here. Of course, none of them should be held responsible for this chapter, for which I take sole responsibility.

2 Source: PovcalNet, iresearch. worldbank.org/PovcalNet/index.htm?1.

3 PovcalNet has data for India for 1983, not 1981.

4 Personal communication.

5 See www.bls.gov/data/inflation_ calculator.htm.

6 One can use PovcalNet, iresearch. worldbank.org/PovcalNet/index.htm, to see what a difference this makes.

7 The Multidimensional Poverty Index (MPI) is published by the Oxford Poverty and Human Development Initiative (OPHI)

and the United Nations Development Programme. See www.ophi.org.uk/ multidimensional-poverty-index/mpi-2014/.

8 The companion volume to *Rethinking Poverty* is entitled *Poor Poverty: The Impoverishment of Analysis, Measurement and Policies*. As the subtitle implies, *Poor Poverty* considers various dimensions of poverty in rather different ways. The volume shows how poverty measurement, analysis and policies have been compromised and undermined. Together, the two volumes offer important challenges to recent thinking on addressing poverty, raising important questions about poverty analysis and poverty reduction policies in recent decades.

References

Blanchard, O., G. Dell'Ariccia and P. Mauro (2010) 'Rethinking macroeconomic policy', IMF Staff Position Note SPN/10/03, 12 February.

Chowdhury, A. (2011) 'How effective is microfinance as a poverty reduction tool?', in K. S. Jomo and A. Chowdhury (eds), *Poor Poverty: The Impoverishment of Analysis, Measurement and Policies*, London/New York: Bloomsbury Academic in association with the United Nations.

FAO (2012) *The State of World Food Insecurity, 2012*, Rome: Food and Agriculture Organization of the United Nations.

Ghosh, J. (2011) 'Poverty reduction in China and India: policy implications of recent trends', in K. S. Jomo and A. Chowdhury (eds), *Poor Poverty: The Impoverishment of Analysis, Measurement and Policies*, London/New York: Bloomsbury Academic in association with the United Nations.

Growth Commission (2008) *The Growth Report: Strategies for Sustained Growth and Inclusive Development*, Washington, DC: World Bank.

Jomo, K. S. and J. Baudot (eds) (2007) *Flat World, Big Gaps: Economic Liberalization, Globalization, Poverty and Inequality*, London: Zed Books.

Jomo K. S. and A. Chowdhury (eds) (2011) *Poor Poverty: The Impoverishment of Analysis, Measurement and Policies*, London/New York: Bloomsbury Academic in association with the United Nations.

Kapur, D., J. P. Lewis J and R. C. Webb (eds) (1997) *The World Bank: Its First Half Century*, Washington, DC: Brookings Institution.

Karnani, A. (2011) 'The bottom of the pyramid strategy for reducing poverty: a failed promise', in K. S. Jomo A. Chowdhury (eds), *Poor Poverty: The Impoverishment of Analysis, Measurement and Policies*, London/New York: Bloomsbury Academic in association with the United Nations.

Khan, M. (2011) 'Governance, growth and poverty reduction', in K. S. Jomo and A. Chowdhury (eds), *Poor Poverty: The Impoverishment of Analysis, Measurement and Policies*, London/New York: Bloomsbury Academic in association with the United Nations.

Meinzen-Dick, R. (2011) 'Property rights for poverty reduction?', in K. S. Jomo and A. Chowdhury (eds), *Poor Poverty: The Impoverishment of Analysis, Measurement and Policies*, London/New York: Bloomsbury Academic in association with the United Nations.

Oxfam (2014) *Even It Up: Time to End Extreme Inequality*, Oxford: Oxfam International.

Reddy, S. (2009) 'The emperor's new suit: global poverty estimates reappraised', in K. S. Jomo and A. Chowdhury (eds), *Poor Poverty: The Impoverishment of Analysis, Measurement and Policies*, London/New York: Bloomsbury Academic in association with the United Nations.

Reinert, E. (2011) 'The terrible simplifiers: common origins of financial crises and persistent poverty in economic theory and the new "1848 Moment"', in K. S. Jomo and A. Chowdhury (eds), *Poor Poverty: The Impoverishment of Analysis, Measurement and Policies*, London/New York: Bloomsbury Academic in association with the United Nations.

Standing, G. (2011) 'How cash transfers promote work and economic security', in K. S. Jomo A. Chowdhury (eds), *Poor Poverty: The Impoverishment of Analysis, Measurement and Policies*, London/New York: Bloomsbury Academic in association with the United Nations.

Stiglitz, J. E., J. A. Ocampo, S. Spiegel, R. French-Davis and D. Nayyar (2006) *Stability with Growth: Macroeconomics, Liberalization and Development*, New York: Oxford University Press.

Taylor, L. (2011) 'Growth, development policy, job creation and poverty reduction', in K. S. Jomo and A. Chowdhury (eds), *Poor Poverty: The Impoverishment of Analysis, Measurement and Policies*, London/

New York: Bloomsbury Academic in association with the United Nations.

Toye, J. (1987) *Dilemmas of Development: Reflections on the Counter-Revolution in Development Theory and Policy*, Oxford: Basil Blackwell.

UN (United Nations) (2005) *The Inequality Predicament: Report on the World Social Situation 2005*, New York: United Nations.

— (2007) *The Employment Imperative: Report on the World Social Situation 2007*, New York: United Nations.

— (2010) *Rethinking Poverty: Report on the World Social Situation 2010*, New York: United Nations.

— (2011) *The Global Social Crisis: Report on the World Social Situation 2011*, New York: United Nations.

UNDP (2014) *Human Development Report 2014*, New York: Human Development Report Office, United Nations Development Programme.

Weisbrot, M., R. Ray, J. Johnston, J. A. Cordero and J. A. Montecino (2009) 'IMF-supported macroeconomic policies and the world recession: a look at forty-one borrowing countries', Washington, DC: Center for Economic Policy Research, October.

Williamson, J. (1990) 'What Washington means by policy reform', in J. Williamson (ed.), *Latin American Adjustment: How Much Has Happened?*, Washington, DC: Institute for International Economics.

World Bank (1997) *World Development Report 1997*, Washington, DC: World Bank.

— (2009) *Global Monitoring Report 2009: A Development Emergency*, Washington, DC: World Bank.

— (2013) 'The state of the poor: where are the poor and where are they poorest?', www.worldbank.org/content/dam/Worldbank/document/State_of_the_poor_paper_April17.pdf.

3 | THE VIEW FROM DEPRIVATION: POVERTY, INEQUALITY AND THE DISTRIBUTION OF WEALTH

Deborah S. Rogers and Bálint Balázs

Introduction

... the gap between the rich and poor is observed to be increasing with time. The causes given to us [in India] were corruption and exploitation of the poor by the rich in various forms.

(Rogers 2012)

In a series of Field Hearings held in communities around Bhopal, India, meeting conveners were told by people that their poverty was caused by decisions and actions of the privileged (Rogers 2012). People in various poverty-stricken communities across Asia and Africa provided similar explanations. Academics and policy analysts tend to ignore this evidence, generating studies instead on the perverse incentives created by provision of assistance, the entrenched culture of poverty, spatial clustering of reduced opportunity, the natural probabilistic distribution of income, the education gap, the technology gap, health disparities, deficits in social capital, and even alleged innate differences in IQ.

But what if the people who spoke at these Field Hearings are right?

In this chapter we consider the possibility that the people living in these poverty-stricken communities are telling us something fundamental: that the decisions and actions of those with money are primary causes of inequality, poverty and impeded development. By this interpretation, we would predict the following:

1 We expect to see positive correlations between poverty and economic inequality – over time and space.
2 We expect that reductions in poverty would occur when reductions in economic inequality (e.g. redistributions) take place.
3 We expect to observe clear mechanisms by which those with wealth perpetuate or enhance levels of inequality and poverty.

In this chapter, we first present qualitative information contributed by people who experience poverty, identifying mechanisms by which the unequal distribution of wealth adds up to generate poverty. We then look at a number of key studies through this lens, concluding that there is clear evidence for the three predictions above, and thus that such interpretation has important explanatory power. Finally, we suggest the implications of this for crafting post-2015 Sustainable Development Goals which would be more effective at reducing poverty and promoting sustainable development.

Bringing in community perspectives

Those who have the most to lose often have the least power to influence research and policy processes. But is it legitimate to bring the perspectives of non-researchers – the subjects themselves – into research addressing policy-related questions? A relatively recent literature on transdisciplinary research, participatory assessments and participatory action research suggests that it is not only legitimate but necessary to meaningful research. Literature on policy analysis increasingly shows that by bringing in the public through participatory and deliberative approaches, policy-making can be successfully influenced by those who are living in poverty, marginalized or excluded. In recent decades participatory methods have become popular in poverty analysis and assessments initiated by NGOs, governments and multinational agencies, and have also occupied the mainstream of development practice to some degree. However, they have only partially succeeded in giving voice to those in poverty.

Approaches such as Participatory Assessments (PAs), Participatory Rural Appraisal (PRA), Rapid Rural Appraisal (RRA) and Participatory Action Research (PAR) have become, according to Chambers, a growing family of methods that enable local people to share, enhance and analyse their knowledge, and to plan and act (Chambers 1997). In such approaches, local realities are captured through local people's perspectives, and are debated in constructive dialogues among stakeholders along issues of common concern. This requires a complete reversal in attitude by the researcher, moving away from the 'cult of expertise' that reproduces social inequalities. According to Chambers, 'self-critical epistemological awareness' is needed for the researcher to act as a facilitator in local knowledge settings (ibid.). The emphasis in participatory arrangements is on how to create communicative arenas open to all stakeholders, and particularly to powerless lay members of local communities, in order to arrive at collective and mutual understanding (Meppem and Gill 1998). Collaborative actions are generated through engagement with all aspects of the research, from problem structuring to reporting (Balázs et al. 2005).

Transdisciplinary research, like participatory research, brings disciplinary researchers and local actors together in a collaborative process. Meaningful cooperation requires strong social and communication skills to integrate different perspectives and action domains. According to Pohl and Hadorn, transdisciplinary research is defined by the need to grasp the complexity of problems, to take into account the diversity of life-world and scientific problem perceptions, to link abstract and case-specific knowledge, and to develop knowledge and practices that promote what is perceived to be the common good (Pohl and Hadorn 2008). In this context, transdisciplinary research proves to be useful in producing normative and practice-oriented knowledge to solve complex life-world problems.

Most participatory research focuses on public health, education, food security and poverty reduction, offering effective and acceptable policy instruments for national and local contexts. Such participatory policy-focused research helps to uncover how social reality is lived and resisted on the grassroots level; therefore policies are considered more transformative than are simple technocratic interventions. Criticisms of participatory arrangements most often point to the lack of principled theory, which implies that practitioners do what they believe will work in various contexts. Structural inequalities and existing institutional and power relations are often blamed, because local realities cannot be readily reconciled with the ideal of broad and equal participation (Bodorkós and Pataki 2009). Binary opposites such as local/global and state/civil society need to be overcome in order for participatory arrangements to be relevant (Mohan and Stokke 2000).

According to Pretty, in such arrangements participation must be considered a right – not a tool to achieve research goals (Pretty 1995). Participation in interactive forms builds on self-mobilization and results in participatory learning processes where groups take control over local decisions, determining how resources are used or how they can have a stake in maintaining practices. A central criticism of participatory arrangements relates to the role of research itself, and to the defined role of the researcher, who at some point must inevitably implement the value-laden process of problem structuration and synthesis of the research.

Another potential problem is the influence of local representation that shapes participatory research; in other words, how to break away from prevailing local structural inequalities through a participatory process which is designed around consensus-building (Chambers 1997). According to Bodorkós and Pataki, hindrances in creating communicative spaces equally open to all can be traced back to the difficulties of changing historically rooted, paternalistic relationships between local people and local establishments, and the lack of a sense of self-efficacy and self-confidence of marginalized people in expressing their wants (Bodorkós and Pataki 2009). Bina Agarwal's work on participatory exclusion argues that hierarchical and patriarchal structures within communities create an environment where 'the poor' may appear to be consulted, but actually cannot express their genuine views, as that would subsequently endanger their situation in the community (Agarwal 2001).

The most prominent and extensive research that emphasized the participatory assessment methodology is the 'Voices of the Poor' project, undertaken by the World Bank in the 1990s (Narayan 2000; Narayan and Petesch 2002; Narayan et al. 2000). The twenty-three-country study compiled interviews from over 60,000 people (in some cases taken from other sources) through Participatory Poverty Assessments (PPAs). Key findings that emerged from the project include the following:

People living in poverty feel they have been bypassed by new economic opportunities. Access to markets and/or links to higher levels of society are hindered by their powerlessness and lack of resources for fair participation. But they view well-being holistically: poverty is much more than income alone. For them, the good life or well-being is multidimensional, with both material and psychological dimensions. People in poverty care about many of the same things all of us care about: happiness, family, children, livelihood, peace, security, safety, dignity and respect (World Bank 2000).

Healthcare is reported as unavailable or too expensive. Education received by young people is inadequate. Gender inequity is widespread, domestic violence pervasive and gender relations stressed: loss of traditional male 'breadwinner' and female 'caretaker' roles (because of changing economic circumstances) is traumatic for both genders, and family breakdown, domestic violence and increased alcoholism among men are often mentioned (ibid.).

According to the findings, insecurity has increased and violence is on the rise, both domestically and in society. A majority of people living in poverty feel they are worse off and more insecure than in the past. Corruption is a key issue: they want governments and state institutions to be more accountable to them. From their perspective, corruption, irrelevance and abusive behaviour ruin the formal institutions of the state (ibid.).

The Equity and Sustainability Field Hearings

The Equity and Sustainability Field Hearings project updates results of the 'Voices of the Poor' project, focusing more directly on equality and equitable development. A global collaboration between academics, NGOs and local communities, the project has worked to ensure that voices from poor and marginalized communities are included in discussions such as the post-2015 Sustainable Development Goals process (Rogers et al. 2014). As argued in *Whose Reality Counts?* (Chambers 1997), sustainable well-being is only possible if shaped from the bottom up. Instead of conducting research on how to achieve sustainable societies – which assumes that researchers know the goals of such a process – the Field Hearings seeks input from local community members on what their goals would be.

In early 2012, following a broad call for partners, Initiative for Equality[1] embarked on this global project along with eighteen local academic and civil society organizations (Rogers 2012). Field Hearings were conducted in thirty-four communities in Bangladesh, China, India, Kyrgyzstan, Mauritius, the Philippines, Malawi, Nigeria, South Africa, Uganda, Hungary and Scotland. Project participants jointly developed a questionnaire or reporting template in English, which local partners then translated and modified to be appropriate for their own communities. Using public meetings, focus groups or individual interviews (depending on what worked best for each community), respondents were asked to assess trends in their community (for health, education, the economy, politics, conflict, families, happiness, circumstances for women and other areas); speculate about the causes of these trends; propose changes needed for their community to become sustainable; describe how privilege and deprivation work in their community; and articulate their wishes for the future of their family and community.

The preliminary results, based on interviews, focus group discussions and public hearings with over 2,700 individuals, provided a surprisingly uniform view of inequality and how it operates in the lives of those living in poverty (ibid.). The gap between wealthy and poor was seen by most Field Hearings participants as increasing. Many expressed concern that growing inequality wipes out any gains made in economic development. Almost every community worried about the growing lack of economic security: jobs are difficult to find and may not last. Economic opportunities are scarce and generally available only to those with connections. Young people do not feel hopeful about their economic future.

The wishes articulated by most respondents were straightforward, basic and sustainable – not acquisitive (ibid.). They want stable incomes and a secure future, with food, healthcare and education for their children; responsive and accountable governments that work to create opportunities for all, regardless of ethnicity or economic class; and access to opportunities and decision-making.

What did community members have to say about poverty and inequality? Those with wealth are viewed as having access to political decision-making, which they use to create further economic opportunities for themselves (ibid.). Some cited racial or ethnic discrimination as a root cause of these problems, while others blamed 'selfishness' by the rich, or the relationship between political power and business opportunities. Corruption and a lack of accountability and transparency on the part of government officials were said to deprive lower income groups of economic opportunities, even when funds have been allocated on their behalf. This is seen as a primary way in which inequality is perpetuated. Furthermore, lack of trust and unity among community members blocks the collaboration necessary for effective problem resolution and new approaches to development and sustainability.

Global and regional poverty

This, then, is what participatory research tells us. How does this tally with hard data on poverty and inequality?

Globally, the total poverty headcount and rate are down from those of several decades ago. According to data released in 2012 by the World Bank's Development Research Group, 1.29 billion people or 22 per cent of the developing world's population lived on $1.25 or less

Box 3.1 Perspectives from Field Hearings community participants (Rogers 2012)

'The level of inequality has increased drastically over the years, which has led the well-being of people at poverty level to a much worse situation.' (Bangladesh)

'The privileged group believes it is their divine right to possess all they want. Deprived groups are left in a helpless situation and cannot escape it without monetary help, which is only accessible from wealthy people. Unfortunately, privileged and rich people are only concerned about their own situation and what they "need".' (Kyrgyzstan)

'They complained that the rich are not creating a favourable environment for the poor to graduate from one level to another economically ... The participants also complained about the greedy mind of the politician, on accumulating riches on their own at the expense of poor people.' (Malawi)

'They do not feel they have chance to influence the decision-making.' (China)

'Corruption, poor governance, wrong economic policy, and political unwillingness are responsible for the wealth inequality and income disparity. This also works as an obstacle to economic progress and social harmony and happiness.' (Nigeria)

'Negative discrimination, as a direct link to human rights violations, appears in every aspect of life; especially in employment and education, as well as in the relationship with the public service providers.' (Hungary)

'They attribute this to the ability of the rich to access better services such as health and education; engagement of the rich in activities that make worse the conditions of the poor such as land grabbing, and degradation of wetlands which would support the livelihoods of the poor; public opinion by the poor often being ignored in planning and decision-making; and unfair competition.' (Uganda) a day in 2008, down from 1.94 billion or 52 per cent in 1981 (World Bank 2012). Preliminary estimates indicate that this number may have fallen to 1.2 billion people by 2012 (Ravallion 2013).

Much of this reduction of extreme poverty took place in China, which had 663 million fewer people living on less than $1.25 a day in 2008 than in 1981 (World Bank 2012). However, even the picture in China is not completely rosy. While rural poverty was falling, studies showed that urban poverty rose during the massive influx of rural migrants to work in urban areas. Even so, it is likely to be an underestimate of urban poverty because these migrants are not counted in the urban census (Meng et al. 2005).

Excluding China, the total extreme poverty headcount has not improved. The headcount in all other developing countries was around 1.1 billion people in 2008, roughly the same as in 1981, though the number had risen and then fallen since 1999 (World Bank 2012). More people fell into poverty in South Asia over this period, despite India's rapid economic growth over the past decade (Broad and Cavanagh 2012). The Asian Development Bank has found that extreme poverty in Asia is not adequately captured at $1.25/day (Asian Development Bank 2014: 10). At the $1.25/day poverty line there are about 733 million people in extreme poverty in Asia, but using the more realistic $1.51/day cut-off raises the extreme poverty rate to 49.5 per cent or 1.75 billion people (ibid.: 11). The share of the population living on less than $2 a day in South Asia has declined since 1990 to about 40 per cent in 2011, but not sufficiently to reduce the absolute number of poor, which rose steadily between 1987 and 2011 (Bigsten and Levin 2005; ESCAP 2014: 14). Throughout the Asia-Pacific region, an additional 933 million people are living on $1.25–$2 a day since 1990 (ESCAP 2014: 14).

Sub-Saharan Africa reduced the $1.25-a-day poverty rate to an estimated 47 per cent of total population in 2008, and has experienced falling absolute numbers of the extreme poor since 2005, reversing a long-run increase since 1981 (World Bank 2012). Resource-rich African nations experienced high rates of economic growth, especially from 2000–11 (Africa Progress Panel 2013). Several African countries successfully reduced the poverty rate; however, others saw level or worsening poverty rates (ibid.).

The Middle East and North Africa region as a whole made substantial reductions in both the poverty rate and headcount over the past two decades. According to the World Bank's PovCal data calculator (World Bank 2013a), the number of people in the Middle East and North Africa region living on under $2/day was 52.9 million in 1990 (23 per cent) and 39.9 million in 2010 (12 per cent).

In Latin America the poverty rate now appears to be significantly lower. An initially high poverty rate, estimated at around 65 per cent in 1950, fell to only 25 per cent by 1980 (Berry 1997). From 1982 through 1993, however, the overall number of persons living in poverty in Latin America increased from 78 to 150 million (Londoño and Szekely 1997). The resumption of moderate economic growth in the 1990s resulted in some progress in reducing poverty (particularly in urban areas). The World Bank's PovCal data calculator (World Bank 2013a) indicates that the number of people in Latin America living on under $2/day was 97.6 million in 1990 (22 per cent) and 60.6 million in 2010 (10 per cent).

Updated figures from the Economic Commission for Latin America and the Caribbean (ECLAC) are not directly comparable because they calculate poverty using a food basket approach (what it costs to feed oneself in each country) rather than the common $1.25/day metric (ECLAC 2014: 54); however, these figures can be compared as to relative trends. ECLAC's figures show that poverty has fallen by 15.7 percentage points since 2002, with extreme poverty also falling significantly (ibid.: 15). By country, poverty levels measured in 2012 ranged from 4.3 per cent in Argentina to 45.3 per cent in El Salvador (ibid.: 17). A multidimensional analysis shows that deprivation of essential needs (housing, sanitation, energy, education) affects from around 5 per cent of the population for Chile to around 70 per cent for Nicaragua – thus there are many who are not categorized as poor in terms of income, but are clearly suffering from deprivation (ibid.: 17).

In eastern Europe and the former Soviet Union, the poverty rate increased from 4 per cent to about 33 per cent during the transition from communism to capitalism from the late 1980s to the early 1990s, representing an increase in headcount from 15 million to over 100 million at a poverty line of $4/day (Milanovic 1995). According to the World Bank's PovCal data calculator (World Bank 2013a), the number of people in the region living on under $4/day has now declined from 130.9 million in 1990 (28 per cent) to 55.7 million in 2010 (12 per cent).

While it seems straightforward to present global poverty rates over time, there are serious conceptual problems with these numbers. Most fundamentally, the very concept of poverty as an expression of monetary income can be challenged. Poverty and well-being are now understood to be multidimensional concepts, including financial assets, access to natural resources, political access, social status and acceptance, location and surrounding environment, health, education, security, vulnerability, self-determination and capabilities, empowerment, and social capital (Alkire and Foster 2011; Chambers 2007; Rogers et al. 2012). A simple measure of monetary income (or consumption) is a very weak proxy for all of these. Furthermore, the same income, even at purchasing parity, means different things in different places. A small income goes much farther in a country where adequate public social services are provided or in a natural environment where food, clean water, housing materials and fuel are freely and equitably available (Broad and Cavanagh 2012). The consumer price index used to calculate purchasing power does not give enough weight to food costs, which are a higher proportion of expenditures for the poor (Cimadamore et al. 2013). Moreover, there are many economic components that do not show up as income at all, including the amount of labour required to earn the income, work outside the monetized economy (often by women), leisure time, and so forth.

The numbers of people in poverty are often presented as averages, but these numbers may hide large movements in the opposite direction (Kanbur 2005). For example, in Mexico during 1990–94, the decrease in national poverty was composed of a drop in urban areas, but an increase in some rural regions. Population growth also affects absolute poverty: in Ghana, for example, while the incidence of poverty was falling at around 1 per cent per year from 1987 to 1991, the total population was growing at almost twice that rate, thus the absolute number of poor grew sizably (ibid.). Finally, the poverty headcount is very sensitive to the numbers used to define poverty. For example, the number of people below \$1.25/day dropped by 32.5 per cent between 1990 and 2008, but numbers below \$2.50 dropped by only 5.3 per cent (Cimadamore et al. 2013). Sensitivity tests also confirm that changes in poverty rates are sensitive to the choice of the poverty line (Naschold 2005).

Global and regional inequality

What do the hard numbers tell us about inequality trends during the past few decades?

Global inequalities between individuals are very high. Calculating global inequalities between the world's individuals, using purchasing power parity rates to assure comparability, results in a Gini coefficient estimate of 70 (Milanovic 2009). Another way of describing global inequality is to divide the income of the world into two halves: the richest 8 per cent of the people will occupy one half, and the other 92 per cent of the population will occupy the other half (Milanovic 2012). From 1988 to 2005, the ratio of the richest 5 per cent to the poorest 25 per cent rose from 185:1 to 297:1 (Cimadamore et al. 2013). The richest 5 per cent of individuals gained an additional 3.49 per cent of income, while the poorest 50 per cent dropped from 3.53 per cent to 2.92 per cent and the poorest quarter dropped from 1.16 per cent to 0.78 per cent (ibid.).

As dramatic as these income inequality measures are, studies which include metrics for wealth, such as financial assets, real estate and savings of various kinds, show an even greater level of inequality globally (Ortiz and Cummins 2011). The International Labour Organization estimates that the global Gini index based on wealth was 89.2 in 2000, significantly higher than the Gini based on global income (ILO 2008). According to UNU-WIDER, the top 10 per cent of adults own 85 per cent of global household wealth (Davies et al. 2008). As Piketty's now famous equation, $r > g$, suggests, when the rate of return on capital, r, significantly exceeds g, the growth rate of the economy, then wealth will be the more significant determinant of inequality (Piketty 2014).

Looked at on the regional or national level, inequality has variously risen, fallen or remained constant. During the 1980s and 1990s, inequality rose in forty-eight out of the seventy-three countries for which sufficient 'high quality' data is available (Cornia and Court 2001). Forty-six out of seventy-three countries analysed had Gini coefficients higher than 0.35–0.40, the threshold beyond which growth and poverty alleviation can be perceptibly affected, while only twenty-nine countries had such high inequality in the early 1980s (ibid.). In contrast, inequality remained constant in sixteen nations, including Brazil, India, Bangladesh and Indonesia, and inequality fell only in nine of the seventy-three sample countries.

For advanced economies (OECD countries), inequality has generally been on the increase. The Gini coefficient stood at an average of 29 in OECD countries in the mid-1980s, but by the late 2000s it had risen to 31.6 (OECD 2011). It rose in seventeen of the twenty-two OECD countries for which long-term data series are available (ibid.). Recent data show that the average income of the richest 10 per cent of the population is about nine times that of the poorest 10 per cent (ibid.).

In the Asia-Pacific region, income inequality grew between 1990 and 2011 in nearly half the countries with comparable data (ESCAP 2014: 14). The Gini coefficient in China increased from 32.4 to 42.1 as reforms led to economic growth (Dollar 2007; ESCAP 2014: 14). In India the Gini rose from 30.8 to 33.9 as growth has bypassed the rural areas where the large majority of the poor live (Cornia and Court 2001; ESCAP 2014: 14). Indonesia's Gini rose from 29.2 to 38.1, while Gini indices for Malaysia (46.2) and the Philippines (43.0) remain among the highest in the region (ESCAP 2014: 14).

Inequality has variously risen, remained level or fallen in the nations of sub-Saharan Africa, starting from initially high levels (Cornia and Court 2001). Many of the resource-rich African countries are highly unequal by international standards. Data developed by the Brookings Institution for Ghana, Nigeria, Tanzania and Zambia (between 1998–2003 and 2005–09) show that the income share taken by the richest decile has increased substantially in each case, while the share going to the other deciles has declined (Africa Progress Panel 2013).

The Middle Eastern and North Africa region has seen some very steep increases in inequality, although this varies from country to country. According to Ortiz and Cummins (2011) using the World Bank's PovCal data calculator (World Bank 2013a), Algeria rose from a Gini of 38.7 in 1990 to 58.7 in 2005, while Turkey stayed level at just under 44.

Inequality has first risen then declined in Latin America over the past few decades. Following the economic crises of the 1980s, inequality rose from already high levels in virtually all countries of Latin America (Cornia and Court 2001; ECLAC 1997). Income inequality has recently fallen in Chile and Mexico, but the richest in these two countries still have incomes more than twenty-five times those of the poorest (OECD 2011). Brazil managed to reduce inequality from a Gini of 60 in 1993 to 54 in 2009 (Birdsall et al. 2011: 11), although it is still far more unequal than any of the OECD countries (OECD 2011). Of the thirteen countries with information available in 2011 or 2012, twelve reported a declining Gini coefficient (ECLAC 2014: 81). Despite this trend, inequality in Latin America still ranks at the top of all regions (Birdsall et al. 2011: 3).

The increase in inequality was universal in eastern Europe and the former Soviet Union, with as much as a twenty-point increase in the Gini coefficient in several countries (Cornia and Court 2001). For example, in Russia the Gini increased from 25.9 in 1989/90 to 40.9 in 1994, immediately after the dismantling of the former communist system. In contrast, in Poland, despite a similar level of 25.5 in 1989/90, the Gini had increased to only 32 by 1995 (Milanovic and Ersado 2008). Between 1990 and 1995 the share of the top decile (region-wide) increased from about 20 per cent of total income to about 25 per cent, while the share of the bottom decile dropped from about 4.5 per cent to 3 per cent of total income (ibid.). Since 1995 the distributions have remained relatively stable or inched slightly upwards (UNU-WIDER 2008).

Prediction 1: Positive correlations between poverty and inequality

During the Equity and Sustainability Field Hearings, people living in poverty told us that the decisions and actions of those with money are a primary cause of poverty and impeded development. If they are right, we would expect to see positive correlations between poverty and economic inequality over time and space. However, in order to analyse the data to look for this relationship, we must first disentangle the influence of other related factors – the most notable of which is economic growth. Growth in per capita income is widely acknowledged to reduce poverty rates, all other things being equal (Ravallion 2005a). When researchers have attempted to untangle the relationship between poverty rates, economic growth (or lack thereof) and distributional inequalities, what have they learned?

In the 1950s, Simon Kuznets found for a cross-section of countries that inequality first increased and then decreased as per capita income increased (Kuznets 1955). The now-famous 'Kuznets Curve' was believed to demonstrate that for poverty reduction to take place in developing countries, it was necessary, at least at first, to accept growing inequality. However, more recent and comprehensive studies have found no evidence that economic growth must be accompanied by rising inequality (Berg and Ostry 2011; Deininger and Squire 1998; Ostry et al. 2014; Piketty 2006; Ravallion and Chen 1997). Rapid growth was associated with falling inequality as often as it was with growing inequality, or with no changes at all (Bigsten and Levin 2005).

Although growth can reduce poverty, growth that is 'distribution-neutral' (i.e. does not alter the fraction of total income obtained by different segments of the population) gives greater gains to the rich. For example, for any growth rate, the income gain to the richest decile in India will be about four times higher than the gain to the poorest quintile; while it will be nineteen times higher in Brazil (Ravallion 2005a). Growth along with changing levels of inequality can either reduce or increase poverty rates, depending on the relative rates of growth and inequality. In the formerly communist transition economies, Milanovic and Ersado (2008) found that growth was often strongly anti-poor, as the acceleration of growth generally left the income share of the poor lower. (This does not necessarily indicate that their average income had gone down, though, since a smaller share might have been counterbalanced by a higher overall income.)

Several studies indicate that high inequality in itself may reduce growth rates and thus block poverty reduction (Aghion et al. 1999; Berg and Ostry 2011; Cornia and Court 2001; Deininger and Squire 1998; Keefer and Knack 2002; Ostry et al. 2014). Rent-seeking and predatory activities tend to rise, and work incentives for the poor are diminished. Rural economies with land concentration in a few hands face very high shirking and supervision costs owing to lack of incentives for untenured agricultural workers, and tend to have lower yields per hectare than do more equitable agrarian systems. High inequality has also been shown to limit progress in education, reproductive health and human capital. High levels of income inequality between classes and among social, ethnic, religious and occupational groups can also increase political instability, crime and social problems, thus negatively affecting growth. From a business perspective, such social tensions tend to erode the security of property rights, augment the threat of expropriation, drive away domestic and foreign investment, and increase the cost of business security and contract enforcement (Cornia and Court 2001).

Empirical data from the past several decades show that, considered in conjunction with growth, higher levels of inequality raise poverty rates while greater equality reduces poverty. For a study of fifty developing countries, the median rate of decline in the proportion of the population living below $1 per day was 1.3 per cent per year in countries with both rising average income and rising inequality, but it was seven times higher – about 10 per cent per year – in the countries that combined growth with falling inequality (Ravallion 2005a). Among contracting economies, when inequality was rising while average living standards fell, the poverty rate rose by a dramatic 14 per cent per year on average, while with falling inequality the poverty rate rose by less than 2 per cent per year (ibid.).

Empirical studies have also found that higher inequality is associated with higher poverty at a given mean income (Fields 2001; Ravallion 2005b). Besley and Burgess, for example, find a significant positive coefficient for inequality when they regress the log headcount index for the $1/day poverty line on both the log mean income and a measure of inequality (Besley and Burgess 2003).

Ravallion assembled data on about 170 'spells' spanning two surveys for each of about seventy developing countries in the 1990s (Ravallion 2005b). For each survey, he calculated a measure of poverty and a measure of inequality. There is a relatively strong *positive* (unconditional) correlation, with a correlation coefficient of 0.31. Poverty incidence does not change, on average, if inequality does not change. Looking just at the subset of growing economies, the relationship is even steeper (ibid.). Higher inequality tends to have more impact on poverty when the incidence of poverty is lower. However, even if one confines the analysis to countries with above-average initial poverty rates (greater than 15 per cent), there is a significant positive correlation between rising relative inequality and rising poverty (ibid.). Across the fifty observations for eastern Europe and Central Asia, the correlation coefficient is 0.62 – even higher than for the full sample. The countries for which poverty rose the most in eastern Europe and Central Asia were those for which inequality rose the most (ibid.).

Over the past three decades, China has had high levels of economic growth, falling poverty rates, and periods of growing inequality (ibid.). On the face of it, this would contradict the hypothesis. However, the periods of more rapid growth did *not* coincide with more rapid increases in inequality. Indeed, the periods of falling inequality (1981– 85 and 1995–98) had the highest growth in average household income. Secondly, the provinces that saw a more rapid rise in rural inequality saw *less* progress against poverty, not more (ibid.).

Naschold estimated the effect of growth versus changes in income distribution on poverty by calculating point elasticities from the cumulative distribution of per capita consumption from individual household surveys, using the PovCal software and the latest available household survey for each country (Naschold 2005). The Gini elasticities all had the expected positive sign, meaning that poverty increases as the distribution of income becomes more unequal (and vice versa).

In the 1990s, several observers noted the close relationship between trends in inequality and trends in poverty in Latin America (Korzeniewicz and Smith 2000). For example, Birdsall and Londoño commented that, in Latin America, at least half of the rise in poverty in the 1980s (50 million additional poor) was due to the deterioration in income distribution (Birdsall and Londoño 1997). During the 1990s, income distribution worsened, exacerbating the negative effects of limited growth on poverty reduction. The impact of deterioration in income distribution during the period 1982–92 was so large that it eclipsed the effects of the subsequent recovery in the growth rates of the region (ibid.). Berry asserted that 'little poverty would exist if the income share of the bottom few deciles were not so low' (Berry 1997). Other analysts acknowledged that economic growth in the 1990s had done far less to ameliorate poverty than stagnation in the 1980s did to deepen it (Tokman 1997). In the past decade, poverty and inequality have been declining across Latin America. For reasons which appear to be related to better education and stronger social protections programmes, of the seventeen countries for which good data are available, twelve have experienced significant declines in inequality (Birdsall et al. 2011: 2).

There is evidence that economic inequality is rising along with economic growth in resource-rich African countries, thus harming the potential for poverty reduction (Africa Progress Panel 2013). Using household surveys to track consumption, poverty and income distribution at two points in time, the Brookings Institution looked at the relationship between growth, inequality and poverty reduction in Ghana, Nigeria, Tanzania and Zambia. In each of the countries there was a significant gap between the anticipated poverty reduction effects of growth, and the actual outcomes (ibid.). In two cases – Ghana and Tanzania – poverty fell, but by less than expected on the basis of the reported growth. In Tanzania, growth based on the initial pattern of income distribution would have been expected to bring another 720,000 people out of poverty. In Zambia, poverty increased despite the fact that the reported increase in consumption was predicted to lift another 660,000 people out of poverty. In the same four-year period in Zambia, the richest 10 per cent saw their share of consumption increase from 33 to 43 per cent, while the consumption share of the poorest 10 per cent fell from 2.6 to 1.4 per cent. In Nigeria, the consumption record pointed to a predicted increase in poverty, but the actual increase was far higher than anticipated, by some 6.7 million people.

Increased inequality explains the apparent discrepancy between anticipated and achieved poverty reduction in Africa. The wealthiest 10 per cent captured a large part of the increase generated by growth, while the poorest 40 per cent saw their share of income decline. In other words, economic growth is driving an increasingly unequal pattern of wealth distribution and weakening the link between growth and poverty reduction (ibid.).

Prediction 2: Reductions in poverty with reductions in inequality

It is clear from the above that poverty is worsened by growing inequality. But can existing poverty be reduced by reductions in inequality? Heltberg explains that a reduction in inequality may reduce poverty for a given level of income, accelerate the poverty-reducing impact of economic growth, and contribute to a larger rate of growth (Heltberg 2005). Although Heltberg does not mention it, reductions in inequality may also be effective at poverty reduction by enhancing the ability of poor people to influence political decision-making, and thereby push for fairer rules that will reduce inequality and poverty even farther.

We can demonstrate the direct impact of increased distributional equality on poverty reduction fairly precisely by analysing actual instances of poverty reduction through increased distributional equality, by considering hypothetical transfers of specific dollar amounts from the very wealthy to the very poor, and by using simple mathematical models to contrast the poverty reductions achieved through growth with those achieved through redistribution.

Real-world instances of poverty reduction show that lowering inequality can have a significant positive impact. Hanmer and Naschold separate a sample of 121 poverty observations into two groups: those with Ginis above 0.43 and those below 0.43 (Hanmer and Naschold 2000). They found that the high-inequality countries needed growth rates around three times as high in order to achieve the same rate of poverty reduction as the low-inequality countries. White and Anderson looked at 143 growth episodes from around the world, breaking down changes in the income taken by the lowest quintile into the effects of growth and those of distribution (White and Anderson 2001). They found that in a substantial number of cases the change in income distribution played a significant role, and in over one quarter of the cases, distribution was more important than overall growth in explaining income growth of the poor.

Looking at the projected impact of hypothetical transfers from the very rich to the very poor, it is clear that this, too, could have an enormous impact on reducing poverty. Pogge and Sengupta explain that if the poorest two-fifths of the global population had gained the 2.9 per cent of global household income that was actually gained by the richest 5 per cent between 1988 and 2008, the income of the poorest one fifth would have nearly doubled already – a gain not expected for another ninety-two years under a realistic growth scenario (Pogge and Sengupta 2014). Likewise, we could bring everyone up over the $2/ day level, a task requiring $300 billion per year, if we took just 1.2 per cent of the income of the richest 10 per cent of humanity (Pogge 2013). In a similar vein, Oxfam researchers recently pointed out that the richest 100 billionaires in the world added $240 billion to their wealth in 2012, enough to end world poverty (at the $1.25/day level) four times over (Slater 2013).

Using simulations to contrast the poverty reductions achieved through growth with those achieved through redistribution leads to a similar conclusion. Using real data for a large number of countries, Dağdeviren and colleagues simulated the effects of hypothetical poverty reduction through distribution-neutral growth versus an equal redistribution of each period's growth increment (Dağdeviren et al. 2005). They concluded that redistribution is far more effective for poverty reduction than are distribution-neutral increases in growth.

We developed our own mathematical simulation[2] to show precisely how much more efficient redistribution is at reducing poverty rates as compared with growth of the economy. Results are presented for three examples.

Example 1: Reducing poverty in a very poor country Using numbers which approximate those of Bangladesh in 1995/96, a redistribution of 3 per cent of the income from the top quintile (reduced from 40.2 to 37.2 per cent) to the bottom quintile (raised from 9.3 to 12.3 per cent) results in a reduction in extreme poverty from 20 to 0 per cent. Attempting to reduce poverty by a similar amount through growth of the economy requires an expansion in total income of approximately 45 per cent. (Model parameters included population (117.487 million;

DESA 2011), mean income (US$662.40/year; UNU-WIDER 2008), distribution of income by quintiles (9.3, 12.9, 16.4, 21.3, 40.2; Ortiz and Cummins 2011), an extreme poverty rate estimated as under $365 per person per year; Ravallion et al. 2009; Sachs 2005) – a number which results in about 23.5 million people in abject poverty.)

Example 2: Reducing poverty in a very rich country Using numbers that approximate those of the USA around 2011, a redistribution of 2 per cent of the income from the top quintile (reduced from 50.05 to 48.05 per cent) to the bottom quintile (raised from 3.4 to 5.4 per cent) results in a reduction of the poverty rate from 15 to 0 per cent. However, attempting to reduce poverty by a similar amount through growth of the economy requires an expansion in total income of approximately 110 per cent – i.e. more than doubling the economy. (Model parameters included population (311.59 million; World Bank 2013b), mean income (48,820 PPP international dollars; ibid.), distribution of income by quintiles (3.4, 8.7, 14.7, 23.15, 50.05; Ortiz and Cummins 2011), and a moderate poverty rate estimated as under $10,000 per person per year[3] – a number which results in about 46.7 million people in poverty; Bishaw, 2012.)

Example 3: Reducing poverty globally Using numbers approximating those of the entire world around 2007/08, a redistribution of 1 per cent of the income from the top quintile (reduced from 82.8 to 81.8 per cent) to the bottom quintile (raised from 1.0 to 2.0 per cent) results in a reduction in the poverty rate from 20 to 0 per cent. Attempting to reduce poverty by a similar amount through growth of the economy requires an expansion of total income of approximately 110 per cent – i.e. more than doubling the world's economy. (Model parameters included population (6.73666 trillion; World Bank 2013b), mean income (10,615 PPP international dollars; ibid.), distribution of income by quintiles (1.0, 2.1, 4.2, 9.9, 82.8; Ortiz and Cummins 2011), and estimated poverty rate of under $730 per person per year (Ravallion et al. 2009) – a number which results in about 1.35 billion people in poverty.)

Prediction 3: Mechanisms by which the wealthy perpetuate inequality and poverty

Our Equity and Sustainability Field Hearings learned that people living in poverty view those with wealth as having greater access to political decision-making, which they then use to divert resources and create further economic opportunities for themselves (Rogers 2012). What do analysts have to say about the mechanisms by which the wealthy enable and protect their own opportunities at the expense of the poor? A review of recent academic and journalistic analyses reveals a multitude of well-recognized mechanisms.

- **Cuts in social spending** (ECLAC 1997; Edwards 1995; Kanbur 2005; Korzeniewicz and Smith 2000; OECD 2011; Ortiz and Cummins 2013; Rosenthal 1996): Dismantling of public welfare provisions, including the recent 'austerity' measures, have had a huge impact on people with inadequate incomes by reducing food, education, housing, healthcare, pension and other benefits that contributed to their well-being. During periods of economic stagnation, the need for these programmes grows larger, and thus the benefits per person are often reduced even when the total spent on government programmes remains large. Ironically, unless explicitly accounted for, public services can be reduced considerably and yet not show up in income- or expenditure-based measures of poverty incidence.

- **Lack of progressive taxation** (Africa Progress Panel 2013; Buchheit 2013; Garofalo 2012; Hujo 2012; OECD 2011): Closely related to cuts in social spending is the lack of, or reversal of, progressive taxation that makes such spending possible. In developed countries, which have seen a move away from highly progressive income tax rates and the elimination of net wealth taxes from the mid-1990s to 2005 (according to the OECD), the reduced redistributive capacity of tax-benefit systems was sometimes the main source of widening household income gaps. At the opposite extreme, very poor countries such as the Democratic Republic of Congo are losing revenues as a result of weak management of concessions, aggressive tax planning by companies, tax evasion and corrupt practices. Meanwhile, numerous tax benefits and loopholes provide a congenial environment for big business, resulting in little or no taxes paid by some of the world's largest companies.

- **Shifts from public to private sector** (Megginson and Netter 2001; Milanovic 1995, 1999; Milanovic and Ersado 2008; Stiglitz 2002: 58): The transfer of resources and functions that were once public into the private sector – including healthcare, pensions, education, industries, physical infrastructure, water, police, prisons, and even military functions – is known to result in greater poverty. In the transition economies of eastern Europe and the former Soviet states, a massive expansion of poverty took place between 1990 and 1995 as this transfer occurred. Increased poverty appears to come about through the loss of public sector jobs, which tend to have a more equal wage scale, and through the need to pay for services that were earlier provided by the state. (Milanovic and Ersado (2008) note that privatization of certain small-scale businesses resulted in more jobs for the poor.) In addition to privatization in the USA and in eastern European transition economies, many developing nations, including India, China (which is nominally communist) and nations in sub-Saharan Africa and Latin America, have followed the trend as well (Megginson and Netter 2001: 322–8).

- **Growing wage inequality** (Cornia and Court 2001; Milanovic 1995; OECD 2011): In developed countries, according to the OECD, the single most important driver of growing inequality has been greater inequality in wages and salaries. The earnings of the richest 10 per cent of employees have grown rapidly relative to the poorest 10 per cent, with the largest gains going to the top 1 per cent. Since the 1980s, there has been a widespread shift towards greater wage flexibility, reduced regulation, erosion of minimum wages, lower unionization, dilution of the wage bargaining power of trade unions and higher labour mobility, all correlated with the recent rises in overall inequality observed in OECD, Latin American and transition economy countries.

- **Transfer of income from wage share to capital share** (Cornia and Court 2001; ILO 2014b; UNICEF and UN Women 2013): In recent years, 'jobless growth' has characterized labour markets across the world. Between the 1980s and the mid-2000s, an estimated three-quarters of countries experienced a fall in the wage share of national income, as high as 13 per cent in Latin America and 10 per cent in the EU (UNICEF and UN Women 2013: 22). Between 2000 and 2008, the unadjusted labour share of income declined in all regions except central and eastern Europe and Central Asia (ILO 2014b: 155). Analyses have identified the rise of capital share (and reduction of labour share) of total income as a key component of overall increases in inequality.

- **Decline of trade unions** (ILO 2014b; UNICEF and UN Women 2013): Decline in labour union membership and collective negotiation coverage has played a role in falling wages and benefits, and weakening of labour standards, regulations and institutions.
- **Informalization of employment** (ILO 2012b, 2014b; UNICEF and UN Women 2013): Employment has become increasingly informalized, even where growth rates have been high. Rates of non-agricultural informal labour averaged 40 per cent, ranging from 6 per cent through over 82 per cent in forty-seven developing countries which were analysed (ILO 2012b: 11; ILO 2014a: 12), exposing workers to risky labour contracts, insecurity and lack of protection or benefits, especially among women, people living in poverty and the unskilled.
- **Job insecurity** (Korzeniewicz and Smith 2000; UNICEF and UN Women 2013): Those in poverty have greater job insecurity, especially during times of economic stagnation, because they can be hired and fired as needed by businesses. Coupled with eroding wages and the gap between the formal and informal work sectors, this leaves people in poverty far less able to protect themselves during economic downturns.
- **Unequal access to credit** (UNICEF and UN Women 2013): Inequalities in access to credit aggravate disparities. The largest companies and most wealthy individuals have easy access to large, cheap credit, while those in poverty have only intermittent access to small, short-term loans at great cost. Because returns to capital increasingly exceed returns to labour, unequal access to credit multiplies inequalities further.
- **Asset inequalities** (Edwards 1995; Korzeniewicz and Smith 2000; Lustig 1995; Morley 1994; Piketty 2014: ch. 7; Ramos 1996; UNICEF and UN Women 2013): Clearly, people living in poverty own far less land, property, resources and financial assets. This drives continued poverty through lack of collateral for loans, and lack of ability to gain returns on investment. Asset or wealth inequality is the outcome of intentional policies, including repealing inheritance taxes, reducing progressive taxation rates in the higher brackets, and blocking land reform efforts, as well as systemic assumptions in our economies that reward capital assets over labour.
- **Loss of land, water and other resources** (Africa Progress Panel 2013; Broad and Cavanagh 2012; De Schutter 2011; Korten

2001; Perkins 2004; Stiglitz 2002): Compounding the initial lack of assets of people in poverty, neocolonial practices across Asia, Africa and Latin America have diverted land and resources away from the control and benefit of local communities, and instead into profitable businesses for outside companies and the local elites who facilitate their activities. Policies of the World Bank and the IMF over the decades have greatly enabled this trend. For instance, the development of profitable cash crops in place of subsistence farming wreaked havoc with the ability of local communities to feed themselves, while extraction of mineral resources has enriched multinational companies while destroying the environment on which local communities depend for their sustenance. In recent years, large agricultural landholdings have been acquired by outside interests in scores of countries, from Angola to Zambia (Land Matrix 2015).

- **Resources directed towards urban, capital-intensive sectors** (Africa Progress Panel 2013; Cornia and Court 2001): Resources, international and national, public and private, are much more frequently directed at urban areas and capital-intensive sectors. For example, increased mineral exports in Tanzania generated growth in average income of 70 per cent over the past decade, but this growth has been directed towards capital-intensive sectors such as mining, telecommunications, financial services and construction, and towards urban centres, leaving other sectors behind. Likewise, growth in Ghana has done little to reduce poverty in the northern region. Between 1999 and 2006, the number of poor rural people in northern Ghana increased from 2.2 million to 2.6 million, even as the overall number of those living in poverty nationally fell by just under one million. In Nigeria, while oil exports have resulted in GDP growth of over 5 per cent a year, the unemployment rate has climbed from 15 per cent in 2005 to 25 per cent in 2011. The rural–urban gap also rose in certain Asian countries during the 1990s. The increase of inequality between regions in China accounts for half of the overall increase in income inequality observed in that country since 1985.

There are other mechanisms as well, both long-standing and relatively recent, which ensure that the rich get richer while the poor get poorer. These include well-known systemic phenomena such as regulatory capture and the relationship between wealth and political campaigns and lobbying (Johnston 2005); the corruption which thrives during the process of privatization of public assets (Bjorvatn and Sbreide 2005; Kaufmann and Siegelbaum 1996; Stiglitz 2002; Tangri and Mwenda 2001); economic globalization and liberalization, which allows the biggest players globally to enter local markets and crowd out small-scale entrepreneurs (Stiglitz 2002); the use of military and police forces to open markets, create lucrative opportunities and protect business interests (Ikelegbe 2005; Johnson 2001; Klein 2008); the cumulative increase of disparities through intergenerational inheritance of wealth (Piketty 2014); the rise of purely financial transactions which result in enormous wealth for those who are successful at this game (Dore 2008; Epstein 2005); and finally, the long-term accumulation and centralization of capital (Piketty 2014).

Conclusions from the analysis

In this chapter we have considered a new interpretation, suggested by people living in poverty themselves: that the decisions and actions of those with money are primary causes of inequality, poverty and impeded development. The results of our literature review, simulation and 'Field Hearings' participatory assessment can be summarized as follows:

- Globally, the extreme poverty headcount is down, but this is primarily due to China's efforts; in the rest of the world, extreme poverty is not much different from what it was in 1981, despite decades of economic growth.
- Globally, inequality levels have greatly increased, although this varies from region to region.
- Higher levels of inequality are clearly correlated with higher levels of poverty, thus supporting our first prediction.
- Steps that reduce inequality (i.e. redistribution of income or wealth) lower poverty more efficiently than does economic growth, thus supporting our second expected finding.
- Numerous clear-cut mechanisms by which inequality and poverty are perpetuated by the policies and activities of those with money have been identified, thus supporting our third expected finding.

In short, our proposed interpretation has important explanatory power and needs to be addressed directly if we intend to end poverty and engage in meaningful sustainable development.

According to World Bank economist Branko Milanovic, more than two-thirds of global inequality between individuals is accounted for by location (country) rather than by economic class (Milanovic 2012). But this analysis – with its implication of manifest destiny for certain regions – is misleading because economic class still determines *who* has the opportunity to engage in the activities that generate the enormous disparities between nations, as well as *how* these opportunities are enabled and protected. The *Africa Progress Report 2013*, for example, documents in great detail the financial transactions between multinational corporations and the elites in mineral-rich African states that lead to huge profits for a few and continued impoverishment for the rest (Africa Progress Panel 2013).

An ideological or theory-driven analysis of wealth, inequality and poverty – whether Marxist, neoliberal or something in between – is more inflammatory than helpful in the global discussion about sustainable development. What is essential is a realistic look at the hard data, facts and implications relating poverty to inequality. With that now in hand, we next take a look at what this might mean for effective Sustainable Development Goals, which are currently shaping up in the multilateral context.

Implications for Sustainable Development Goals

What are the implications of these findings from research on poverty, wealth and power for crafting Sustainable Development Goals that would be effective at reducing poverty and promoting sustainable development in the post-2015 era? To date, there has been an attempt to achieve poverty reduction without altering fundamental systemic drivers of inequality or diminishing the privileged status of national and international elites. Our analysis above shows that this approach has been self-defeating, because it continues to generate increasing inequality, which then locks in poverty.

The goals of our Equity and Sustainability Field Hearings respondents – those most in need of sustainable development – included stable incomes and a secure economic future, with food, healthcare and education for their children; responsive and accountable governments that work to create opportunities for all, regardless of ethnicity or economic class; and access to opportunities and decision-making (Rogers 2012). These goals are completely compatible with the concepts of sustainable development and equity, and could readily be framed within a new set of post-2015 Sustainable Development Goals (SDGs). How could the new SDGs respond to these wishes and effectively address inequality and poverty?

In the following, we make some proposals based on the literature, to tackle the poverty–wealth–power nexus:

- The new SDGs must confront inequality directly through a strongly worded stand-alone goal on equality, with strong supporting targets and indicators. This has been recommended by the Inequalities Consultation Advisory Group, one of the Global Thematic Consultations on the Post-2015 Development Agenda, and others (Save the Children 2012; UNICEF and UN Women 2013). Indeed, the Field Hearings network led the successful drive to include Goal 10 of the Open Working Group's outcome document, which explicitly addresses inequality (UN Open Working Group 2014). On the other side of the same coin, Oxfam calls for an end to extreme wealth as one component of the need to address inequality and poverty (Slater 2013).
- Equality must also be incorporated into all the other goals and targets. Since poverty is multidimensional and entangled with all aspects of life, it is necessary to address all types of inequalities (violence and security, gender, health, education, discrimination, human rights, and many others) in order to address poverty effectively (Save the Children 2012; UNICEF and UN Women 2013).
- Furthermore, in order to make the targets meaningful with respect to equality, all monitoring data must be disaggregated by social and economic groups (which might include the lower income or wealth groups, women, excluded minorities, and others who experience significant disadvantages). Otherwise, significant inequalities can hide beneath apparently improving averages (Save the Children 2012; UNICEF and UN Women 2013).
- The following crucial issues must be the subject of strong targets under the primary goal on overcoming inequalities (Goal 10) and other relevant goals, in order to address the main goals of our Equity and Sustainability Field Hearings respondents:

  (1) Stable incomes and a secure economic future

  - Establish a 'social protection floor' below which no one is allowed to fall, funded through public spending; this should be made more explicit in the targets under Goal 1 on poverty reduction (UN Open Working Group 2014; ILO 2012a; Jones 2009; Ortiz and Cummins 2011; UNICEF and UN Women, 2013)

- Policies and programmes generating full employment, including favouring high-employment industries, and public works programmes if needed to make up the gap (Ortiz and Cummins 2011; UNRISD 2010)
- Protection of labour rights, organizing and collective bargaining, worker safety; organizing the informal sector; addressing unpaid work; protection against exploitation, trafficking and slavery (Cornia and Court 2001; UNICEF and UN Women 2013; UNRISD 2010)
- Asset (especially land) redistribution has been shown to be effective at bringing people out of poverty without backsliding; at an international level this should include the return of land as well as appropriate compensation for resources extracted (Cornia and Court 2001; Dağdeviren et al. 2005; Jones 2009; Ortiz and Cummins 2011; UNICEF and UN Women 2013; UNRISD 2010)
- Land grabs and resource extraction benefiting only outsiders and the elites must be stopped, as they are one of the primary mechanisms impoverishing local communities; resource extraction businesses must include contractual guarantees of local benefits (Ortiz and Cummins 2011; UNICEF and UN Women 2013)
- Global economy requires protection of local communities and businesses from harmful practices and impacts of direct foreign investment, non-productive financial transactions, monopolistic practices, etc. (Cornia and Court 2001; UNICEF and UN Women 2013)

(2) Food, healthcare and education

- Public sector spending should include provisions for meeting universal education, health, child and elder care, pensions, physical infrastructure including water and sanitation, policing and other primary needs (Cornia and Court 2001; Jones 2009; Ortiz and Cummins 2011; UNICEF and UN Women 2013; UNRISD 2010)

(3) Responsive and accountable governments

- Broadly inclusive democratic participation in decision-making is crucial to poverty elimination because it allows greater political influence by those experiencing poverty. Targets under Goal 16 on inclusive societies (UN Open Working Group 2014) must include political access and empowerment, publicly funded elections, a free news media, rights to participation by all, rule of law, transparency and accountability of governments, effective anti-corruption policies and enforcement (Jones 2009; Ortiz and Cummins 2011; UNRISD 2010)

(4) Access to opportunities and decision-making

- Targeted action such as quotas, affirmative action and special expenditures and protections for disadvantaged groups that have been excluded for various reasons (Jones 2009; UNRISD 2010)
- Equitable and democratic ownership and control of financial and business enterprises; this could be accomplished through cooperative ventures, municipal development corporations, state-owned banks and industries, or other arrangements (Alperovitz 2005)
- Credit access is critical for those living in poverty, who are generally without collateral, to invest and build up equity in property and businesses (Dağdeviren et al. 2005; Ortiz and Cummins 2011; UNRISD 2010)

(5) Resources to fund the above activities

- Taxation must be direct and progressive, including inheritance taxes; loopholes, tax evasion and offshore schemes must be ended (Cornia and Court 2001; Jones 2009; Ortiz and Cummins 2011; UNICEF and UN Women 2013; UNRISD 2010)
- Debt relief, particularly of sovereign debts that were incurred for the benefit of the few (Ortiz and Cummins 2011)
- New international sources of development finance to redistribute wealth between countries; suggestions have included taxing the arms trade, global environmental taxes (carbon-use tax), and taxing speculative short-term currency flows (the so-called 'Tobin tax') (Ortiz and Cummins 2011)

People who bear the brunt of poverty and inequality are telling us something vital, and their observations are corroborated by hard data. It's time to hear them clearly, and respond effectively.

Acknowledgements

We gratefully acknowledge the many local partners who organized and conducted Equity and Sustainability Field Hearings in 2012, and the thousands of community members who participated by sharing their perspectives – www.initiativeforequality.org. Research conducted by Bálint Balázs received partial funding from the EU FP7 CONVERGE (Rethinking globalisation in the light of contraction and CONVERGEnce; Grant agreement no. 227030) project and the EU FP7 PERARES (Public Engagement with Research and Research Engagement with Society; Grant agreement no. 244264) project.

Notes

1 Initiative for Equality (IfE) is a global network of advocates, academics and community members working together to ensure that poor, socially excluded and marginalized communities are empowered to participate in sustainable development dialogues, decision-making and follow-up monitoring for accountability (www.initiativeforequality.org/).

2 These examples were obtained by running a straightforward mathematical calculation (using MatLab) as follows:

We specify the values for population, mean income and distribution of income to quintiles as mentioned in the text.

We assume that, within each quintile, the income is distributed to each 1 per cent of the population according to a straight-line slope reflecting the percentage increase between the share of income for that quintile and the next highest. For the top quintile, the slope is the same as for the fourth quintile. This assumption is a gross simplification, but in the absence of actual data it is a reasonable estimate.

For calculations involving only growth of the economy, we assume that the additional income is distributed exactly as originally specified; thus, each quintile receives the same fraction of the income as before, but the total absolute amount increases by the specified percentage growth.

For calculations involving only redistribution, we assume that the overall economy does not grow, but that fraction of the income received by the top quintile is reduced by the specified percentage redistribution, while the fraction of income received by the bottom quintile is increased by that same specified percentage.

3 This reference provides statistics on the numbers of people in poverty in the USA; the poverty line cut-off used by the US government is actually a calculation based on numbers of people in the household. We use the approximation of $10,000/person/year in our model in order to obtain the approximate number of people in poverty.

References

Africa Progress Panel (2013) 'Equity in extractives: stewarding Africa's natural resources for all', in *Africa Progress Report 2013*, Geneva: Africa Progress Panel.

Agarwal, B. (2001) 'Participatory exclusions, community forestry and gender', *World Development*, 29(10): 1623–48.

Aghion, P., E. Caroli and C. García-Peñalosa (1999) 'Inequality and economic growth: the perspective of the new growth theories', *Journal of Economic Literature*, 37(4): 1615–60.

Alkire, S. and J. Foster (2011) 'Counting and multidimensional poverty measurement', *Journal of Public Economics*, 95: 476–87.

Alperovitz, G. (2005) *America beyond Capitalism: Reclaiming Our wealth, Our Liberty, and Our Democracy*, Hoboken, NJ: John Wiley & Sons.

Asian Development Bank (2014) *Key Indicators for Asia and the Pacific 2014*, Mandaluyong City, Philippines: Asian Development Bank.

Balázs, B., G. Bela, B. Bodorkós, K. Milánkovics and G. Pataki (2005) 'Preserving bio- and sociodiversity through Participatory Action Research', *Living Knowledge, International Journal of Community Based Research*, 5: 11–13.

Berg, A. G. and J. D. Ostry (2011) *Inequality and Unsustainable Growth: Two Sides of the Same Coin?*, Washington, DC: International Monetary Fund.

Berry, A. (1997) 'The income distribution threat in Latin America', *LARR*, 32(2): 3–40.

Besley, T. and R. Burgess (2003) 'Halving global poverty', *Journal of Economic Perspectives*, 17(3): 3–22.

Bigsten, A. and J. Levin (2005) 'Growth, income distribution, and poverty: a review', in A. Shorrocks and R. van der Hoeven (eds), *Growth, Inequality, and Poverty: Prospects for Pro-poor Economic Development*, Oxford: Oxford University Press.

Birdsall, N. and J. L. Londoño (1997) 'Asset inequality does matter: lessons from Latin America', OCE Working Paper no. 344, Washington, DC: Inter-American Development Bank.

Birdsall, N., N. Lustig and D. McLeod (2011) 'Declining inequality in Latin America: some economics, some politics', Working Paper, Washington, DC: Center for Global Development.

Bishaw, A. (2012) 'Poverty: 2010 and 2011', American Community Survey Briefs, ACSBR/11-01.

Bjorvatn, K. and T. Sbreide (2005) 'Corruption and privatization', *European Journal of Political Economy*, 21: 903–14.

Bodorkós, B. and G. Pataki (2009) 'Local communities empowered to plan?: applying PAR to establish democratic communicative spaces for sustainable rural development', *Action Research*, 7: 313–34.

Broad, R. and J. Cavanagh (2012) 'What do the new World Bank poverty statistics really tell us?', triplecrisis.com/what-do-the-new-world-bank-poverty-statistics-really-tell-us.

Buchheit, P. (2013) '16 giant corporations that have basically stopped paying taxes – while also cutting jobs!', *Alternet*, www.alternet.org/corporate-accountability-and-workplace/16-giant-corporations-have-basically-stopped-paying-taxes.

Chambers, R. (1997) *Whose Reality Counts? Putting the First Last*, London: Intermediate Technology Publications.

Chambers, R. (2007) ' Poverty research: methodologies, mindsets and multidimensionality', IDS Working

Paper no. 293, Brighton: Institute of Development Studies, University of Sussex.

Cimadamore, A. D., R. Deacon, S. Grønmo, G. Koehler, G. T. Lie, K. O'Brien and A. St Clair (2013) 'Poverty and the Millennium Development Goals (MDGs): a critical assessment and a look forward', CROP Policy Brief, Bergen.

Cornia, G. A. and J. Court (2001) 'Inequality, growth and poverty in the era of liberalization and globalization', in *U. W. I. f. D. E. Research* (ed.), Helsinki: UNU-WIDER, pp. 45.

Dağdeviren, H., R. van der Hoeven and J. Weeks (2005) 'Redistribution does matter: growth and redistribution for poverty reduction', in A. Shorrocks and R. van der Hoeven (eds), *Growth, Inequality, and Poverty: Prospects for Pro-poor Economic Development*, Oxford: Oxford University Press.

Davies, J., S. Sandström, A., Shorrocks and E. Wolff (2008) 'The world distribution of household wealth', Discussion Paper no. 2008/03, Helsinki: UNU-WIDER.

De Schutter, O. (2011) 'How not to think of land-grabbing: three critiques of large-scale investments in farmland', *Journal of Peasant Studies*, 38(2): 249–79.

Deininger, K. and L. Squire (1998) 'New ways of looking at old issues: inequality and growth', *Journal of Development Economics*, 57: 259–87.

DESA (2011) 'World population prospects, the 2010 revision', esa.un.org/unpd/wpp/Excel-Data/population.htm.

Dollar, D. (2007) 'Poverty, inequality and social disparities during China's economic reform', World Bank Policy Research Working Paper 4253, World Bank.

Dore, R. (2008) 'Financialization of the global economy', *Industrial and Corporate Change*, 17(6): 1097–1112.

ECLAC (1997) *La brecha de la equidad: América Latina, el Caribe y la cumbre social*, Santiago: United Nations Economic Commission on Latin America and the Caribbean.

— (2014) *Social Panorama of Latin America 2013*, New York: Economic Commission for Latin America and the Caribbean.

Edwards, S. (1995) *Crisis and Reform in Latin America: From Despair to Hope*, New York: Oxford University Press.

Epstein, G. A. (2005) *Financialization and the World Economy*, Cheltenham: Edward Elgar.

ESCAP (2014) *Statistical Yearbook for Asia and the Pacific 2014*, Bangkok: UN Economic and Social Commission for Asia and the Pacific.

Fields, G. S. (2001) *Distribution and Development: A New Look at the Developing World*, Cambridge, MA: MIT Press.

Garofalo, P. (2012) '26 major corporations paid no corporate income tax for the last four years, despite making billions in profits', Think Progress, thinkprogress. org/economy/2012/04/09/460519/major-corporations-no-taxes-four-year/.

Hanmer, L. and F. Naschold (2000) 'Attaining the international development targets: will growth be enough?', *Development Policy Review*, 18: 11–36.

Heltberg, R. (2005) 'The growth elasticity of poverty', in A. Shorrocks and R. van der Hoeven (eds), *Growth, Inequality, and Poverty: Prospects for Pro-poor Economic Development*, Oxford: Oxford University Press.

Hujo, K. (ed.) (2012) *Mineral Rents and the Financing of Social Policy: Opportunities and Challenges*, UNRISD and Palgrave Macmillan.

Ikelegbe, A. (2005) 'The economy of conflict in the oil rich Niger Delta region of Nigeria', *Nordic Journal of African Studies*, 14(2): 208–34.

ILO (2008) 'Income inequalities in the age of financial globalization', *World of Work Report 2008*, Geneva: International Institute for Labour Studies (International Labour Organization).

ILO (2012a) *Social Protection Floors Recommendation*, Rule 202, 101st ILC session, International Labour Organization, www.ilo.org/dyn/normlex/en/f?p=NORMLEXPUB:12100:0::NO::P12100_INSTRUMENT_ID:3065524.

ILO (2012b) *Statistical Update on Employment in the Informal Economy*, Geneva: International Labour Organization.

ILO (2014a) *Employment Policies for Sustainable Recovery and Development*, Geneva: International Labour Organization.

ILO (2014b) *World of Work Report 2014: Developing with Jobs*, Geneva: International Labour Organization.

Johnson, C. (2001) *Blowback: The Costs and Consequences of American Empire*, New York: Macmillan.

Johnston, M. (2005) *Syndromes of Corruption: Wealth, Power, and Democracy*, Cambridge: Cambridge University Press.

Jones, H. (2009) 'Equity in development: why it is important and how to achieve it', Working Paper 311, London: Overseas Development Institute.

Kanbur, R. (2005) 'Economic policy, distribution, and poverty: the nature of disagreements', in A. Shorrocks and R. van der Hoeven (eds), *Growth, Inequality, and Poverty: Prospects for Pro-poor Economic Development*, Oxford: Oxford University Press.

Kaufmann, D. and P. Siegelbaum (1996) 'Privatization and corruption in transition economies', *Journal of International Affairs*, 50(2): 419–58.

Keefer, P. and S. Knack (2002) 'Polarization, politics and property rights: links between inequality and growth', *Public Choice*, 111: 127–54.

Klein, N. (2008) *The Shock Doctrine: The Rise of Disaster Capitalism*, New York: Macmillan.

Korten, D. C. (2001) *When Corporations Rule the World*, San Francisco, CA: Berrett-Koehler.

Korzeniewicz, R. P. and W. C. Smith (2000) 'Poverty, inequality, and growth in Latin America: searching for the high road to globalization', *Latin American Research Review*, 35(3): 7–54.

Kuznets, S. (1955) 'Economic growth and income inequality', *American Economic Review*, 45: 1–28.

Land Matrix (2015) 'The online public database on land deals', www.landmatrix.org/en/.

Londoño, J. L. and M. Szekely (1997) 'Distributional surprises after a decade of reforms: Latin America in the nineties', Occasional Papers of the Office of the Chief Economist, Washington, DC: Inter-American Development Bank.

Lustig, N. (ed.) (1995) *Coping with Austerity: Poverty and Inequality in Latin America*, Washington, DC: Brookings Institution.

Megginson, W. L. and J. M. Netter (2001) 'From state to market: a survey of empirical studies on privatization', *Journal of Economic Literature*, 39(2): 321–89.

Meng, X., R. Gregory and Y. Wang (2005) 'Poverty, inequality, and growth in urban China, 1986–2000', IZA Discussion paper series 1452, Bonn: Institute for the Study of Labour.

Meppem, T. and R. Gill (1998) 'Planning for sustainability as a learning concept', *Ecological Economics*, 26: 121–37.

Milanovic, B. (1995) 'Poverty, inequality, and social policy in transition

economies', Policy Research
Working Paper 1530, Policy Research
Department, Transition Economics
Division.

— (1999) 'Explaining the increase
in inequality during transition',
Economics of Transition, 7 (2):
299–341.

— (2009) 'Global inequality recalculated:
the effect of new 2005 PPP estimates
on global inequality', Policy Research
Working Paper 5061, World Bank
Development Research Group,
Poverty and Inequality Team.

— (2012) 'Global income inequality by
the numbers: in history and now – an
overview', Washington, DC.

Milanovic, B. and L. Ersado (2008) 'Reform
and inequality during the transition:
an analysis using panel household
survey data, 1990–2005', Policy
Research Working Paper 4780, World
Bank, Development Research Group,
Poverty Team & Europe and Central
Asia Region Human Development
Network.

Mohan, G. and K. Stokke (2000)
'Participatory development and
empowerment: the dangers of
localism', *Third World Quarterly*, 21(2):
247–68.

Morley, S. A. (1994) *Poverty and Inequality
in Latin America: Past Evidence, Future
Prospects*, Washington, DC: Overseas
Development Council.

Narayan, D. (2000) *Voices of the Poor: Can
Anyone Hear Us?*, New York: Oxford
University Press.

Narayan, D. and P. Petesch (2002) *Voices
of the Poor: From Many Lands*, New
York: Oxford University Press.

Narayan, D., R. Chambers, M. K. Shah and
P. Petesch (2000) *Voices of the Poor:
Crying out for Change*, New York:
Oxford University Press.

Naschold, F. (2005) 'Growth, distribution,
and poverty reduction: LDCs are
falling further behind', in A. Shorrocks

and R. van der Hoeven (eds), *Growth,
Inequality, and Poverty: Prospects
for Pro-poor Economic Development*,
Oxford: Oxford University Press.

OECD (2011) 'Divided we stand: why
inequality keeps rising', Organisation
for Economic Co-operation and
Development.

Ortiz, I. and M. Cummins (2011) 'Global
inequality: beyond the bottom
billion – a rapid review of income
distribution in 141 countries', Social
and Economic Policy Working Paper,
New York: United Nations Children's
Fund (UNICEF).

— (2013) 'The age of austerity: a review of
public expenditures and adjustment
measures in 181 countries', Working
Paper, New York and Geneva:
Initiative for Policy Dialogue and the
South Centre.

Ostry, J. D., A. G. Berg and C. G.
Tsangarides (2014) *Redistribution,
Inequality, and Growth*, Washington,
DC: International Monetary Fund.

Perkins, J. (2004) *Confessions of an
Economic Hit Man*, San Francisco, CA:
Berrett-Koehler Publishers.

Piketty, T. (2006) 'The Kuznets' Curve,
yesterday and tomorrow', in
Banerjee, A. V., R. Benabou and D.
Mookherjee (eds) *Understanding
Poverty*, Oxford: Oxford University
Press.

— (2014) *Capital in the Twenty-first
Century*, trans. A. Goldhammer,
Cambridge, MA: Belknap Press.

Pogge, T. (2013) 'Poverty, human rights
and the global order: framing the
post-2015 agenda', in M. Langford,
A. Sumner and A. Yamin (eds),
*Millennium Development Goals and
Human Rights: Past, Present and
Future*, Cambridge: Cambridge
University Press.

Pogge, T. and M. Sengupta (2014)
'Rethinking the post-2015
development agenda: eight ways

to end poverty now', *Global Justice: Theory, Practice, Rhetoric*, 7: 3–11.

Pohl, C. and G. H. Hadorn (2008) 'Methodological challenges of transdisciplinary research', *Natures Sciences Sociétés*, 16: 111–21.

Pretty, J. (1995) 'Participatory learning for sustainable agriculture', *World Development*, 23: 1247–63.

Ramos, J. R. (1996) 'Poverty and inequality in Latin America: a neostructural perspective', *Journal of Interamerican Studies and World Affairs*, 38 (2/3): 141–58.

Ravallion, M. (2005a) 'Growth, inequality, and poverty: looking beyond averages', in A. Shorrocks and R. van der Hoeven (eds), *Growth, Inequality, and Poverty: Prospects for Pro-poor Economic Development*, Oxford: Oxford University Press.

— (2005b) 'A poverty–inequality trade off?', *Journal of Economic Inequality*, 3: 169–81.

— (2013) 'Two goals for fighting poverty', Development Series blog.

Ravallion, M. and S. Chen (1997) 'What can new survey data tell us about recent changes in distribution and poverty?', *World Bank Research Observer*, 11: 357–82.

Ravallion, M., S. Chen and P. Sangraula (2009) 'Dollar a day revisited', *World Bank Economic Review*, 23 (2): 163–84.

Rogers, D. S. (ed.) (2012) *Waiting to be Heard: Preliminary Results of the 2012 Equity & Sustainability Field Hearings*, Rapid City, SD: Initiative for Equality.

Rogers, D. S., A. K. Duraiappah, D. C. Antons, P. Munoz, X. Bai, M. Fragkias and H. Gutscher (2012) 'A vision for human well-being: transition to social sustainability', *Current Opinion in Environmental Sustainability*, 4: 1–13.

Rogers, D. S., B. Balazs, T. Clemente, A. da Costa, P. Obani, R. Osaliya and A. Vivaceta de la Fuente (2014) 'The Field Hearings Participatory Monitoring for Accountability Platform: utilizing Initiative for Equality's "Equity & Sustainability Field Hearings" network to help achieve more equitable and sustainable development', in UNICEF (ed.), *Thematic Consultation on Participatory Monitoring and Accountability*, United Nations.

Rosenthal, G. (1996) 'On poverty and inequality in Latin America', *Journal of Interamerican Studies and World Affairs*, 38 (2/3): 15–38.

Sachs, J. D. (2005) *The End of Poverty: How We Can Make It Happen in Our Lifetime*, London: Penguin.

Save the Children (2012) 'Born equal: how reducing inequality could give our children a better future', London: Save the Children.

Slater, J. (2013) 'The cost of inequality: how wealth and income extremes hurt us all', Oxfam Media Briefing 02/12.

Stiglitz, J. E. (2002) *Globalization and Its Discontents*, New York: Norton.

Tangri, R. and A. Mwenda (2001) 'Corruption and cronyism in Uganda's privatization in the 1990s', *African Affairs*, 100: 117–33.

Tokman, V. (1997) 'Jobs and solidarity: challenges for post-adjustment in Latin America', in L. Emmerij (ed.), *Economic and Social Development into the XXI Century*, Washington, DC: Inter-American Development Bank.

UN Open Working Group (2014) 'Proposal of the Open Working Group for Sustainable Development Goals', sustainabledevelopment. un.org/sdgsproposal.

UNICEF and UN Women (2013) 'Addressing inequalities: synthesis report of global public consultation', in *Global Thematic Consultation on the Post-2015 Development Agenda*, United Nations.

UNRISD (2010) 'Combating poverty and inequality: structural change, social

policy and politics', UNRISD/2010/4,
Geneva: United Nations Research
Institute for Social Development
(UNRISD).

UNU-WIDER (2008) UNU-WIDER
World Income Inequality Database,
Version 2.0c, May, www.wider.unu.
edu/research/Database/.

White, H. and E. Anderson (2001)
'Growth versus distribution: does
the pattern of growth matter?',
Development Policy Review, 19(3):
267–89.

World Bank (2000) 'Listen to the voices',
go.worldbank.org/NTVCW2JYW0,
accessed 19 December 2014.

— (2012) 'New estimates reveal drop
in extreme poverty 2005–2010',
Press release, econ.worldbank.
org/WBSITE/EXTERNAL/EXTDEC/
0,,contentMDK:23129612~pagePK:
64165401~piPK:64165026~theSitePK:
469372,00.html.

— (2013a) 'PovcalNet: the on-line tool
for poverty measurement developed
by the Development Research
Group of the World Bank', iresearch.
worldbank.org/PovcalNet/index.
htm.

— (2013b) 'World Bank country profiles
for 2000–2011', data.worldbank.
org/data-catalog/country-profiles.

PART TWO

DEVISING AND REFINING DEVELOPMENT GOALS

4 | THE QUEST FOR SUSTAINABLE DEVELOPMENT: THE POWER AND PERILS OF GLOBAL DEVELOPMENT GOALS

Maria Ivanova and Natalia Escobar-Pemberthy

Sustainable development has been an overarching goal for the international community – countries and international organizations – for over twenty years. The Brundtland Commission Report introduced the concept into the international political discourse in 1987 and governments adopted it officially at the 1992 Rio Earth Summit (UN 1992; WCED 1987). It has, however, remained mostly a 'creatively ambiguous' aspiration (Kates et al. 2005). The 2012 United Nations Conference on Sustainable Development, Rio+20, set out to review accomplishments along the three dimensions of sustainable development – environmental, economic and social – and catalyzed a process to create a new set of global goals, Sustainable Development Goals (SDGs), to guide governments on a more concrete pathway for achieving sustainable development.

While the debate about whether Rio+20 was a success or a failure might not be settled (Ivanova 2013), many observers agree that one of the most important outcomes of the conference was the agreement to set Sustainable Development Goals (Correa do Lago 2013; Griggs et al. 2013; Melamed and Ladd 2013). The vision first articulated by the governments of Colombia and Guatemala, which others continue to develop, is for these goals to frame the core of a revamped sustainable development vision – the nexus between basic human needs, economic growth, environmental sustainability, social equity and governance instruments. Despite the existing debates around the balance between economic growth and environmental sustainability (Ekins 2002; Martens 2010), discussions about the SDGs aimed to create both a comprehensive (covering all three dimensions of sustainable development) and universal (applicable to all countries) set of goals. In August 2014, the Open Working Group on Sustainable Development Goals, comprising seventy governments negotiating the substance and scope of the SDGs, presented an official report to the UN General Assembly launching a debate about the specific goals and targets in a process that is scheduled to conclude by the seventieth session of the UN General Assembly in September 2015 (UN General Assembly 2014).

The decision to design Sustainable Development Goals constituted an important signal that policy processes must integrate environmental, economic and social concerns at the national and international levels. However, even after the Open Working Group submitted its proposal, questions remained about the relationship between this new approach and the Millennium Development Goals (MDGs), the goals that governments agreed upon in 2001 to guide them in eradicating poverty and attaining key development indicators. The MDGs successfully motivated the international community to support action towards a set of common aspirations and generated political momentum to continue global goal-setting, and are set to expire in 2015. As the international community finalizes another set of global goals, what are the main lessons from the MDGs process? How could the SDGs be implemented to avoid some of the flaws associated with the MDGs process? How will the SDGs integrate the MDGs process and achievements in a post-2015 context? These are some of the questions that governments and scholars have been grappling with (CROP 2013; ECE et al. 2012; Evans and Steven 2012; Griggs et al. 2013; Iguchi et al. 2012).

In this chapter, we reconstruct the different stages in the creation of global development goals since the 1990s and articulate key implications for the Sustainable Development Goals process in light of the steps taken so far by the United Nations and the proposal presented by the Open Working Group to the UN General Assembly. In 1995, the Organisation for Economic Co-operation and Development (OECD) called for new strategic instruments to improve development assistance and provided the core elements for goals for sustainable development. The MDGs emerged from those ideas and the current SDGs are conceived as the next iteration of powerful, impactful global goals. The power of goals to give meaning, purpose and guidance translates into political attention at a planetary level. On the other hand, the perils of global goals include a narrow focus that neglects areas not covered by the goals, potentially distorted risk and investment preferences, and misleading measurement practices (Dervis 2005; Hulme 2009; Kusek et al. 2003). Any new stage in the process of defining international goals needs to accord specific attention to the strategic definition of the goals so as to boost the motivation of the actors involved, promote improvement of the capacity of countries to undertake the necessary measures, minimize structural constraints, and, ultimately, ensure implementation.

We begin the analysis with an overview of the historical evolution of global development goals demonstrating the continuity of the process and its cumulative nature. Section 2 analyses the strengths and challenges in the design and implementation of a goal-setting development strategy of global character. Section 3 outlines the contemporary political process for the design of Sustainable Development Goals and some of the distinctive, integrative features of the goals proposal in comparison to previous global goal-setting efforts. Our argument is that decisions about the SDGs have two equally important dimensions: the articulation of goals and the implementation of these goals. The political process around the articulation of the Sustainable Development Goals has recaptured the spirit of integration of economic, social and environmental variables. The political process around the implementation of the SDGs would need to do so as well. To this end, the process of translating the current proposals into policy decisions and identifying relevant targets and indicators would be critical and would require innovative and effective governance at all levels.

The evolution of global development goals

The evolution of a common international development agenda dates back to the end of the Second World War. Governments began conceptualizing development as a strategy to not only reduce poverty but to guarantee security and stability in the international system (Duffield and Waddell 2006; OECD 1995). Given that it was a human development strategy, the expectation was that global development goals would contribute to peace, security and to the stability of the international system by providing for basic needs, the absence of which could cause conflict and instability (Binagwaho and Sachs 2005). In an initial stage, OECD identified poverty reduction as 'the central challenge', proposing a global partnership around the goals that had been defined by United Nations summits and the increasing concerns around poverty, debt and the environmental consequences of globalization and economic growth (Boutros-Ghali 1995; Michel

2005). The 1995 OECD report 'Development partnership in a new global context' recognized the need to improve the effectiveness and efficiency of international aid, not only as a way to reduce poverty but also as a strategy to guarantee the stability of the international system (Hulme 2009). The OECD member states, however, went a step farther, and in 1996 the High Level Meeting of the Development Assistance Committee adopted a more strategic approach, a 'set of concrete, medium-term goals, all based on the recommendations of major United Nations conferences, to be pursued on the basis of agreed principles', defined in the report 'Shaping the 21st century: the contribution of development co-operation'. The report included a specific list of strategies around the three dimensions of sustainable development and set timelines for their attainment – from 2005 to 2015 (see Table 4.1).

TABLE 4.1 Indicators to measure the success of a global development partnership, OECD DAC

Economic Well-being	Social Development	Environmental Sustainability and Regeneration
• Reduction by one-half in the proportion of people living in extreme poverty by 2015	• Universal primary education in all countries by 2015 • Demonstrated progress toward gender equality and the empowerment of women by eliminating gender disparity in primary and secondary education by 2005 • Reduction by two-thirds in the mortality rates for infants and children under age 5 and a reduction by three-fourths in maternal mortality, all by 2015 • Access through the primary health-care system to reproductive health services for all individuals of appropriate ages as soon as possible and no later than the year 2015	• The current implementation of national strategies for sustainable development in all countries by 2005, so as to ensure that current trends in the loss of environmental resources are effectively reversed at both global and national levels by 2015

Source: Michel (1998)

In preparation for the 2000 UN Millennium Summit, and as a way to broaden the international efforts towards poverty reduction, the UN

Secretary-General, the Secretary-General of the OECD, the managing director of the IMF and the president of the World Bank agreed on producing a joint report to offer guidelines in the goal development process. 'A better world for all' presented a set of seven International Development Goals (IDGs) as a 'common framework to guide our policies and programmes and to assess effectiveness' (IMF et al. 2000). Twenty indicators articulated the seven goals at a more detailed level (see Table 4.2). The institutions designed their development plans based on integrative measures of development rather than an exclusive focus on income (Hulme 2009), and promoted the idea of prioritizing quality of life over economic growth. Importantly, the IDGs sought to provide goals for all developing countries. Designed by the donor community, however, they were never completely accepted by developing countries, which were especially concerned with issues such as economic growth, development and increasing inequality (Fukuda-Parr and Hulme 2011; IMF et al. 2000; UNDP 2003).

The transition from the IDGs into the 2000 UN Millennium Assembly was not an easy process. In April 2000, the UN secretary-general's report 'We the peoples: the role of the United Nations in the 21st century' called for a new international development agenda (UN Secretary-General 2000). The IDGs informed the subsequent political discussions and provided the core framework of what would become the MDGs, but financing, baselines for indicators and differing perspectives among developed and developing countries remained contentious (Hulme 2009). The initial proposal was followed by the UN General Assembly's adoption of the Millennium Declaration as a new mandate for the definition, financing and implementation of international development as a global strategy (UN 2000). This process led to the articulation and approval of the Millennium Development Goals in 2001 as a global strategy to improve human development, incorporating concerns of both donor and aid recipient countries but creating a framework applicable exclusively to developing nations.

The MDGs comprise eight global goals that lie at the core of the international development agenda (see Figure 4.1). Ambitious, yet concrete, the MDGs offer a multidimensional perspective on poverty. They represent a set of global goals that incorporate different policy areas ranging from education and health to gender equality, environmental sustainability and foreign aid. Importantly, these core areas were all

TABLE 4.2 Evolution of global development goals from IDGs to SDGs

		IDGs		MDGs		SDGs	
		Goals	No. of Indicators	Goals	No. of Targets	Goals	No. of Targets
Economic well-being		Goal 1: Reducing extreme poverty: The proportion of people living in extreme poverty in developing countries should be reduced by at least one-half between 1990 and 2015.	3	Goal 1: Eradicate extreme poverty and hunger	3	Goal 1: End poverty in all its forms everywhere	7
						Goal 2: End hunger, achieve food security and improved nutrition and promote sustainable agriculture	9
						Goal 8: Promote sustained, inclusive and sustainable economic growth, full and productive employment and decent work for all	12
						Goal 9: Build resilient infrastructure, promote inclusive and sustainable industrialization and foster innovation	8

Goal 2: Universal primary education: There should be universal primary education in all countries by 2015.	3	Goal 2: Achieve universal primary education	1	Goal 4: Ensure inclusive and equitable quality education and promote lifelong learning opportunities for all	8
Goal 3: Gender equality: Progress towards gender equality and the empowerment of women should be demonstrated by eliminating gender disparity in primary and secondary education by 2005.	2	Goal 3: Promote gender equality and empower women	1	Goal 5: Achieve gender equality and empower all women and girls	9
Goal 4: Reducing infant and child mortality: The death rates for infants and children under the age of five years should be reduced in each developing country by two-thirds between 1990 and 2015.	2	Goal 4: Reduce child mortality	1	Goal 3: Ensure healthy lives and promote well-being for all at all ages	13
Goal 5: Reducing maternal mortality: The rate of maternal mortality should be reduced by three-quarters between 1990 and 2015.	2	Goal 5: Improve maternal health	2		
Goal 6: Reproductive health: Access should be available through the primary healthcare system to reproductive health services for all individuals of appropriate ages, no later than 2015.	2	Goal 6: Combat HIV/AIDS, malaria and other diseases	3		
				Goal 10: Reduce inequality within and among countries	10

Social development

TABLE 4.2 (Continued)

IDGs Goals	No. of Indicators	MDGs Goals	No. of Targets	SDGs Goals	No. of Targets
Goal 7: Environment: There should be a current national strategy for sustainable development, in every country by 2005, so as to ensure that current trends in the loss of environmental resources are effectively reversed at both global and national levels by 2015.	6	Goal 7: Ensure environmental sustainability	4	Goal 6: Ensure availability and sustainable management of water and sanitation for all	8
				Goal 7: Ensure access to affordable, reliable, sustainable and modern energy for all	5
				Goal 11: Make cities and human settlements inclusive, safe, resilient and sustainable	10
				Goal 12: Ensure sustainable consumption and production patterns	11
				Goal 13: Take urgent action to combat climate change and its impacts	5
				Goal 14: Conserve and sustainably use the oceans, seas and marine resources for sustainable development	11
				Goal 15: Protect, restore and promote sustainable use of terrestrial ecosystems, sustainably manage forests, combat desertification, and halt and reverse land degradation and halt biodiversity loss	

Environmental sustainability and regeneration

| Global partnership | Goal 8: Develop a global partnership for development | 6 | Goal 16: Promote peaceful and inclusive societies for sustainable development, provide access to justice for all and build effective, accountable and inclusive institutions at all levels | 12 |
| | | | Goal 17: Strengthen the means of implementation and revitalize the global partnership for sustainable development | 19 |

Sources: IMF et al. (2000); OECD (1995); UN General Assembly (2014); UN (2013b)

Note: The Sustainable Development Goals have not been approved by the United Nations General Assembly. The goals included here are based on the proposal developed by the Open Working Group on Sustainable Development Goals submitted to the General Assembly in September 2014.

present in the original articulation of the IDGs as evidenced in Tables 4.1 and 4.2.

The eight goals are further disaggregated into a set of targets and indicators providing the necessary monitoring and assessment instruments (Manning 2009; Waage et al. 2010). They include economic, social and environmental dimensions of sustainable development but reflect them as independent factors, do not establish links among them, and do not recognize that attaining some of the targets is a prerequisite to progress in several of the goals (ECE et al. 2012). In the case of environmental sustainability, for example, environmental degradation and natural resource management also affect poverty, health and development. The twenty-one targets establish 'learning goals', intermediary benchmarks that allow for planning, monitoring and evaluation, and change of course, but they retain the silo approach rather than an integrated agenda.

The SDGs proposal has attempted to account for these deficiencies. While maintaining the same core as the IDGs and MDGs in policy areas such as poverty reduction, education, health and environmental sustainability, the proposal adopts a more integrated approach to poverty reduction and sustainable development. Moreover, it expands the scope of goals and targets substantively, making them relevant to all countries. For example, while both the IDGs and the MDGs focused only on poverty reduction under the economic well-being category, the SDGs include productive employment, decent work, inclusivity

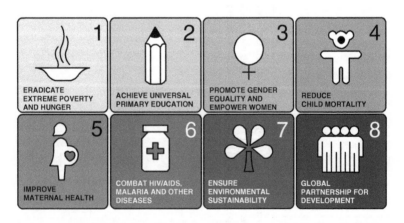

4.1 Millennium Development Goals

and innovation. The social development category retains the main focus from previous global goals, and while it decreases the number of health goals, it increases the number of health-related targets, which cover a wide range of issues. Through the significant number of targets, the focus on women's and girls' empowerment evolved from simply the provision of education to a number of measures such as the elimination of discrimination and violence against all women and girls everywhere, the promotion of women's full and effective participation and equal opportunities for leadership at all levels of decision-making, and reforms to give women equal rights to economic resources and access to ownership. Importantly, through a new target, reproductive health, which was eliminated as a goal in the MDGs owing to political pressures, is integrated into the SDGs. Governments are urged to 'ensure universal access to sexual and reproductive health-care services, including for family planning, information and education, and the integration of reproductive health into national strategies and programmes by 2030'. The proposal also features a new goal within the social development category – the reduction of inequality within and among nations.

Perhaps the greatest evolution from the IDGs and MDGs is in the environmental sustainability category. There are now seven discrete goals that recognize the importance of various ecosystems and the services they provide; they emphasize the need for 'urgent action to combat climate change and its impacts', add a focus on energy, sustainable production and consumption, and cities.

In the area of global partnership, the SDGs also expand by articulating two ambitious goals: 'promote peaceful and inclusive societies for sustainable development, provide access to justice for all and build effective, accountable and inclusive institutions at all levels', and 'strengthen the means of implementation and revitalize the global partnership for sustainable development'. The SDGs, therefore, extended into the area of governance across levels identifying a number of targets for countries (see Table 4.2).

Creating a set of global Sustainable Development Goals was a political process building on previous international efforts and integrating the lessons learned. It has been connected to the process of rethinking the development agenda post-2015, but also independently driven by the constituencies engaged in the sustainability agenda. In 2010, the High-level Plenary Meeting of the General Assembly on the

MDGs requested that the UN secretary-general initiate a process on the future of the development agenda after the 2015 deadline of the MDGs. Governments, international agencies, academics and NGOs established formal and informal dialogues to examine possibilities for enhancing the international development agenda after the MDGs, the so-called post-2015 development agenda. To this end, UN Secretary-General Ban Ki-moon created the System Task Team to serve as a consultation mechanism with stakeholders. It brought together more than sixty UN agencies and international organizations that provide 'analytical inputs, expertise and outreach' (ECE et al. 2012) to define new stages in international efforts for development. The Division of Development Policy and Analysis within the UN Department of Economic and Social Affairs coordinated this global conversation.

At the same time, at the 2012 United Nations Conference on Sustainable Development – Rio+20 – governments recognized the need to reaffirm sustainable development as the foundational principle for the global development agenda beyond 2015. 'A realistic development agenda can no longer neglect the link among the economic, social and environmental dimensions of development. Long-term development will thus require integrated policy making, where social equity, economic growth and environmental protection are approached together' (ibid.). The government of Colombia (later in partnership with Guatemala) urged governments to create a mechanism for political commitment to sustainable development, through goals that consider the balance between economic growth, social development and the use of environmental resources as well as the specific needs and characteristics of individual countries (República de Colombia 2012). Over forty governments were convened by Colombia's Ministry of Foreign Affairs to support a proposal for a comprehensive development agenda that includes and addresses the economic, social and environmental dimensions (Castro 2012; Uribe 2013).

The outcome of Rio+20 initiated an intergovernmental process to define a set of Sustainable Development Goals to contribute to the 'full implementation of the outcomes of all major summits in the economic, social, and environmental fields' (UN 2012b) according to the three dimensions of sustainable development and the connections between them. As defined, these goals constitute an instrument for the international community to prioritize the issues required for improving socio-economic development and responsible environmental management, as did the mandate of the 1992 Rio Declaration and the objectives defined in Agenda 21. In particular, the draft proposal submitted by Colombia to Rio+20 included references to such topics as poverty, consumption patterns, human settlements, biodiversity, forests, oceans, hydrological resources, food security and energy, including renewable resources (República de Colombia 2012). However, as the Rio+20 outcome document also reflected, additional work was required in defining priorities and establishing the specific elements for goals that would advance sustainable development.

A major point of contention during the Rio+20 negotiations was whether the process of SDGs articulation was to be expert-driven or political. While an expert-driven process was expected to bring technical knowledge into the design of indicators and progress methodologies, a political process would guarantee the commitment of governments and international organizations to the implementation of the goals. The Rio+20 outcome document called for an Open Working Group under the aegis of the UN General Assembly and open to all stakeholders. On 22 January 2013, the UN General Assembly adopted decision 67/555 establishing the Open Working Group, which would comprise thirty representatives from the five UN regional groups, nominated by member states (see Table 4.3). Selecting thirty countries, however, proved more difficult than expected, as most member states requested that they be engaged in the process. The final composition of the group therefore grew from thirty to seventy countries as several countries agreed to share seats, creating a constituency-based system of representation and breaking the usual political negotiating blocks (G77, European Union, etc.). The mandate of the Open Working Group was twofold. The group had to articulate the scope and form of the SDGs and provide the required mechanisms for full participation of stakeholders from civil society, the scientific community and agencies from the UN system. Although the composition of the group was political, government representatives were urged to engage experts, take into account lessons from the MDGs, and ensure that the new set of goals included all three dimensions of sustainable development, mainstreaming the environment at the core of the goals both collectively and individually.

TABLE 4.3 Membership of the SDGs Open Working Group

Africa Group	Asia Pacific Group	Latin America and the Caribbean Group GRULAC
1. Algeria / Egypt / Morocco / Tunisia 2. Ghana 3. Benin 4. Kenya 5. United Republic of Tanzania 6. Congo 7. Zambia / Zimbabwe	8. Nauru/Palau/Papua New Guinea 9. Bhutan/Thailand/Viet Nam 10. India/Pakistan/Sri Lanka 11. China/Indonesia/Kazakhstan 12. Cyprus/Singapore/United Arab Emirates 13. Bangladesh/Republic of Korea/Saudi Arabia 14. Iran (Islamic Republic of)/Japan/Nepal	15. Colombia/Guatemala 16. Bahamas/Barbados 17. Guyana/Haiti/Trinidad and Tobago 18. Mexico/Peru 19. Brazil/Nicaragua 20. Argentina/Bolivia (Plurinational State of)/Ecuador
Western European and Others Group	Eastern European Group	
21. Australia/Netherlands/United Kingdom of Great Britain and Northern Ireland 22. Canada/Israel/United States of America 23. Denmark/Ireland/Norway 24. France/Germany/Switzerland 25. Italy/Spain/Turkey 26. Hungary	27. Belarus/Serbia 28. Bulgaria/Croatia 29. Montenegro/Slovenia 30. Poland/Romania	

Following its mandate, the Open Working Group on Sustainable Development Goals held thirteen discussion sessions between March 2013 and July 2014. Using inputs from member states, the UN system and major groups, governments discussed different policy issues from a technical perspective. A technical support team prepared issue briefs on topics ranging from poverty eradication to sustainable agriculture and population dynamics. As requested, the group presented a report to the 68th session of the UN General Assembly in 2014. The proposal comprised seventeen goals and 169 targets seeking to establish an integrated sustainable development agenda across economic, social and environmental dimensions at all governance levels (see Table 4.2). Markedly, the proposal includes a stronger environmental perspective. While the MDGs had one general and rather elusive goal, 'attain environmental sustainability', the SDGs feature seven environmental goals articulated in concrete terms and with concrete impacts on economic, social and environmental factors across countries.

Debates, however, persist on the structure, content and implementation hurdles for the SDGs at both the global and national levels. Particularly, concerns have emerged about the large number of goals and targets and about the way in which countries should approach the process of articulating concrete goals at the national level and of ensuring implementation (Schwabe 2014). While some countries propose a universal approach in which all targets apply to all countries, others advocate a 'dashboard' approach in which each country selects which goals and targets to implement along with their baselines and deadlines. Furthermore, scholars, NGOs and policy-makers have raised concerns about the way in which the goals will be approached by the UN system (Bernstein et al. 2014; Open Working Group on Sustainable Development Goals 2014; Third World Network 2014). The institutional role of the United Nations in the implementation and monitoring process will be central to the success of a new development agenda. In relation to that, the Secretary-General's report about the 2015–30 agenda, 'The road to dignity by 2030: ending poverty, transforming all lives and protecting the planet', proposes a new agenda around the concept of sustainable development, focusing on rights and the planet. Six elements – dignity, people, prosperity, planet, justice and partnership – are defined to reinforce the sustainable development agenda and to guarantee that the vision defined by the UN and its member states reaches the country level and public opinion (UN Secretary-General 2014). Finding a way to connect the SDGs with the broader UN development agenda will guarantee that the SDGs fulfil their purpose 'to envision a more holistic and integrated agenda for advancing human well-being that is equitable across individuals, populations and generations; and that achieves universal human development while respecting the Earth's ecosystems and critical life support systems' (UN 2013a).

Power and perils of global development goals

The power of the Millennium Development Goals lies in their simplicity and brevity (Open Working Group on Sustainable

Development Goals 2013a). Some of the main challenges include a narrow focus, the possibility of distorted risk and investment preferences, and the potential to generate misleading measurements. Ultimately, at the country level, performance against a set of goals is a function of effort and ability (Ordóñez et al. 2009) but it is also shaped by structural constraints and the political economy of development. Effort is determined by motivation, and ability by resources. They are therefore variables that countries can manipulate. Structural constraints and political economy are much more difficult to influence and need to be taken into account when setting expectations about implementation and delivery. The MDGs have provided a structure to focus advocacy and spur motivation as well as to target investment and thereby improve ability (Bourguignon et al. 2008; Haines and Cassels 2004; Manning 2009; Michel 2005). They have not addressed structural constraints, however, and have not had significant influence on the political economy dynamics in countries.

The ultimate purpose of the MDGs was to engender substantial improvements in the quality of life of the most vulnerable populations (Binagwaho and Sachs 2005). To this end, they set out to motivate action and improve the ability of countries to deliver on core development indicators. Several of the goals stand out because they have directed attention, effort and action towards relevant activities needed to attain an improved level of development. The simplicity of the MDGs offered a clear and concise message that was easy to communicate. Indeed, the MDGs emerged as the main point of reference for the international development agenda and 'galvanized action and political will towards a core set of development priorities' (Open Working Group on Sustainable Development Goals 2013a), helping raise awareness about the moral unacceptability of poverty and about the need for a strong global partnership to achieve development. The use of concrete targets and indicators has proved to be an effective instrument for focusing the efforts of numerous actors, monitoring the evolution of the different strategies, and prompting global political mobilization around concrete targets for development (Manning 2009; Melamed and Scott 2011; Waage et al. 2010). Political commitment and action have been forthcoming, and improvements in some indicators are visible (see Box 4.1).

Box 4.1 Progress in the implementation of the MDGs

- Extreme poverty has been reduced across all regions, including sub-Saharan Africa. In total, the percentage of people living with less than $1.25 a day has gone from 47 per cent in 1990 to 24 per cent in 2008, meaning that 0.8 billion people no longer live in these conditions.
- The proportion of people with access to improved sources of water increased from 76 per cent in 1990 to 89 per cent in 2010, achieving the target of halving the proportion of people without sustainable access to safe drinking water.
- Parity in primary education between girls and boys has been achieved. Since 2000, most of the world's children have been enrolled in school. Girls' enrolment grew from 91 per cent in 1997 to 97 per cent in 2010.
- The number of deaths of children under five years old decreased from more than 12 million in 1990 to 7.6 million in 2010.
- The global incidence of malaria has decreased by 17 per cent since 2000.

Source: UN (2012a)

In addition, the use of targets and indicators motivating policy action helps to create a culture of monitoring and evaluation, which, despite the need for further improvement, has brought to the international community more and better data about poverty, education, health, gender equality, etc., particularly in developing regions in Latin America and Asia. Indicators of education enrolment, disease incidence, access to safe water, and gender empowerment, among others, are now carefully measured as part of states' commitments to the MDGs. At the same time, various agencies within the United Nations, together with national governments and statisticians, and other organizations in charge of the development of data, formed the Inter-Agency and Expert Group (IAEG) on MDG Indicators to improve the methodologies and technical issues related to data production and to promote better documentation and standards in the compilation of data at the national level.

Nevertheless, debates on the achievements in specific issue areas persist, and a more critical assessment of the actual implications the MDGs have had for development is necessary. While the UN recognizes important progress in the poverty rate, educational coverage, maternal health, disease prevention and access to safe water (UN Secretary-General 2013), independent analyses conducted by external organizations show a worrying lack of success in addressing the deeper issues of inequalities, environmental change, hunger and unemployment (CROP 2013) (see Box 4.2). Furthermore, inadequate capacity and structural constraints on enacting the necessary measures at the national level have hindered countries' trajectories towards goals such as eradicating poverty, reducing child mortality and combating infectious diseases, and many of the MDGs remain unfulfilled. Indeed, the UN Millennium Development Goals Summit emphasized that 'without substantial international support, several of the Goals are likely to be missed by many developing countries by 2015' (UN 2010).

Box 4.2 Challenges in the implementation of the MDGs

- Reduction in unemployment is not sustained. Fifty-eight per cent of the employment in developing regions is classified as vulnerable, while women and youth are still holding insecure and poorly remunerated positions.
- Important changes have been achieved in terms of maternal health, but progress is still slow. Problems with adolescent pregnancies and limited access to contraceptive methods still persist.
- The improvement of access to safe sources of water in rural areas is still poor. Nearly half of the population in developing regions also suffers from limited access to improved sanitation facilities.
- 850 million people still live in hunger despite progress in poverty reduction and child under-nutrition.
- The absolute number of people living in slums increased from 650 million in 1990 to an estimated 863 million in 2012.
- Gender inequality persists at the education, employment and government participation levels. Violence against women continues, affecting the achievement of these goals.

Source: UN (2012a)

Traditional forms of development had been the primary focus for the MDGs, resulting in lack of recognition for the interconnections among the three dimensions of sustainable development, and in a superficial treatment of the environmental and social dimensions. Conceptualized as one of eight goals (MDG7), environmental sustainability was construed in terms that are too broad as a goal and too limiting as targets. The fact that only three environmental issues – biodiversity, water and urbanization – were addressed in the targets of this goal, and the absence of concrete initiatives around the incorporation of sustainable development in different policy areas, are examples of the weaknesses of MDG7 formulation. In the social sphere, issues such as security, human rights and governance were neglected. In addition, the MDGs do not consider the differing initial conditions of countries in terms of international development and do not recognize special situations within countries where the goals are adopted.

Nevertheless, the MDGs have become the overarching development strategy steering investment – through ODA or other funds – into sectors identified as important, by shaping risk and investment preferences. However, targets for several dimensions are imprecise, making it complex to measure and implement them. Precious resources can therefore easily be steered into developing measurements tactics rather than invested in development strategies. Even though the MDGs improved the culture of data collection and measurement, the emphasis in monitoring proved to be contentious. Despite the improvement in some of the targets and indicators, it is also argued that so much emphasis on monitoring has neglected action to address the structural reasons for the current problems. At the same time, focus on results or outcomes failed to account for the progress achieved by some countries that have not reached the targets but have moved forward considerably. Little to no attention has been accorded to the quality or sustainability of the results achieved. The lack of accountability mechanisms presents a significant shortcoming. Finally, and perhaps most contentiously, since they are applicable only to developing countries, the MDGs did not recognize the monetary and moral responsibility of developed countries and offered a weak approach to addressing the issues of social justice, equality, vulnerability and exclusion.

In this context, as governments debate the proposal for Sustainable Development Goals as a new set of global goals, and will then set out to implement them, the lessons from the MDGs will be important.

Furthermore, the key question is how to integrate the goals into the overall sustainable development agenda in a process that guarantees not only the implementation of the mandates of the international community, but the broader goals of human well-being and sustainable development.

Sustainable Development Goals: the synergy agenda

In essence, the SDGs process debated the creation of a coherent vision that recognizes the interlinkages between the three dimensions of sustainable development. Governments participating in the Open Working Group, scholars and others engaged in the process suggested multiple topics around which the goals should be constructed (see Boxes 4.3 and 4.4). The final proposal, presented to the 68th session of the UN General Assembly, incorporated some of these elements (see Table 4.2). The concurrence with the post-2015 process raises the challenge of the integration of the SDGs into the global development discourse. Ultimately, the overall goal is the same: the attainment of long-term sustainable development (UN Secretary-General 2014). As the High-Level Panel of Eminent Persons on the Post-2015 Development Agenda expressed in its Monrovia Communiqué from 1 February 2013, the global development agenda should aim 'to end extreme poverty in all its forms in the context of sustainable development and to have in place the building blocks of sustained prosperity for all' (HLP-P2015 2013: 5). In this context, the SDGs explicitly recognize that such development cannot be achieved without safeguarding the ability of the planet to maintain the conditions critical to human well-being (UN Secretary-General 2014). Effective integration of the two processes would likely result in a rigorous agenda emphasizing the connection between poverty eradication and environmental sustainability, efficient use of resources, and meaningful contribution from multiple stakeholders. Fragmentation into multiple policy processes, on the other hand, can cause fatigue and reduced commitment to implementation from states and other actors (Committee for Development Policy 2012).

There are several scenarios for synergy between the SDGs and the global development agenda. One option is the creation of a comprehensive set of goals that recognizes integration as a cross-cutting principle, and comprises traditional human development goals alongside sustainable development goals. Another possibility is for each goal to incorporate multiple targets associated with each of

Box 4.3 Topics included in the Open Working Group agenda

- Cities
- Conflict prevention, peace, rule of law and governance
- Consumption and production
- Economic growth and macroeconomic stability
- Education and culture
- Employment
- Energy
- Gender equality
- Health
- Human rights
- Oceans, seas, forests and biodiversity
- Population dynamics
- Social protection
- Transportation
- Youth

Source: Open Working Group on Sustainable Development Goals (2013b)

Box 4.4 The proposal of the High-Level Panel of Eminent Persons on the Post-2015 Development Agenda

- Goal 1: End poverty
- Goal 2: Empower girls and women and achieve gender equality
- Goal 3: Provide quality education and lifelong learning
- Goal 4: Ensure healthy lives
- Goal 5: Ensure food security and good nutrition
- Goal 6: Achieve universal access to water and sanitation
- Goal 7: Secure sustainable energy
- Goal 8: Create jobs, sustainable livelihoods and equitable growth
- Goal 9: Manage natural resource assets sustainably
- Goal 10: Ensure good governance and effective institutions
- Goal 11: Ensure stable and peaceful societies
- Goal 12: Create a global enabling environment and catalyze long-term finance

Source: HLP-P2015 (2013)

the dimensions of sustainable development – economic, social and environmental. Alternatively, each goal could be associated with one of the dimensions of sustainable development independently (Le Goulven 2013). Each one of these options would have different consequences for the design and implementation of the goals.

The discussions of the Open Working Group focused on the possibility of creating a comprehensive set of goals that recognize integration as a cross-cutting principle, and comprise traditional human development goals alongside sustainable development goals. The current SDGs proposal thus offers a list of seventeen topics as potential global goals and significantly improved articulation of the connections between economic, social and environmental issues beyond the specific variables of poverty eradication, education, health and others included in the MDGs. The scope of the SDGs currently under negotiation includes governance mechanisms, values and lifestyles, and equality. The targets also draw attention to the process of data production and collection, emphasizing the role of science in the SDGs process. Ultimately, the challenge will be to design targets and indicators that can be measured and monitored universally while being relevant to and informed by different national realities.

Indeed, the SDGs, as proposed by the Open Working Group, truly exemplify the integration between the three dimensions of sustainable development while adding specific targets to create the necessary frameworks, policies and partnerships to ensure implementation. The fundamental connections among environment, economic well-being and social development are reflected in the range of targets associated with each goal. Table 4.4 illustrates this dynamic by showing the number of targets across the economic, social and environmental dimensions for each of the seventeen goals. Goal 17, referring to the means of implementation for global partnership, is a new one and has the largest number of targets, nineteen, incorporating finance, technology, capacity-building, trade, institutional coherence, partnerships and data, monitoring and accountability.

Definition of adequate targets and indicators, measurement of progress, and support for implementation are elements critical to success (UNEP 2012). Concrete measurement strategies and mechanisms provide governments and international organizations with the necessary data and science-based information to evaluate advancement and take corrective measures as required. An adequate

TABLE 4.4 Integrating the dimensions of Sustainable Development through targets

SDGs Goal	SDGs Targets				
	Economic	Social	Environmental	Finance & Governance	Total
Goal 1: Poverty	2	2	1	2	7
Goal 2: Hunger	2	2	1	3	8
Goal 3: Healthy lives		8	1	4	13
Goal 4: Education	1	5	1	3	10
Goal 5: Gender equality		6		3	9
Goal 6: Water and sanitation		2	4	2	8
Goal 7: Energy		1	2	2	5
Goal 8: Economic growth and employment	4	5	1	2	12
Goal 9: Infrastructure	3	1	1	3	8
Goal 10: Inequality	2	5		3	10
Goal 11: Cities	1	3	3	2	10
Goal 12: Consumption and production	2	1	5	3	11
Goal 13: Climate change		1	2	2	5
Goal 14: Oceans	2	1	5	2	10
Goal 15: Terrestrial ecosystems/biodiversity	1	1	7	3	12
Goal 16: Peaceful societies		3		9	12
Goal 17: Means of implementation	cross-cutting				19

Source: The authors

baseline for measurement, adequate methodology for gathering data, and availability of information are other variables to consider in the design of the new set of global goals (Waage et al. 2010). Developing countries have advocated strongly for a transparent and open assessment process, including the creation of a stakeholders' review process or a sounding/monitoring system that guarantees effective implementation. Australia and Switzerland emphasized the use of official statistics and the need to design a process of data collection that guarantees the necessary input to measure the baseline and monitor implementation (Iguchi et al. 2012). These issues will be critical to the success of the SDGs as a new political agenda.

Ultimately, the Sustainable Development Goals need to be simple yet comprehensive and, importantly, universal (HLP-P2015 2013; UN 2013a). The SDGs must communicate clearly to countries and stakeholders the meaning of sustainable development and the mechanisms to implement it. Obligations under the SDGs need to extend to all countries, regardless of their level of development, as all states are accountable for the implementation of the outcome of the Rio+20 mandate. That is why universality in particular is a key characteristic of the proposed set of goals. Contextualized specific national and regional targets can be used to measure progress at the different levels, to complement the general approach of global goals (Nayyar 2012). The definition of the new framework also requires transparency, participation and engagement from all groups, including vulnerable populations. As indicated in Agenda 21 – and in Rio Principle 10 – twenty years earlier, all concerned citizens are entitled to, and should participate in bringing about, sustainable development (UNCED 1992). The proposal by the Open Working Group provides a solid foundation for the articulation of a new global vision and governments are now poised to take it to the level of implementation across scales and geographies.

Conclusion

Global goals became an important development tool for the international community after the end of the Cold War. With increasing awareness of planetary interconnectedness and political interdependence, governments sought to create a common vision and strategy that would ensure economic welfare, environmental integrity and social justice. The historical evolution from international development goals to Millennium Development Goals to Sustainable Development Goals shows 'the power of global goals and a shared purpose' (UN 2012a) to bring together states and stakeholders on the same path of action (Hulme 2009; Michel 2005). Sustainable Development Goals are thus part of a long timeline of international cooperation mechanisms and constitute a key opportunity to revive and re-envision the original global strategy for sustainable development when the idea of an international development agenda based on targets and indicators was first proposed.

The original vision for the international development goals of the 1990s might indeed be the right launching point for the integration across the three dimensions of sustainable development that is necessary. The process that started with the IDGs and moved into the MDGs and subsequently into the current debate is grounded in a set of common values that are still relevant – applicability, universality, transparency, comprehensiveness and inclusiveness (UN 2013a). The concerns and objectives of the development agenda during the 1990s, which led to the International Development Goals, could still inform a contemporary approach that merges a stronger environmental dimension with traditional development priorities.

Across the mechanisms derived from the process of goal-setting, different analysts have also debated the expansion of the human development discourse and its relation to sustainability and human security (Gasper 2011; Koehler et al. 2012). In this context, the Sustainable Development Goals represent a chance to design an international instrument that recognizes the multidimensional nature of the sustainable development challenge and the interconnections between different variables. While the MDGs have been successful in focusing attention on and motivating action towards a set of common global aspirations, there is a general consensus on the need to expand into a new framework 'centered on human well-being, with measurable metrics, keeping in mind the need for the coherent and balanced integration of environmental, economic and social dimensions' (UNEP 2012: 459). These new global goals would apply across the board and provide a common vision. Through differentiated targets and indicators, however, the SDGs could be responsive to the characteristics, capacities and priorities of different countries. As suggested by Colombia, a multilevel framework would be necessary, including internationally defined indicators as well as country- or region-specific indicators and additional measurements that guide national action to address local problems.

Building on the political momentum of Rio+20 to design and implement the SDGs and the mandate to assess the MDGs experience to articulate a post-2015 development agenda, governments have an opportunity to move forward to a more transformative global agenda that restores the concept of sustainable development as the core of human well-being. Maintaining the instrumental value and simplicity of the MDGs while addressing sustainable development and the reality of individual countries will be critical. Leaders, governments, business, academia and civil society have been challenged to identify different elements that are relevant in the construction of a new set of goals, and the UN General Assembly has the challenge of a more systematic approach to address the complexity of the sustainable development agenda. If they succeed, the mandate of Rio+20 and the broader goal of sustainable development will be fulfilled.

References

Bernstein, S., J. Gupta, S. Adresen, P. M. Haas, N. Kanie, M. Kok ... and C. Stevens (2014) 'Coherent governance, the UN and the SDGs', in POST2015/UNU-IAS Policy Brief no. 4, Tokyo: United Nations University Institute for the Advanced Study of Sustainability.

Binagwaho, A. and J. D. Sachs (2005) *Investing in Development: A Practical Plan to Achieve the Millennium Development Goals*, New York: Earthscan.

Bourguignon, F., A. Bénassy-Quéré, S. Dercon, A. Estache, J. W. Gunning, R. Kanbur ... and A. Spadaro (2008) 'Millennium Development Goals at midpoint: where do we stand and where do we need to go', in European Commission (ed.), *Mobilising European Research for Development Policies*, Brussels.

Boutros-Ghali, B. (1995) *An Agenda for Development 1995: With Related UN Documents*, New York: United Nations.

Castro, C. (2012) 'Colombia propone fijarse Objetivos de Desarrollo Sostenible', *Revista Semana*.

Committee for Development Policy (2012) *The United Nations Development Strategy Beyond 2015*, New York: UN.

Correa do Lago, A. (2013) 'The outcome of the Rio+20 mandate and UNEP's Governing Council', Video interview, Nairobi: Center for Governance and Sustainability at UMass Boston.

CROP (2013) 'Mobilizing critical research for preventing and eradicating poverty', in CROP Brief no. 13, Bergen: International Social Science Council/ University of Bergen.

Dervis, K. (2005) 'Bridging the gap: how the Millennium Development Goals are uniting the fight against global poverty', *Sustainable Development Law & Policy*, 6(1): 3.

Duffield, M. and N. Waddell (2006) 'Securing humans in a dangerous world', *International Politics*, 43(1): 1–23.

ECE, ESCAP, UNDESA, UNEP and UNFCCC (2012) 'Building on the MDGs to bring sustainable development to the post-2015 development agenda', in *UN System Task Team on the Post-2015 UN Development Agenda*, New York: UN.

Ekins, P. (2002) *Economic Growth and Environmental Sustainability: The Prospects for Green Growth*, London and New York: Routledge.

Evans, A. and D. Steven (2012) *Sustainable Development Goals – a Useful Outcome from Rio+20*, New York: NYU Center of International Cooperation.

Fukuda-Parr, S. and D. Hulme (2011) 'International norm dynamics and the "end of poverty": understanding the Millennium Development Goals', *Global Governance*, 17(1): 17–36.

Gasper, D. (2011) 'The human and the social: a comparison of the discourses of human development, human security and social quality', *International Journal of Social Quality*, 1(1): 91–108, doi: 10.3167/IJSQ.2011010108.

Griggs, D., M. Stafford-Smith, O. Gaffney, J. Rockström, M. C. Öhman, P. Shyamsundar ... and I. Noble (2013) 'Policy: sustainable development goals for people and planet', *Nature*, 495(7441): 305–7.

Haines, A. and A. Cassels (2004) 'Can the Millennium Development Goals be attained?', *British Medical Journal*, 329(7462): 394–7.

HLP-P2015 (2013) *A New Global Partnership: Eradicate Poverty and Transform Economies through Sustainable Development*, New York: High-Level Panel of Eminent Persons on the Post-2015 Development Agenda.

Hulme, D. (2009) 'The Millennium Development Goals (MDGs): a short history of the world's biggest promise', Brooks World Poverty Institute Working Paper Series, 100.

Iguchi, M., S. Hoiberg Olsen and I. Miyazawa (2012) 'Current outlook on the Sustainable Development Goals (SDGs): a brief analysis of country positions', Tokyo: Tokyo Tech/IGES/UNU–IAS.

IMF, OECD, UN and World Bank Group (2000) 'A better world for all – progress towards the international development goals', Washington, DC, and New York.

Ivanova, M. (2013) 'The contested legacy of Rio+20', *Global Environmental Politics*, 12(3): 1–11.

Kates, R. W., T. M. Parris and A. A. Leiserowitz (2005) 'What is sustainable development? Goals, indicators, values, and practice', *Environment: Science and Policy for Sustainable Development*, 47(3): 8–21.

Koehler, G., D. Gasper, R. Jolly and M. Simane (2012) 'Human security

and the next generation of comprehensive human development goals', *Journal of Human Security Studies*, 1(2): 75–93, www.jahss. org/journals/JOHSR_vol1-2.pdf.

Kusek, J. Z., R. C. Rist and E. M. White (2003) *How Will We Know the Millennium Development Goal Results When We See Them?*, Washington, DC: World Bank Group.

Le Goulven, K. (2013) 'Doing development in a changing world', Presentation for the University of Massachusetts Boston, Boston, MA.

Manning, R. (2009) 'Using indicators to encourage development: lessons from the Millennium Development Goals', DIIS Reports, Danish Institute for International Studies.

Martens, J. (2010) *Thinking Ahead: Development Models and Indicators of Well-being beyond the MDGs*, Dialogue on Globalization: Friedrich-Ebert-Stiftung, International Policy Analysis.

Melamed, C. and P. Ladd (2013) 'How to build Sustainable Development Goals: integrating human development and environmental sustainability in a new global agenda', Research Report, London: Overseas Development Institute.

Melamed, C. and L. Scott (2011) *After 2015: Progress and Challenges for Development*, London: Overseas Development Institute.

Michel, J. H. (1998) 'Shaping the 21st century: the contribution of development co-operation', in OECD (ed.), *Sustainable Development: OECD Policy Approaches for the 21st Century*, Paris: OECD, pp. 29–36.

— (2005) 'The birth of the MDGs', *DACNews*, www.oecd.org/dac/ thebirthofthemdgsdacnewssept-oct2005.htm, accessed 20 May 2013.

Nayyar, D. (2012) *The MDGs after 2015: Some Reflections on the Possibilities*,

UN System Task Team on the Post-2015 UN Development Agenda, New York: UN.

OECD (1995) 'Development partnerships in the new global context', 3/4 May, www.oecd.org/dataoecd/31/61/2755357.pdf, accessed 18 February 2012.

Open Working Group on Sustainable Development Goals (2013a) *Issues Brief – Conceptual Issues*, New York: Technical Support Team, UN.

— (2013b) *Programme of Work 2013–2014*, New York: UN.

— (2014) *Issues Brief – Means of Implementation*, New York: Technical Support Team, UN.

Ordóñez, L. D., M. E. Schweitzer, A. D. Galinsky and M. H. Bazerman (2009) 'Goals gone wild: the systematic side effects of over-prescribing goal setting', Working Paper no. 09-83, Cambridge, MA: Harvard Business School.

Republica de Colombia (2012) 'Rio+20 Objetivos de Desarrollo Sostenible (ODSs)', Input to the United Nations Conference on Sustainable Development Rio+20, Bogotá.

Schwabe, D. (2014) 'Too many SDGs?', Institute Notes, Washington, DC: Bread for the World Institute.

Third World Network (2014) 'SDG negotiations reveal the hard fight for means of implementation', www.globalpolicy.org/component/content/article/252-the-millenium-development-goals/52671-means-of-implementation-nearly-toppled-process-of-sdgs-agenda.html.

UN (United Nations) (1992) *Rio Declaration on Environment and Development*, A/CONF.151/26, Rio de Janeiro: United Nations Conference on Environment and Development.

— (2000) *United Nations Millennium Declaration: Resolution*, A/RES/55/2, New York: UN.

— (2010) *Keeping the Promise: United to Achieve the Millennium Development Goals*, A/RES/65/1, New York: UN.

— (2012a) *Millennium Development Goals Report 2012*, www.un.org/en/development/desa/publications/mdg-report-2012.html, accessed 20 March 2013.

— (2012b) *The Future We Want*, A/RES/66/288, Outcome Document from Rio+20, United Nations Conference on Sustainable Development, Rio de Janeiro.

— (2013a) Initial input of the Secretary-General to the Open Working Group on Sustainable Development Goals, A/67/634, New York: UN.

— (2013b) *Millennium Development Goals Report 2013*, www.un.org/millenniumgoals/pdf/report-2013/mdg-report-2013-english.pdf, accessed 14 April 2014.

UN General Assembly (2014) *Report of the Open Working Group of the General Assembly on Sustainable Development Goals*, A/68/970, New York: UN.

UN Secretary-General (2000) *We the Peoples – the Role of the United Nations in the 21st Century*, A/54/2000, New York: UN.

— (2013) Special Message from the Secretary-General of the United Nations, *Acronym – WFUNA*, 2(1): 2.

— (2014) *The Road to Dignity by 2030: Ending Poverty, Transforming All Lives and Protecting the Planet*, A/69/700, Synthesis report of the Secretary-General on the post-2015 sustainable development agenda, New York: UN.

UNCED (1992) Agenda 21, New York: UN.

UNDP (2003) *Human Development Report 2003 – Millennium Development Goals: A Compact among Nations to End Human Poverty*, New York: UN.

UNEP (2012) *Global Environmental Outlook 5*, Nairobi: UN.

— (2013) 'Embedding the environment in Sustainable Development Goals', in

U. N. E. Programme (ed.), *UNEP Post-2015 Discussion Paper 1*, Nairobi: UN.

Uribe, J. G. (2013) 'The outcome of the Rio+20 mandate and UNEP's Governing Council', Video interview, Nairobi: Center for Governance and Sustainability at UMass Boston.

Waage, J., R. Banerji, O. Campbell, E. Chirwa, G. Collender, V. Dieltiens

... and E. Unterhalter (2010) 'The Millennium Development Goals: a cross-sectoral analysis and principles for goal setting after 2015', *The Lancet*, 376(9745): 991–1023.

WCED (1987) *Our Common Future – the Brundtland Report*, www.un-documents.net/wced-ocf.htm.

5 | GOING BEYOND THE ERADICATION OF EXTREME POVERTY: DEBATING THE SUSTAINABLE DEVELOPMENT GOALS IN BRAZIL

Rômulo Paes-Sousa and Paulo de Martino Jannuzzi

Brazil's socio-economic dynamics have changed substantially since the start of the century, with numerous studies highlighting their ability to combine economic growth with social inclusion. Brazilian social protection policy has contributed to this in two ways: by increasing revenue levels and stimulating human capital development among the poorer population.

Since the *Fome Zero* (Zero Hunger) strategy was launched in 2003, the focus of Brazil's social protection policy has shifted significantly from an initial emphasis on food and nutritional security to increasing revenue levels and access to other social protection programmes. In 2010, at the close of President Lula's second term, the *Bolsa Família*, a conditional cash transfer programme, covered 12.8 million families, i.e. more than 51 million people.

In 2011, President-Elect Rousseff launched *Brasil Sem Miséria* (Brazil without Extreme Poverty, BWEP), a strategy to eradicate extreme poverty by 2014. The new strategy deploys twenty ministries involved in 120 undertakings, targeting 16 million extremely poor Brazilians. BWEP aims at the promotion of rights in the core concept of its political narrative, thus promoting the following political goals: to raise per capita household income of the target population; increase their access to public goods and services; and increase their job opportunities.

BWEP is founded first and foremost upon the *Bolsa Família* programme. The plan is based on the conception of poverty as a multidimensional phenomenon.[1] BWEP aims therefore to combat the multidimensions of poverty by developing those human capabilities necessary for breaking the poverty cycle definitively.

BWEP is thus based both on the idea of poverty as a multidimensional phenomenon, and on the related concept of social development: it includes strategies to promote better access to the job market and to primary education. It is also grounded on the idea of social justice with a focus on the most dispossessed.

Although theoretically the Brazilian government endorsed a multidimensional conception of poverty, it has in actuality chosen a one-dimensional criterion to identify the extreme poverty line (those living on less than US\$1.25 a day), using preliminary data from the 2010 demographic census to estimate the social demands. This criterion nevertheless has the advantage of being consistent with both the *Bolsa Família* programme and the UNDP's Millennium Development Goal indicators. Besides, at the time of BWEP formulation, as was illustrated by 2010 census publications, many social indicators were still highly correlated to income levels or monetary poverty rates.

The use of the international extreme poverty line, computing indicators by 2010 census data, benefited the plan, as follows:

- it made international comparisons possible;
- MDS (the Ministry of Social Development) has accumulated knowledge that could be drawn upon when using the poverty line for the *Bolsa Família* programme; and
- it allowed for producing estimates at the municipal level.

However, as a result of Brazilian economic growth, the one-dimensional conception of extreme poverty has become less helpful: while monetary extreme poverty has decreased, it is important to understand the dynamics of the other dimensions of extreme poverty. This has challenged Brazil to revise its one-dimensional concept of poverty; to produce credible evidence from its ambitious multi-sectorial policy approach; and to describe the indicators of success for its new public policy interventions. In this chapter, we will describe the available alternatives for assessing the decline of monetary poverty in Brazil and discuss how the objectives of sustainable development can help the Brazilian government reshape its policy indicators for estimating the effects of its inclusive growth strategy. That process can also lead to the emergence of a more integrative and effective public intervention for poverty eradication.

The reduction of monetary poverty and extreme poverty in Brazil (1981–2009): what comes next?

Different conceptual and analytical approaches have been used in international literature in the last ten to twenty years to study and measure the phenomenon of hunger, poverty and extreme poverty. A brief account of such approaches can make important contributions to the studies on new indicators to be adopted in the post-2015 Development Goals Agenda after 2015. In spite of all achievements related to monetary poverty, much more remains to be done.

There are four main conceptual/analytical approaches to poverty: poverty as a lack of income for the consumption of a basket of basic goods and services (i.e. monetary poverty); poverty as a lack of basic needs – both monetary and non-monetary (multidimensional poverty); poverty as a relative, rather than absolute, deprivation of income or other socio-economic dimensions (relative poverty); and poverty as a self-perception of each individual (subjective poverty) (Feres and Vilatoro 2011).

Poverty as income insufficiency seems to be the most widely used approach (Alkire and Foster 2011). Under this approach, a family is considered poor if its available income or its total expenditure is below a set monetary value (i.e. poverty line), which is calculated according to the costs of all products and basic services necessary for the survival of all members within a family. The dominance of this approach is certainly due to the World Bank´s mission advocacy and its studies that led to the definition of the international US\$1.25 a day per person.

The multidimensional approach to poverty, or poverty MPI, represents a complementary concept for monetary poverty, inasmuch as it also identifies the minimal list of goods and services (public and private) needed for survival, including access to safe drinking water, housing, sanitation, food in adequate quantity and diversity, and school attendance. International organizations adopt the multidimensional approach to poverty because it allows the identification of specific needs and targeted groups. This allows the incorporation of certain dimensions that are intrinsically associated with the measurement of poverty, such as low income.

The UNECLAC – United Nations Economic Commission for Latin America and the Caribbean – has adopted the multidimensional approach to poverty for thirty years, and researchers and international centres, such as the Oxford Poverty and Human Development Initiative

(Kageyama and Hoffmann 2006), have constructed measurements that follow this approach.

In the Brazilian case, as will be evident later on this chapter, with the virtual elimination of extreme monetary poverty, and especially with the design of strategies to mitigate symptoms and determinants of poverty, there will certainly be a need to adopt a multidimensional indicator of poverty. Such a poverty index should reflect, besides the availability of income levels, the progressive access to social services and opportunities provided by BWEP actions and programmes.

The concept of relative poverty is linked to the inequality of individuals and families in relation to access to goods and services or availability of income. This is different from the idea of monetary poverty or the poverty line, where a certain number of individuals do not have a certain level of income to buy a basket of products; and it is also different from the idea of multidimensional poverty, where a certain number of individuals do not have access to basic goods and services. Relative poverty, on the contrary, assesses how society distributes public and private resources, including income, goods and services, and how low-income citizens get access to resources. In general, the poor are those individuals who come from the lowest deciles in terms of income per capita or those with more precarious access to goods or services considering a certain relative threshold (based on positional measures such as median, quartiles, etc.). This approach is more suitable for developed countries, where minimum subsistence is guaranteed for a majority share of the population, and where, therefore, the emphasis of social policy is directed at reducing social inequalities between population groups (Atkinsons 2002).

Besides these analytical approaches based on more objective indicators, there is also the subjective approach to poverty, based on self-perception of poverty. In the studies adopting the subjective approach to poverty in underdeveloped countries, poverty is measured according to the individual responses to questions on the ability to cover home maintenance and daily life expenses. Eurostat (1998) sponsored these studies in the most developed European countries; the scope of information to characterize poverty was broader, and encompassed questions on the level of satisfaction not only of basic needs, but also of other sociocultural aspirations (Jannuzzi 2001).

None of these approaches is more valid or legitimate than the others in measuring poverty or evaluating the target actions or plans for overcoming poverty in any situation. The four approaches are complementary – each one has its own meritorious aspects and also its shortcomings and limitations. Naturally, depending on the design of a specific policy or programme, one or other approach may be more adequate. Monetary poverty indicators are sensitive measures of cash transfer programmes; on the other hand, a multi-sectorial strategy to overcome poverty requires a multidimensional perspective to evaluate its effects.

It is worth noting that poverty measurement depends not only on the adopted conceptual/analytical perspective, but also on methodological difficulties such as collecting information about income and other dimensions of living conditions in sample surveys. It is well known that refusals to participate in and non-responses to questionnaires, under-reporting of income sources and income volatility add significant difficulties to the estimation of poverty and extreme poverty.

In fact, in the Brazilian case, different conceptual/analytical approaches as well as different methodologies to deal with survey data lead to different estimations of poverty and extreme poverty for 2009/10 (Figure 5.1).[2] The calculation of 21 million people in poverty (the largest number) was obtained from the concept of monetary poverty according to the World Bank criterion of US$2 dollars a day per capita, adjusted by purchasing power parity (PPP); the lowest estimation is obtained by the Oxford Poverty and Human Development Initiative (OPHI) methodology of multidimensional poverty: 5.2 million poor people. By using 2010 census data it is possible to obtain five different estimations – between 13 and 18 million – according to procedures of data processing with zero household income, and allocation and use of micro data of the surveys' Universe or Sample (within the limit of R$70.00 monthly per capita). According to the definition of undernourishment adopted by the Food and Agriculture Organization (FAO), there are 13 million malnourished Brazilians; according to the monetary poverty's criterion of consumption, the Consumer Expenditure Survey identified 11.3 million people, which is similar to the number that were classified as being in Severe Food Insecurity and people considered in extreme poverty by living on under US$1.25 PPP per day.

As presented, the methodologies used for poverty measurement are complex. Yet which of these measures are more adequate to analyse the evolution of poverty over the course of the past decades, for the

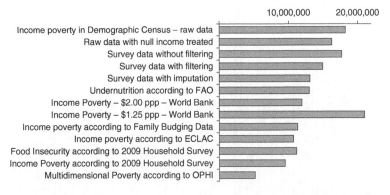

5.1 Estimates of poverty according to different concepts, methodologies and data calculation sources, Brazil, 2009/10 (*sources*: FAO, World Bank, OPHI, IBGE, Cepal)

purposes of monitoring the Millennium Development Goals and fighting against hunger? Which of these measurements better reflect the strategies adopted by the Brazilian government in its fight against hunger and poverty in the last two decades?

From a pragmatic perspective, considering the similar estimates of 'extreme poverty' by the FAO and the National Household Sample Survey of 2009, and also the extension of the available historical series, the World Bank's US$1.25 PPP income poverty indicator is the indicator we adopt for the analysis presented in this section.[3] Certainly, such an indicator has downsides: it does not adequately reflect the conception of poverty currently adopted by Brazilian public policy for the fight against hunger; it does not include, for instance, information about children's access to the National School Feeding Programme, which has significant effects on poverty. It also does not include information on access to other specific programmes for distribution of food baskets or food supplements for pregnant women and newborns.

Typically, the indicator is an approximate measure that identifies families with insufficient resources to buy a monthly basket containing basic food that guarantees the minimum daily calorie intake to all its members.

In fact, analysis of the indicator between 1981 and 2009 is consistent with historical progress regarding access to basic food in Brazil during

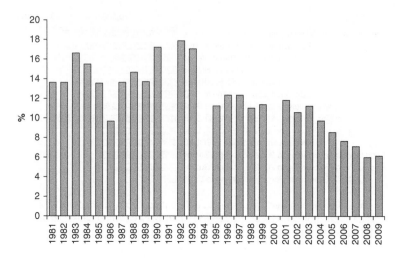

5.2 Evolution of extreme monetary poverty ($1.25 dollar PPP), Brazil, 1981–2009 (*source*: World Bank)

that same period (Figure 5.2). In a context of unemployment and no other governmental interventions for combating hunger (besides the National School Feeding Programme), the level of extreme poverty and starvation was fairly stable during the 1980s (around 15 per cent of the population). In 1986 there was a modest yet relevant decrease, which is explained by the better economic situation brought about by *Plano Cruzado*, which combined a minimum wage increase with stable food prices. The increase in inflation in the early 1990s, in addition to economic and employment retraction, as well as the interruption of food assistance programmes created ten to twenty years before, has certainly aggravated extreme poverty and hunger (extreme poverty has increased two percentage points, to 17 per cent of the population).

From 1993 onwards, with economic recovery, a successful monetary stabilization policy (i.e. *Plano Real*) and a stronger food supply (via increased food imports and higher agricultural productivity), the population that was subjected to unstable food supply gained better access to food. Between 1994 and 2002, the extreme poverty percentage remained around 11–12 per cent of the population.

Since then, under the influence of Lula's social development policies (i.e. *Fome Zero* and *Bolsa Família*, as mentioned above), the promotion of the internal market and its redistributive impacts, extreme poverty dropped to 6.1 per cent in 2009, a third of the figure in 1991.

The decrease in extreme poverty and the expansion of the *Bolsa Família* programme are closely connected. Indeed, between 2003, when the *Bolsa Família* programme was created, and 2010, the programme expanded from 3.6 million to 12.5 million beneficiary households.[4] Furthermore, the figures for extreme poverty have decreased faster in the north-east and north of Brazil, which are also the areas with the greatest expansion of programme coverage. *Bolsa Família* has thus greatly impacted the fight against hunger.

In addition, the *Fome Zero* strategy increased access to water and food: for example, it has built cisterns in the semi-arid region, has distributed food to schools for free with the help of philanthropic organizations, and has strengthened families' agriculture by expanding the network of food security equipment. This has thus contributed to reducing the risk of food insecurity and malnutrition, and a 55 per cent reduction in infant mortality in the north-east region between 2000 and 2010 also reinforces this point (Martignoni 2012).

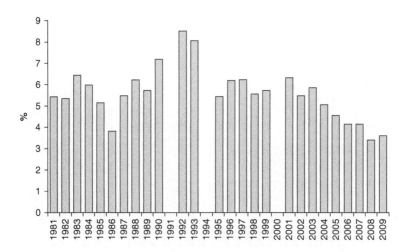

5.3 Evolution of the extreme poverty monetary gap ($1.25 dollar PPP), Brazil, 1981–2009 (*source*: World Bank)

The evolution of the indicator for the intensity of extreme poverty in the decade from 2000 is further evidence of the impact of the *Bolsa Família* programme in reducing extreme poverty. This indicator can be understood as the relative distance of average income per capita of the extreme poor households from the US$1.25 PPP per capita line.[5] As expected of a programme focusing on the poorest (Soares and Satyko 2009), and of income transfers for a larger number of families with children, the beneficial effects of the programme have a strong impact on reducing the extreme poverty gap. While for twenty years, from 1981 to 2001, the indicator remained at the same level, with oscillations resulting from economic policies, between 2003 and 2009 the gap was reduced by 40 per cent, from 5.1 to 3.6 per cent.

Another confirmation of the *Bolsa Família* programme's impact on poverty reduction can be evaluated by the evolution of the income appropriation share of the poorest 10 per cent. During the 1980s there was a regressive movement in income distribution, penalizing the poorest 10 per cent. Since 2002, there has been a reversal of the historical trend, i.e. progressive increases; and by the end of 2009, the poorest 10 per cent received just under 0.8 per cent of national income.

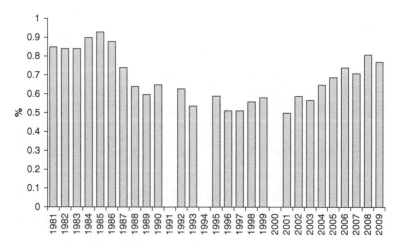

5.4 Evolution of income appropriation of the poorest 10 per cent, Brazil, 1981–2009 (*source*: World Bank)

A 2011 paper, 'Eradicate extreme poverty: a goal within the reach of Brazil', from the Institute of Applied Economic Research, discusses additional effects of the *Bolsa Família* programme on poverty and inequality. It presents a historical series of indicators from 1995 to 2009, based on the National Household Sample Survey. Since 2003, there has been a clear and steady downward trend in poverty, inequality and poverty's intensity (i.e. relative distance from the line of R$70.00) (Osorio et al. 2011).

A similar discussion can be found in another paper from the same institute, in which the authors tested, through a simulation using 2009 National Household Survey data, the possible effects of revoking *Bolsa Família* on beneficiary families. The revocation would raise the number in extreme poverty from 11.9 million to 17.8 million – that is, an additional nearly six million people in extreme poverty (Souza et al. 2011).

A more robust analysis of the importance and magnitude of the *Bolsa Família* programme – and other income transfer programmes in the world – is given by the World Bank. The authors analysed the evolution of poverty in Brazil and several other countries between 2001 and 2009, using different poverty lines – US$4.00, US$2.50, and $1.25, adjusted by purchasing power parity; they also scaled the contribution of different factors and sources of income in their analysis. In the Brazilian case, and with reference to the extreme poverty line of US$1.25, the study points out that a significant poverty reduction was linked to a wage increase and social transference contributions. In terms of the other two poverty lines, labour income is again the main poverty reduction factor in the country, social transferences being a secondary yet still significant factor. In reality, the policy of recovering the purchasing power of the minimum wage and employment creation over the period are the reasons for the improvement in various life-related aspects in Brazil (Azevedo et al. 2013).

The BWEP Plan is the last step towards the inclusion of the extreme poor, aiming at a minimum level of consumption of goods and services. Additionally, it offers a set of opportunities for sustainable development to the extremely poor.

BWEP sets the goal of eradicating extreme income poverty. This is the adopted eligibility criterion, and also the indicator measuring the Plan's success. Nevertheless, the BWEP public policy agenda is multi-sectoral in nature. Despite the limitations of a one-dimensional model, the eradication of extreme income poverty is achievable.

The goal of eradicating extreme poverty is feasible taking into account the commitment to eligibility and assessment parameters: the eradication of extreme monetary poverty leads to financially improved living conditions for the beneficiaries. BWEP's multidimensional scope favours, however, a larger range of social protection and services promotion. So, once the associated target is achieved, BWEP will move towards the concept of multidimensional poverty, incorporating its criteria and indicators. In other words, the eradication of extreme financial poverty will help reduce de facto extreme poverty and also redefine poverty and the public policies addressing it.

Can sustainable development goals help future social protection policy in Brazil?

The game-changing proposal to adopt a set of global SDGs was formalized in the Latin America and Caribbean Preparatory Meeting for the Rio+20 Conference in Santiago (Chile) in September 2011, by the governments of Colombia and Guatemala (Colombia Rio+20 2011). Since then, the debate and consensus-building around the SDGs has attracted a great deal of attention from international agencies, governments, NGOs and academics, as well as other actors. The SDGs, which consider poverty eradication, gender equality, food security, adaptation to and mitigation of climate change, and finance for development, *inter alia*, are now set to define the global policy development agenda for the next fifteen years.

These essential items of development policy are also present in the BWEP Plan. However, closer observation of these policy recommendations can help Brazil to respond to and surmount the challenges posed by the Plan (Paes-Sousa 2013).

As mentioned earlier, the criterion for selecting the potential beneficiaries of the Plan is one-dimensional: nominal income. This under-represents the contribution, or lack of it, of non-monetary income[6] and other dimensions of poverty. In reality, Brazil has already eradicated extreme poverty as defined by monetary means alone. A *comprehensive* concept of poverty – including the broad range of goals identified by the BWEP – is required to push this new policy thrust towards a more advanced and effective sustainable human development model anchored in social protection. Brazil's current and future challenges lie beyond the monetary dimension of poverty. They include long-standing demands for good-quality public services, such as better health, improved education services and a more comprehensive and safer public transportation system.

Having achieved success in taking 22 million people out of monetary-based extreme poverty (living on less than US$1.25 per day), Brazilian public policies now must start to pay more attention to the poor and the new but lower middle class, rather than focusing solely on the extreme poor.[7] However, the risk of falling back into extreme poverty still hangs over those who have recently ascended to a higher social stratum. Concepts such as resilience and sustainability are now critical for enriching the Brazilian anti-poverty policy framework.

In one of the most urbanized countries among the emerging powers, 84.3 per cent of Brazil's population is distributed across 5,700 cities; and only 15.7 per cent live in rural areas. However, according to the 2010 Population Census, there is a high concentration of extreme poverty in rural areas: 46 per cent of those living in extreme poverty live in rural areas. Focusing on the poorest sectors of the population dispersed in both small cities and rural areas is a challenge: the drivers can differ significantly. As a result the BWEP aims to promote their inclusion, at the state level; moving beyond the traditional approach adopted in the past, which saw municipal governments as the main policy brokers.

Brazil has championed a broader view of goals and indicators for the post-2015 agenda. On the eve of achieving its main task, i.e. the eradication of extreme monetary-based poverty, it now faces the challenge of adopting a similar approach for its internal agenda, an agenda defined by broader goals and indicators consistent with a maturing of socio-economic policies.

As an emerging power and a reference country for public policy, Brazil has effectively used its internal experience to shape its international message in relation to SDGs. Revising its internal policies, similarly, in the light of international discourse, can help Brazil to anticipate possible pathways towards an updated development objective for the eradication of all forms of poverty compatible with the next phase of the public policy agenda.

Notes

1 Issues such as social justice, equity, capabilities, empowerment, democracy and moral principles were present in the formative debate of the BWEP. The concepts of Amartya Sen were very influential. For a better understanding of the philosophical perspective of Sen on social needs and public policies, see

Development as Freedom (1999), published by Oxford University Press.

2 All data in this section were obtained from FAO (2012).

3 This value conforms with what from 2011 onwards in Brazil has been called the extreme poverty line, and it is also the parameter used in the *Bolsa Família* programme to allocate the basic benefit. It is near the estimated value for the international extreme poverty line given by the World Bank, which is US$1.25 PPP, and lies between other regional extreme poverty lines calculated by investigators such as Sonia Rocha. See also www.iets.org.br/article.php3?id_article=915.

4 That expansion, in such a short period of time, would not have been possible without the city halls' involvement in the programme's administration, in hiring staff for the registration of potential beneficiaries, delivery of cards and monitoring of its

conditional rules. In fact, the Census Bureau's Annual Social Assistance System – SUAS Census – shows that the number of municipal officers involved in the operation of the *Bolsa Família* programme and social assistance programmes (*Serviço de Proteção Integral à Família*, social and educational activities, etc.) in SUAS public basic facilities more than doubled between 2007 and 2011, when it reached nearly sixty thousand workers.

5 Thus, if a family has, for instance, a per capita income of $35.00, its income should be increased by another $35.00, or 100 per cent, to overcome extreme poverty.

6 Some examples of non-monetary income are house ownership and self-production of food.

7 The sector of the population with a per capita income of between US$1.25 and US$2.50.

References

Alkire, S. and J. Foster (2011) 'Counting and multidimensional poverty measurement', *Journal of Public Economics*, 95(7): 476–87.

Atkinsons, A. B. (2002) *Social Indicators: The EU and Social Inclusion*, Oxford University Press (On Demand).

Azevedo, J. P. et al. (2013) 'Is labor income responsible for poverty reduction? A decomposition approach', Policy Research Working Paper 6414, New York: World Bank.

Colombia Rio+20 (2011) 'Sustainable Development Goals. A proposal from Colombia and Guatemala', Bogotá: Ministerio das Relaciones Exteriores.

Eurostat (1998) 'Income distribution and poverty in EU', in CEPAL, *Poverty Statistics*, Santiago, pp. 169–82.

FAO (2012) *The State of Food Insecurity*, Rome: World Bank Country Database,

OPHI Database, IBGE, Microdata processing.

Feres, J. C. and P. Vilatoro (2011) 'La viabilidad de eradicar la extrema pobreza: un examen conceptual y metodológico', *Estudios Estatísticos y Prospectivos*, 78, Santiago: Cepal.

Jannuzzi, P. M. (2001) 'Indicador de pobreza auto-declarada: discussão e resultados para RMSP em 1998', *Pequisa & Debate*, 12(2): 41–65.

Kageyama, A. and R. Hoffmann (2006) 'Pobreza no Brasil: uma perspectiva multidimensional', *Economia e Sociedade*, 15(1): 79–112.

Osorio, R. G., S. Soares and P. H. Souza (2011) 'Eradicate extreme poverty: a challenge within the reach of Brazil', Texts for Discussion no.1619, Brasilia: IPEA.

Martignoni, E. M. (2012) 'Infant mortality by region and household income levels per capita in 2000 and 2010 Censuses', Technical Study no. 5, Brasilia: SAGI.

Paes-Sousa, R. (2013) 'New strategy for poverty eradication in Brazil: the emergence of the Brasil *Sem Miséria* plan', Brasilia: IPC-IG.

Soares, S. and N. Satyko (2009) 'The *Bolsa Família* program: institutional design, impact and future possibilities', Discussion Paper no. 1424, Brasilia: IPEA.

Souza, P. H., R. G. Osorio and S. Soares (2011) 'Methodology to simulate *Bolsa Família*', Texts for Discussion no.1654, Brasilia: IPEA.

6 | THE MDGS VERSUS AN ENABLING GLOBAL ENVIRONMENT FOR DEVELOPMENT: ISSUES FOR THE POST-2015 DEVELOPMENT AGENDA

Manuel F. Montes

This chapter argues that the practice of international cooperation has clearly disregarded the internationally agreed meaning of sustainable development. Specifically the dominance of the MDG approach unduly focuses on individual-level social development, discounting the economic and genuinely environmental aspects of sustainable development, which are unattainable without macroeconomic development and structural change. It examines the manner in which mechanisms in international trade and finance and premature external 'openness' hinder development in developing countries. These matters have been taken up under the topics of Means of Implementation and the Global Partnership for Development in the debates over the Sustainable Development Goals.

Systemic obstacles to development

In 2015, the international community was preoccupied with political discussions on the alternatives to the Millennium Development Goals (MDGs) after 2015 and the design of the Sustainable Development Goals (SDGs), as mandated by the Rio+20 conference. It is timely to consider the question of whether development is a matter mostly of individual effort on the part of states or whether there are features of the international economic system that could serve as significant obstacles to the development ambitions of communities and countries. If there are obstacles in the international economic system, it is important that the post-2015 development agenda and the SDGs wrestle with and exhibit significant progress in the elimination or reduction of these obstacles.

The limited number of successfully developing countries since the 1950s has produced a debate over whether their success was mostly due to their effective avoidance of international obstacles to development. The following discussion does not have to take one position or the other. It confines itself to evaluating specific features of the international system on the basis of how they are conducive to enabling long-term investment towards economic diversification, a key requirement for sustainable development.

Terminologies of previous development orthodoxies litter the development literature – 'import substitution industrialization', 'basic needs', 'structural adjustment', 'Washington Consensus' and 'Millennium Development Goals' (MDGs). Each of these orthodoxies tended to be a reaction to perceived weaknesses or missing elements from the one immediately preceding it. For example, the 'basic needs' strategy responded to the view that import substitution strategies focused too much on modern, capital-intensive activities, and not enough on raising the average standard of living. The most recent orthodoxy, as exemplified by the MDGs, is that development is about poverty eradication.

This chapter presents the view that poverty eradication is an overly narrow, possibly misleading, overarching objective of development. Poverty eradication is a desired outcome of development but its achievement is permanent only with the movement of a significant proportion of the population from traditional, subsistence jobs to productive, modern employment. The association of development with poverty eradication affords the donor community pride of place in economic policy-making in developing countries. But this place can be at the cost of absolving much of the responsibility of donor countries for supporting an enabling international environment for development in trade, finance and technology, even setting aside such issues as human migration. The poverty eradication approach favours ascribing development failures to errors in domestic policy-making of the aid-receiving countries, drawing attention away from the treacherous features of the international system whose structure serves mainly the economic and political interests of powerful factions in donor countries.

The group of donor countries overlaps practically on a one-to-one basis with the group of countries with dominant voting weights in power centres of global governance, such as the IMF. This group not only overlaps with the group of former colonial powers and the list of Annex I countries in the UN Framework Convention on Climate Change with the largest accumulated discharges in CO_2 over the last two centuries, it overlaps substantially with the group of creditor countries and the headquarters sites of private sector creditors to developing countries. Aid recipient countries have to contend with instabilities in their exchange rates provoked by the monetary policies of donor countries. Episodes of developing country debt distress have seen the starkest instances of development reversals. The group of aid-receiving countries must navigate an unpredictable and arbitrary developing country debt process in the event of debt distress. In the MDGs, issues of global economic governance and burden-sharing are crammed into 'MDG8', the so-called global partnership for development, with a very selective and poorly defined set of targets.[1] Even if more developing countries that are now aid recipients switch into becoming aid donors, such new donors will still have to contend with the instabilities and traps in the global system whose reform they have limited initiative over.

Sustainable development requires not just higher levels of income, nutrition, education and health outcomes but in the first place involves higher levels of productivity and capabilities. Higher levels of productivity and capabilities are possible only with structural transformation of the economy. In turn, in most societies, such a structural transformation has been 'associated with a shift of the population from rural to urban areas and a constant reallocation of labour within the urban economy to higher-productivity activities' (UNCTAD 2011: 6). Structural transformation is possible only with substantial and sustained investment over decades in new activities and products, not just in anti-poverty programmes. In fact, as expounded in the UN (2011a), the need to respond urgently to climate change will require accelerated introduction of new activities and products in developing countries because they have the largest mitigation potential and the greatest adaptation requirements. Fast-tracked climate action will require transfers of financing and technology to developing countries (see ibid.: ch. VI). Climate change will also require achieving sustainable consumption, particularly in developed countries, since their consumption is greatly served by exports produced in 'dirty' industries in developing countries.

Where the international economic system is hostile to investment in new, productivity-enhancing economic activities is where its features create obstacles to development. For example, aid volatility has been shown to create as much as 8 per cent of lost macroeconomic performance (Kharas 2008). Developed countries are host to the largest financial centres, whose operations are intimately linked to tax haven jurisdictions, which are properly called 'offshore financial centres' (OFCs) (Economist 2013); the same *Economist* article, which reports that an estimated $20 trillion is 'stashed away' in OFCs, suggests that it is *onshore* financial centres, 'from the City of London to Delaware', which do not have an interest in shutting down tax havens. The Tax Justice Network (2014) estimates that such illicit flows from developing countries, which could instead have been additional government tax revenues or investment by the wealthy in their own countries, came to $991 billion, or almost $1 trillion, in 2012.

Capital and technological investments are required to overcome the enormous productivity gap between developing and developed countries which characterizes the world economy. In 2008, the ratio of the average gross national income (GNI) per worker in the OECD as compared to those in the least developed countries (LDCs) was 22:1 in favour of the OECD (UNCTAD 2010: 174). This imbalance has worsened by a factor of five in comparison to the earliest days of capitalist development. In the nineteenth century, taking the Netherlands and the United Kingdom (UK) as the richest countries and Finland and Japan as the poorest, the productivity gap was only between 2:1 and 4:1 (Chang 2003).

Commodity dependence and instability in trade and finance

The international economic system is lacking crucial mechanisms for delivering long-term, stable resources required by developing countries to upgrade their capabilities. This is already partly reflected in the existence of MDG8, incomplete as it is, but has also been incorporated in many previous international agreements, for example in the Monterrey Consensus (UN 2003). For example, both the Monterrey Consensus (through paragraph 47, 'Debtors and creditors must share the responsibility for preventing and resolving unsustainable debt situations') and MDG8 (Target 8.B is 'Deal comprehensively with the debt problems of developing countries') recognize the need to overhaul the sovereign debt restructuring mechanism. Countries dependent on commodity exports have experienced sizeable increases in debt liabiliites during booms and have subsequently suffered debt servicing difficulties during the commodity busts.

Dependence on commodity exports sustains the productivity gap between developed and developing countries. Abundant global liquidity and growing trade imbalances fuelled a commodity boom in the 2000s which benefited many developing countries, including many LDCs. All previous global liquidity booms have ended with serious economic crises in developing countries (Akyüz 2012a, 2013). The more recent commodity price boom did not introduce an enduring improvement in macroeconomic balances, especially for low income countries (LICs). While in the 2000s LDCs experienced the strongest growth rates since the 1970s, more than a quarter of LDCs actually saw GDP per capita decline or grow slowly in the 2002–07 global boom (UNCTAD 2010). Even in the middle income region of Latin America, Izquierdo et al. (2007) present evidence of insignificant structural improvement in fiscal and current account balances.

Previous commodity boom periods had similarly not been an occasion for structural change in LDCs. UNCTAD (2009: 145) suggests that between the 1970s and 1997, manufacturing as a proportion of GDP increased by less than two percentage points in LDCs as a group, a period which saw various episodes of commodity and global liquidity booms. When considering LDCs from Africa alone, and including Haiti, manufacturing fell from 11 to 8 per cent of GDP during the same period.

Developing countries extensively liberalized their trade regimes in the 1980s. In the aftermath, UNCTAD (2010: 174) found that some LDCs have more open trade regimes than other developing countries, and others are more open than even developed countries. These policies had been intended to facilitate economic diversification. Instead, more trade liberalization has been associated with a more concentrated structure of exports (see Figure 6.1).

In Latin America and the Caribbean, the phenomenon of '*reprimarización*', a restoration of reliance on primary exports, is unmistakable (see Figure 6.2).

Based on an analysis of the clustering of major breaks in the growth process in the developing world, Ocampo and Parra (2006) contend that unstable macroeconomic performance in developing countries is mostly explained by external events in trade and financing emanating from the economic performance and policies in the developed countries. In the case of smaller economies, these are more susceptible to growth collapses (Ros 2005) and external shocks are a larger proportion of their achieved economic size. Changes in external conditions set in train disorderly debt restructuring, disruptive balance-of-payments

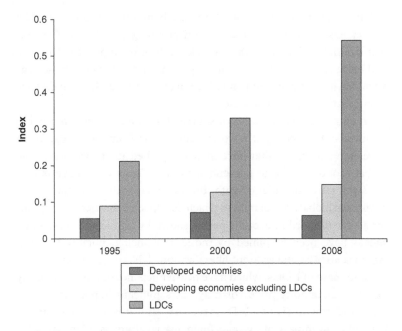

6.1 Concentration of exports (*source*: UNCTAD (2010: 17, Chart 8))

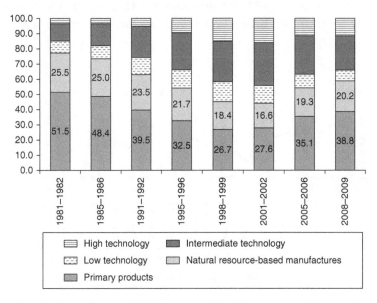

6.2 Structure of exports, Latin America and Caribbean since 1980 (percentages of total value) (*source*: UNECLAC (2010 : 74, Figure II.12))

(BOP) adjustments, widespread private bankruptcies, social conflict and extensive institutional and political changes and policy experimentation, which amplify these breaks in the growth process. Ocampo and Parra (2006) suggest that the 1950s and early 1960s can be seen as a 'golden age' of development coinciding with a much lower incidence of international economic crises.

International trade is a major source of instability. Figure 6.3 traces a pattern of large changes in world trade growth from the 1970s, which developing countries that have increasingly tied their fortunes to the global economy have to contend with. The figure also suggests that the swings are coincidental with, but much larger in amplitude than, changes in global growth rates in which developed countries still account for a large proportion over the period shown by the graph. These trade shocks have been amplified by induced financing, notably in Latin America after capital account liberalization (UN 2008: viii–x).

In the case of LDCs, which have heavier dependence on commodity exports, commodity price volatility has significant impact on investment and growth (UNCTAD 2010: 191). But it is also important to highlight the impact of aid and financing volatility as a key driver of their external debt crises. Aid is as volatile as 'private flows and the volatility increases with aid dependence' (Akyüz 2008: 15–16; also UN 2005: ch. IV). Kharas (2008) indicates that aid volatility imposes

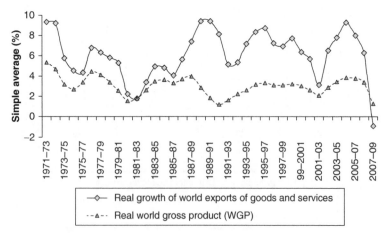

6.3 Growth rates of world trade and world GDP (*source*: UN (2010: 74, Figure IV.1))

through the channel of macroeconomic volatility deadweight losses of 15–20 per cent of the total value of aid, or about 1.9 per cent of GDP for the average aid recipient. Akyüz (2008: 16) deems aid for the most part to be more volatile than 'either output or fiscal revenues', citing IMF-commissioned studies by Robe and Pallage (2001) for volatility and procyclicality with respect to output (especially for African countries) and Bulíř and Hamann (2003), Bulíř and Lane (2004) and Hill (2005) with respect to fiscal revenues.

Instability in private financial flows to developing countries is another significant source of external instability for developing countries. The scale of these flows is amplified by the ability of residents to move their assets abroad to avoid taxes or in the face of looming balance-of-payments difficulties. Figure 6.4 demonstrates a pattern of three distinct boom–bust periods measured through the pattern of net private capital flows to developing countries: the first ended with the Mexican debt crisis in 1982, the second with the Asian financial crisis in 1997, and the third with the Lehman collapse in 2008.

Since the1997 Asian financial crisis, major emerging economies have accumulated international reserves by purchasing developed country financial assets either from their export earnings (in the case of net exporters) or from external borrowing (in the case of net importers) as a form of self-insurance against volatile private portfolio flows.

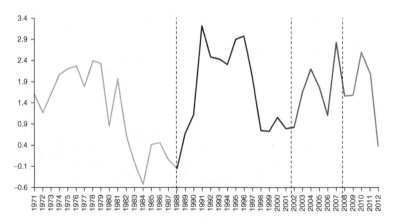

6.4 Net private capital flows to developing countries (percentage of GDP) (*source*: Updated from Akyüz (2012a: 68, Figure 2))

These 'investments' by the developing country authorities reduce the ability of these countries to undertake counter-cyclical policies and build their domestic financial sectors. These 'investments' also impose an opportunity from forgone financing for domestic investment. This mechanism created the ironic pattern just before the 2007/08 crisis of developing country authorities being significant net investors in developed country economies (UN 2010).

It is important to point out that macroeconomic volatility and periodic crises have a long-lasting impact on growth and employment in developing countries, in contrast to the case of developed countries. Figure 6.5 demonstrates this in the case of Turkey, but similar patterns are found for Brazil, Chile, Indonesia and Malaysia (ibid.: ch. V). Growth volatility and investment volatility interact strongly and undermine efforts to spark sustainable private investment. These crises also destabilize public sector balances.

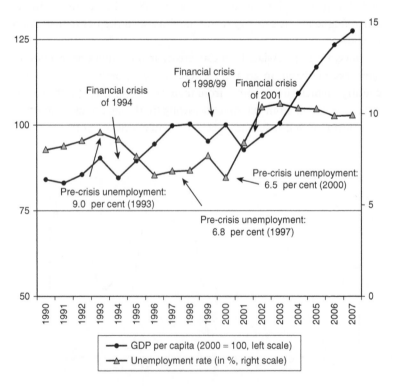

6.5 Medium-term employment impact of crises in Turkey (*source*: UN (2010: 31, Figure II.4))

Investment volatility closely tracks variability in GDP growth rates (see Figure 6.6). In middle-income countries (MICs) where private investment has a larger macroeconomic impact, the causation could flow both ways, either originating from the instability of financing or the cyclicality of growth itself determining the timing of private investment. In the case of LICs and LDCs, the government impact on the macroeconomy is larger. Government spending can be highly volatile when governments are forced to respond in a procyclical manner to reduced export earnings or to meet fixed public deficit targets in structural adjustment programmes. Such abrupt changes in public spending in turn increase the perceived risk of private investment and cause private investment to fall.

The obstacles posed by the international economic architecture to development objectives could be summarized as follows:

1 Economic development requires significant and long-term investment in new activities and the absorption of substantial segments of the population in these activities. Development requires a steady progression towards structural change. One important input to structural change is steady overall economic growth, which impels private investment and risk-taking.

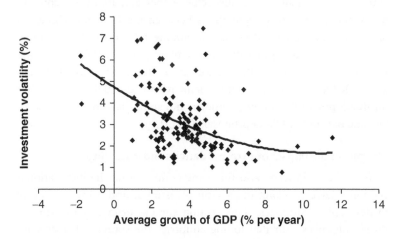

6.6 Growth of GDP and investment volatility among developing countries, 1971–2000 (*source*: UN (2010: 61, Figure III.5)). Investment volatility is measured by the coefficient of variation (CV) of the annual growth rate of gross capital formation at 2000 prices in 1971–2006. The coefficient of variation is defined as the standard deviation divided by the mean for the period.

2 Outcomes and policies in international trade and finance have undermined macroeconomic stability in developing countries. Periodic crises induced by the international economy have thwarted the needed investment.

3 An enabling environment for long-term investment in developing countries will require two things: (1) the reform of international mechanisms, including possibly the introduction of missing ones, and (2) developing countries' capacity to reduce and insulate themselves from harmful international influences.

The Open Working Group proposal for Sustainable Development Goals (OWG 2014) for the seventeen Sustainable Development Goals (SDGs) includes some proposals for means of implementation and global partnership for development. For example, under Goal 10, 'Reduce inequality within and among countries', Subgoal 10.5 calls for moves to 'improve regulation and monitoring of global financial markets and institutions and strengthen implementation of such regulations'. Goal 17, 'Strengthen the means of implementation and revitalize the global partnership for sustainable development', includes items such as Subgoal 17.3, 'enhance global macroeconomic stability including through policy coordination and policy coherence'. These kinds of text, as patchy and unspecific as they are, are the outcome of heavy and contentious negotiations between the G77 and China on one hand and developed countries (among others, the USA, Japan, Australia, Germany and new EU members such as Poland and the Czech Republic) on the other. A core group in the G77 and China had a fully fledged list of means of implemention and a global partnership for development for the negotiations, and some elements managed to become part of the OWG proposals (2014).

Mitigating the impact of external deficits and instability

Instabilities in trade and financing coming from the international economy have a strong impact on investment and growth stability in developing countries. This section surveys proposals to mitigate these influences. For developing countries the sources of instability can be grouped into the following areas: (1) commodities, (2) trade, and (3) external finance, including ODA and private flows. These areas are the key sources of macroeconomic instability in developing countries.

OWG (2014) incorporates some relevant international outcomes from previous agreements, such as the Brussels Plan of Action for LDCs, the MDGs. For example, Subgoal 17.10, 'promote a universal, rules-based, open, non-discriminatory and equitable multilateral trading system under the WTO including through the conclusion of negotiations within its Doha Development Agenda', comes from the Millennium Declaration of 2000 (Paragraph 13). Subgoal 17.11, 'increase significantly the exports of developing countries, in particular with a view to doubling the LDC share of global exports by 2020', comes from the Istanbul Programme of Action (UN 2011b: para. 65a). The core of Subgoal 17.12, 'realize timely implementation of duty-free, quota-free market access on a lasting basis for all least developed countries consistent with WTO decisions, including through ensuring that preferential rules of origin applicable to imports from LDCs are transparent and simple, and contribute to facilitating market access', comes from paragraph 47 of WTO (2005), the WTO 2005 ministerial outcome.

Commodities In the case of commodities, developing countries fall into different categories, according to differences in commodity needs and whether the country imports or exports them.

In the case of foodstuffs as internationally traded commodities, the main problems have been the following (Khor 2012; South Centre 2007; FAO 2010):

1 A pattern of decades-long insufficient investment in food production and in rural areas, which has in turn been linked to an overemphasis on external trade to cover domestic food requirements and low prospective returns on investment in the face of continuing agricultural subsidies in developed countries.
2 A publicly subsidized shift to biofuel production since the early 2000s, which has now significantly reduced the capacity for food production.
3 Increasing dependence on events emanating from the financial markets for the determination of international prices of basic food.

OWG (2014) reflects some of these concerns; how the agreed text will be fleshed out in the future is uncertain and also a matter of the determination of developing countries and support from international civil society. Goal 2, 'End hunger, achieve food security and improved nutrition, and promote sustainable agriculture', manages to have some notable Subgoals. For example, 2.4: 'by 2030 ensure sustainable food production systems and implement resilient agricultural practices that increase productivity and production, that help maintain ecosystems, that strengthen capacity for adaptation to climate change, extreme weather, drought, flooding and other disasters, and that progressively improve land and soil quality', and 2.b, 'correct and prevent trade restrictions and distortions in world agricultural markets including by the parallel elimination of all forms of agricultural export subsidies and all export measures with equivalent effect, in accordance with the mandate of the Doha Development Round'.

For the petroleum, minerals and metals sector, the question of commodity booms and busts and the differentiation between short-term and long-terms trends are critical (Erten and Ocampo 2012). Financial markets have also been seen to have had an important impact on the volatility of prices in these sectors.

Booms and busts in commodity prices have strong macroeconomic and investment effects on commodity-dependent exporters. Busts in commodity prices (or increases in international food and energy prices) provoke periods of external borrowing on the part of commodity exporters (or net importers of food and energy). In 1963, the IMF established a compensatory fund which permitted non-conditional financing for periods of falling commodity prices, to be paid back when commodity prices recovered. It was the largest special IMF facility and accounted for a quarter of total IMF credit extended between 1976 and 1985 (Kumar 1988).

In the 1990s, the compensatory non-conditional financing from the IMF for shocks that were purely external in nature was increasingly in conflict with structural adjustment programmes (SAPs) and poverty-reduction and development policy reform programmes. By 1998, the IMF's financial facilities were effectively folded into the poverty-reduction strategy programmes, which transformed them into conditional financing carrying interest, a modality inappropriate to the purpose and expensive to potential users. Following the 2009 G20 summit, rules were amended to relax conditionality procedures and implement an increase in borrowing levels. What is still lacking is a stable, non-conditional, international facility for compensatory financing for external shocks.

Trade Given the high rates of growth in global trade since the end of the Second World War, Lewis (1979), in his Nobel lecture, suggested that moving towards export-led growth would be a reasonable gamble. This challenge had been taken up by most developing countries since the start of the 1980s. While the volume of trade is much higher than in 1980, and the size of the developing economies as a proportion of the total world economy has increased, only a few countries have succeeded in changing the structure of their economic relationship with the global economy in the period of intensified trade engagement since the 1980s (as also reflected in Figures 6.1 and 6.2 in the previous section).

In some countries, such as China – which is counted among those whose gamble on export-dependent[2] growth has 'paid off' – there are serious concerns that this pattern of growth is unsustainable (Akyüz 2012a) and that a reorientation towards domestic demand is already required. The unprecedented growth rates in output and income recognized by Lewis (1979) were those achieved in the era of import substitution and internationally sanctioned state controls over private capital flows, not during the era of export promotion and deregulation of private finance. Export-reliant growth for most countries did not lead to the required scale and timing of economic diversification.

The most dynamic system and rule-making arena has been in free trade agreements (FTAs) and bilateral investment treaties (BITs), involving reductions in tariff rates, lower state regulation, and strengthened protection for intellectual property and investors' rights. The process of negotiation and accession towards economic partnership agreements (EPAs) with the European Union is one of these growing issues. EPAs, which have been agreed and begun to be put into force in many Caribbean countries, require participating countries to eliminate tariffs on 80 per cent of the value of trade within fifteen years.

African countries have offered instead to liberalize 60 per cent over twenty years; the European Commission rejected the proposal. In many countries in Africa, between 50 and 70 per cent of exports to the EU 'are made up of only one product' – petroleum accounting for 90 per cent of Nigerian exports, gold and diamonds 96 per cent of Botswana's exports, coffee 67 per cent of Burundi's exports (South Centre 2010: 2). The challenge posed by the EPA tariff coverage is that African countries must rapidly establish competitive industries in other products and sectors within fifteen years. The danger is that the EPA will 'lock African countries into their current patterns of production, i.e. low levels of manufacturing capacity' (ibid.: 2).

The structure of economic openness should depend on the level of countries' economic development, something the present free trade paradigm does not recognize (Akyüz 2009b). This would have to involve a degree of non-reciprocity, so that countries could shield some economic activities from external competition until they are competitive. This could involve low or no tariffs on imports for machinery and other inputs to new production activities while having protective tariffs for activities that are being developed.

WTO obligations limit policies that have been traditionally applied for structural transformation and catch-up, a situation Chang (2003) has characterized as 'kicking away the ladder', since the now developed countries had the scope to apply these policies in their own development.

Disciplines on investment measures under the Agreement on Trade-Related Investment Measures (TRIMS) inhibit WTO members from imposing domestic content requirements on investors. Intellectual property rights – which are enforceable under the Agreement on Trade-Related Aspects of Intellectual Property Rights (TRIPS) through trade sanctions – hinder reverse engineering and other activities to adapt foreign technologies to local conditions. Moreover, the threat of trade sanctions on key exports discourages efforts in developing countries to undertake reverse engineering activities even when such actions could potentially reduce the import bill or foreign exchange outflow and/or are supportive of the start-up of new economic activities.

There are few signs that these developing country obligations undertaken in exchange for promised but unrealized actions on the part of developed countries, particularly in the elimination of agricultural subsidies, can be moderated or renegotiated soon, under the WTO's Doha development agenda. The WTO Bali ministerial meeting in December 2013 did not advance these issues.

Based on these considerations, the following elements are important in reshaping the international trade regime:

1 *There is an urgent need to dramatically shrink, if not eliminate, subsidies* in developed countries that disadvantage developing countries through trade. The most flagrant of these are agricultural subsidies.

2 *The principle of non-reciprocity on the basis of development level must be revived and strengthened in trade.* This is an application of the principle of common but differentiated responsibilities in the area of trade.

The principal challenge is the revival and elaboration of non-reciprocity based on the level of development, which can take many forms. One well-known approach is the provision of longer adjustment periods. Unfortunately, conditions for accession often ignore the applicant country's level of development. Moreover, adjustment periods have been stipulated as a fixed number of years, rather than being based on the development level, as is the case at present for the intellectual property exemption for LDCs. Another problem is that exclusions from international disciplines, such as those for environment and research and development (R&D), actually tilt the playing field in favour of developed countries, since these have more resources and human capacities to undertake such interventions. R&D and environmentally motivated activities require public sector financing which is in short supply in developing countries since their tax and revenue systems are not as well developed as those of developed countries. The underlying issue is that the expansion of international commerce requires a steady increase in the number of countries that can participate in trade without increasing their debt to other countries. Restoring flexibility in the setting of tariff rates by developing countries is critical.

This can be done within a framework of progressive trade openness in the long term by returning to earlier approaches of measuring openness based on average rates across tariff lines. This will allow countries to raise or lower tariff rates according to which industries they seek to promote at a particular stage of development. The current approaches of setting percentages of tariff lines that either must be bound or set to zero within a particular time frame are either inimical to development or require high government capabilities to undertake rapid sectoral development interventions if the country is to escape being locked into its current pattern of production.

Financial flows In the 2013/14 United Nations General Assembly discussions on Sustainable Development Goals, the 'means of implementation' became an arena of debate between developed and developing countries. Developed countries took the position that private capital can be mobilized for developing financing with the removal of controls on capital flows, while developing countries were more sceptical that foreign private flows could by themselves provide the long-term finance needed for developmentally oriented investment. At the global level, capital and financial market liberalization was expected to enable developing countries to acquire increased access to investment financing. Based on investment rates on fixed capital, there is no evidence that the increased volume of capital flows can be associated with increased investment (see UN 2010: chs 2 and 5). Instead, since the 1980s, in response to the removal of capital account controls, private flows have been mostly short-term, leading to increased volatility and uncertainty, and these appear to have destabilized long-term investment actions critical for structural transformation and development.

For many LDCs, notably in Africa, ODA represents a large proportion of public resources, as much as 40 per cent for some. Volatility in ODA flows induces volatility in public spending, which in turn induces volatility in demand in the whole economy. One can group the required reforms into two main categories (Akyüz 2009a): crisis prevention and crisis resolution.

Crisis prevention

Crisis prevention mechanisms are crucial for reducing the vulnerability of developing countries to external financial instability, while preserving their national policy autonomy to set their pace of international trade integration. Three areas require attention for crisis prevention (ibid.; see also UN 2009, Ocampo 2011):

1 Effective multilateral discipline over financial, macroeconomic and exchange rate policies in systemically important countries, particularly those economies whose currencies are components of the IMF's special drawing rights – the United States, the eurozone countries, Japan and the UK. Such countries should be precluded from quantitive easing when its extent floods the international economy with liquidity which developing countries have to fend off to safeguard the levels of their exchange rates and international competitiveness.
2 Establishment of an international reserves system not based on a national currency or currencies.
3 Effective regulation and supervision of financial markets and capital flows.

To achieve the first goal, the international system must establish monetary and financial disciplines on reserve-issuing economies. Large swings in macroeconomic policies and financial conditions in developed economies have imposed boom–bust cycles on developing economies. 'International spillovers from macroeconomic, exchange rate and financial policies in advanced economies are much more damaging ... than shocks from their trade policies. But, unlike trade, there is no effective multilateral discipline in money and finance' (Akyüz 2009a: 12). Because of the absence of obligations on the part of the USA as a reserve-issuing currency, there was no mechanism, including in the IMF, to prevent the explosion of risks in the US financial sector, whose failure has caused a global crisis.

A fundamental change in the reserve system is the second key requirement of crisis prevention. Effectively, the current global reserve system depends on the national currency of the USA. Liquidity booms and busts experienced by developing countries have been induced by policy changes in the USA in pursuit of its own macroeconomic imperatives. The system is also inherently unstable owing to the 'Triffin dilemma', which requires the reserve-issuing country to run current account deficits to provide liquidity to underpin increasing global trade. This system had been anchored in a fixed rate of gold convertibility and unsurprisingly collapsed in 1971 when the USA abandoned convertibility because of the threat of its gold stock running out.

The Asian crisis in the second half of 1990s demonstrated the inherent instability of the system and the vulnerability of developing countries to financial flows. Instability in international financial flows has resulted in developing countries undertaking significant self-insurance by accumulating reserves. This is itself a source of additional instability since it generated financing for deficits undertaken by the USA in the lead-up to the crisis.

The current crisis has restarted discussion on increasing the use of the Special Drawing Rights (SDRs) of the IMF to uncouple global liquidity from the US dollar. There are technical and governance issues that must be addressed in increasing the use of SDRs (UN 2010, 2012; Akyüz 2009a) but this approach provides the most accessible path to reducing dependence on a national currency and removing a source of imbalance leading to a crisis.

The effective regulation of financial markets and capital flows is the third pillar of crisis prevention. The present crisis demonstrates that financial claims are highly vulnerable to cumulative processes that do not correct themselves except through discontinuous crises with large policy and social dislocation. Moreover, financial instability emanating from large financial centres has adverse international spillovers, in both the boom and bust phases.

In practice, applying common but differentiated responsibility in international financial regulation will require that developing countries do not undertake the same degree of liberalization of financial services under the WTO; at a minimum, this will require that the positive list approach in scheduling international services to be liberalized must be continued. In practice, developing countries must also protect their sovereign right to impose controls on capital flows as provided for in the IMF's Articles of Agreement. The IMF (2012) recently published an 'institutional view' of capital account liberalization and management which recognized this right. Developing countries will need to exercise this right in the face of the generally 'hostile' (Gallagher 2011: 12) view that IMF staff have had of capital account management tools since the 1990s.

Financial crisis resolution
Financial crises have been occasions for dramatic development reversals in the developing world. Avoiding these reversals will require orderly and equitable approaches to crisis resolution which the international system does not provide at present.

The standard approach has been fraught with controversy. IMF-led programmes involve new financial injections and public sector austerity, which are mainly intended to keep debtor countries up to date on their debt service obligations with external private debtors. These programmes insist on keeping the capital account open, even with significant capital outflows and losses in reserves. Under these programmes, the burden of adjustment falls almost exclusively on debtor countries. These programmes often require the public sector to assume the external debt obligations of the private sector (often including those of operations of foreign companies resident in the debtor country). This approach exempts external creditors from market discipline and propagates moral hazard in private financial lending activities to developing countries.

The underlying objective of crisis resolution must be to restore as quickly as possible the ability of the affected country to resume economic activities, as is the case in crisis resolution in domestic contexts. This will require the sanctioning of standstills during the period of debt-resolution negotiation and the provision of resources for critical current account needs (Akyüz 2009a). Beyond a standstill, a growth-oriented resolution could also require restrictions on capital account flows and import restrictions during the period of debt resolution in order to conserve foreign exchange.

The absence of an orderly, non-arbitrary process of sovereign debt resolution is an important development obstacle. Countries are subjected to litigation which ties up their external economic transactions; a proper crisis-resolution mechanism will include a standstill on such litigation. There is a need to involve neutral parties in the resolution process, such as arbitration panels made up of experts, as in the WTO's dispute settlement process, since the lead role played by the IMF in these episodes creates conflict-of-interest concerns as the IMF and its sister organization the World Bank are themselves creditors.

Rebuilding domestic 'policy space'[3]

The radical application of SAPs and Poverty Reduction Strategy Papers (PRSPs) in the developing world hinged essentially on reliance on private incentives and markets to address social problems and underdevelopment based on profound suspicions concerning the capacity of other institutions, particularly the government, to deal with these issues (see Montes 2013: section 1). The MDG framework requires governments to invest in social sectors while keeping low tariffs and taxes which induce fiscal deficits. It is also assumed this should be done while keeping the emphasis on international competitiveness, and progressive opening of the capital account. Since the MDGs provided social targets as responsibilities of developing country governments, Nayyar (2011: 19) characterized the resulting division of responsibilities thus: 'In fact, the emphasis on social development meant that governments in LDCs relied on external resources to finance expenditure on social sectors but did not mobilize domestic resources to finance investment in infrastructure, agriculture or productive activities.'

The global deregulation of financial markets has made large private sector portfolio managers the principal arbiters of real sector outcomes, in sharp contrast to the situation in the 1950s and 1960s. The original Bretton Woods economic system of 1944 assigned a definite priority to the real sector, as opposed to the financial sector, as the driver of growth. The Bretton Woods system mandated controls over capital movements, which were eventually eroded when countries eliminated policies on their capital account. The resulting system is that private portfolio managers can immediately react through capital movements to policy changes by developing country governments and their central banks. Developing country policy-makers find their policy options limited to those that will not provoke adverse reactions on the part of international portfolio managers.

Since the 1980s, international priorities have shifted away from policies that promote expanded employment, trade and production. While in the past developing countries sought to protect domestic industries from competition from imports to build their competitiveness, the proliferation of international disciplines, including those in FTAs such as under the EU's economic partnership agreements, reduces the number of industries they can seek to develop and protect (by binding the tariff at zero, for example, for 80 per cent of tariff lines). FTAs require accelerated trade liberalization and limit the period and the resources public authorities can utilize to build domestic industries to enable them to expand their participation in external trade in subsequent years. The accompanying shift in international economy policy towards decisive control by private financial markets over economic decisions as a result of national and international policies towards financial deregulation has reduced public resources and mechanisms for addressing international boom–bust cycles. Financial markets have attained enormous influence on commodity prices and access to credit.

There are two sources of restrictions of policy space in developing countries: (1) restraints originating in the overall status of 'openness' in the international economy; and (2) constraints arising from international commitments. In an ethos that privileges openness, these two sources, of course, interact. For example, the openness of commodity-dependent economies makes them more susceptible to the procyclicality of international prices. During price booms, many commodity-exporting countries have greater access to external debt, and many take it on. During periods of commodity-price downturns, these economies are more subject to conditionalities in stand-by programmes with international financial institutions, which have most often resulted in restrictions on policy space in the name of enhancing openness to the international economy.

Nature and degree of economic 'openness' International trade and investment provide important advantages to developing countries. However, the nature and degree of economic openness themselves have a direct impact on the amount of policy space available to authorities in developing countries. The term 'openness' refers to the extent to which states have degraded their capacity to regulate private sector actions to achieve national or developmental goals.

The most significant loss of policy tools for developing countries has come from liberalization of the capital account. The degree of capital-account openness severely restricts the scope for monetary policy and exchange-rate policy. While it would be preferable to use exchange-rate policy to achieve exchange-rate stability in order to meet trade and domestic industrial development objectives, surges in external capital flows can overwhelm the resources of monetary authorities to intervene in exchange-rate markets. With fully open capital accounts, authorities also lose the ability to use interest rates to determine credit availability and adopt a counter-cyclical policy.

Under the IMF Articles of Agreement, capital controls legally remain a sovereign right of member states. However, member states have given up some of these rights via BITs. They have also given up many of the tools to regulate capital accounts as part of SAP commitments.

In many emerging markets, authorities have shown reluctance to recover capital-account management tools. In the years after their economic crises in the late 1990s, capital accounts in Asian countries were more open than they were before (Akyüz 2012a). For many countries in Latin America, accepting exchange appreciation through open capital accounts has played a role in meeting inflation targets, but this is at the expense of medium- and long-term goals in productivity growth, employment and industrial development.

There is a channel through which open capital accounts increase the risk of lending to developing countries, which is contrary to the widely held view that open capital accounts reduce the risks to lenders by offering greater assurance of being able to recover their claims. Because most developing countries cannot borrow abroad in their own currencies, 'during recessions the real value of their currency tends to decline, raising the cost of servicing foreign debt exactly when the capacity to pay is diminished' (UNCTAD 2011: 41).

Developing countries must recover a capacity to regulate their capital accounts. Among regulations on capital accounts, 'macro-prudential' tools and policies apply to protect the prudential integrity of domestic financial systems. However, a significant proportion of capital flows, such as portfolio positions in the local stock markets and the foreign purchase of local bonds, are not undertaken in the banking system (though banks might serve as conduits for these transactions) and are not normally part of financial supervisory activities. In fact, because previous BOP crises have been followed by widespread collapses in financial sectors in developing countries, it would be advisable for even 'macro-prudential' policies to be undertaken beyond prudential reasons with a view to eliminating the build-up of external imbalances and an increased risk of BOP crises.

Capital controls are the most critical when countries are facing a payments crisis, since international reserves are necessarily finite. As discussed in the section on crisis resolution, developing countries must have the capacity to impose orderly standstills and have access to external finance in these situations.

At the international level, improved regulation of source markets and greater stability in exchange rates and interest rates in reserve-issuing countries have the potential significantly to reduce capital surge pressures in developing countries and facilitate capital account regulation.

International commitments In the original Millennium Declaration (UN 2000: para. 13), UN member countries declared: 'We are committed to an open, equitable, rule-based, predictable and non-discriminatory multilateral trading and financial system,' thus incorporating equity as a standard for the international system. When the MDGs were formulated, in theory drawn from the Millennium Declaration, the standard of equity was not carried over and target 8A under MDG8 requires only further development of an 'open, rule-based, predictable, non-discriminatory trading and financial system'. A clear lacuna in the international system is the poorly developed conception of what equity in the design, application and practice of a rules-based international trade and financial system entails.

How equity is built into the rules and practices of international governance is key to assigning differential responsibilities in sustaining a development-enabling global system.

In the case of external imbalances, the international financial system provides for enforceable adjustments only on debtor countries, the country grouping most populated by developing countries. Adjustment programmes for debtor countries are the favoured domain of policy conditionality, which has subsequently provoked extensive international debate within the framework of aid effectiveness. Under SAPs, occasioned by the developing country debt crises of the 1980s, conditionality proliferated and reached extensively into development policies and strategies, going beyond what might be considered donors' legitimate concern to prevent the wasteful use of resources provided to debtors in support of their adjustment programmes. The OECD-led aid-effectiveness effort initially appeared to incorporate ambitious intentions to reform the system of policy conditionality towards genuine partnership between donors and recipients and the realization of 'country ownership' of development programmes.

The framework for country ownership starts with debtor/recipient countries taking the lead in deciding on and designing their own development programmes. In practice, the design of many of the programmes involved aligning country policies to policies favoured by international financial institutions (UNCTAD 2011). An earlier, delicately worded, finding of a report of the World Bank's (2004: viii) evaluation office on PRSP states: 'The Bank management's process for presenting a PRSP to the Board undermines ownership. Stakeholders perceive this practice as "Washington signing off" on a supposedly country-owned strategy.'

A very important form of policy space constriction comes from the growing area of BITs and private investor protections incorporated in the FTAs. Developed countries, notably the United States and European countries, have required investor protection in negotiating FTAs and EPAs. Under BITs, private investors obtain the standing to lodge disputes directly with states for violations of investors' rights, which have been interpreted broadly to include policies that impact expected future earnings. This permits the private parties, mostly international companies, extraordinary influence over the policies of their host governments, well beyond domestic political processes and accountability. While both developing and developed countries are party to these treaties, the asymmetry derives from the more limited resources of developing countries, the greater incidence of international companies which are in fact based in developed countries, and the greater need for development interventions in poorer countries. Obligations under these treaties can subject developing countries to penalties if, for example, a government imposed restrictions on capital outflows during a BOP crisis (Montes 2012).

The international community must acknowledge the role of these asymmetries as obstacles to development, recognizing that national policy space is indispensable for all countries, developed or developing. Scoring trends using indicators of these asymmetries would be a valuable activity for civil society and international research institutes.

Taking on international obligations is a sovereign national decision. In theory, these commitments sustain the value of the multilateral system for all participants in the system, although some benefit more than others. In exchange for a derogation of sovereign powers, global rules protect countries from arbitrary treatment in economic matters, such as their exports in foreign markets. The issue of international commitments arises when they are inequitable in nature, application or practice,[4] meaning that they demand more in terms of performance and contribution on the part of poorer and weaker economies compared to developed economies. Beyond inequality among classes and people, inequitable rules among nations are an obstacle to development and poverty eradication. 'It is also clear that unfair rules of the game in the contemporary world economy would encroach upon policy space so essential for development' (Nayyar 2011: 19).

In trade, developed countries have retained their agricultural subsidies. Developing countries have fewer resources to sustain agricultural subsidies and have taken on commitments to limit restrictions on agricultural imports. Newly acceding countries to the WTO have been required to place a ceiling on or to eliminate agricultural subsidies. In the WTO, existing members have the right to impose obligations on countries seeking membership which they themselves do not fulfil. There is a wide range of sizes of economies, markets and levels of development in the WTO. Developing countries trying to draw from the General Agreement on Tariffs and Trade (GATT) well-defined tradition of 'special and differential treatment' (SDT) have found it difficult to make measurable progress on the Doha Declaration's agreement 'that all special and differential treatment provisions shall be reviewed with a view to strengthening them and making them more precise, effective and operational' (WTO 2001: para. 44).

Conclusions

While developing countries hold primary responsibility for their own development, the fortunes of their economies are now even more severely dependent on structures and events in the international economy. The international system can serve as an obstacle to development in two ways: (1) missing, defective or perverse international institutional arrangements; and (2) restrictions on national policies from an undifferentiated proliferation of international obligations and policy rules.

Focusing development cooperation on poverty eradication can be misleading, especially if such a focus absolves economically powerful countries of responsibility for eliminating systemic obstacles to development. Many of these obstacles have the potential of 'biting back' and causing damage to developed countries themselves. Many analysts look upon the current unresolved troubles of the eurozone as another instance of the error of resolving external debt crises through adjustment only on the part of indebted countries. As well as 'biting back', the international community needs to recognize the adverse medium- and long-term economic, social and environmental implications of anaemic development from a poorly structured international system. In the 1950s and 1960s, development progress was more robust, but this was also a period of more effective development cooperation and national policy space. Many of the elements needed to reform global mechanisms and restore the balance between international disciplines and national policy space are found in the outcomes of existing UN agreements but are poorly put into practice.

Some of the elements of effective development cooperation emerged in the SDGs (OWG 2014). Among the list of malfunctioning international mechanisms mentioned in the SDGs are the following areas:

1 Strengthening compensatory finance for commodities-dependent developing countries; Subgoal 2.c requires international food commodity markets to 'adopt measures to ensure the proper functioning of food commodity markets and their derivatives, and facilitate timely access to market information, including on food reserves, in order to help limit extreme food price volatility'.
2 Strengthening special and differential treatment in WTO rules and enlarging the non-reciprocal content of trade agreements, including FTAs, to permit developing countries greater ability to diversify their

domestic economies; Subgoal 10c: 'implement the principle of special and differential treatment for developing countries, in particular least developed countries, in accordance with WTO agreements'.

3 Arriving at equitable and effective disciplines over agricultural subsidies in developed countries; Subgoal 2c as discussed above.

4 Restoring flexibility in the setting of tariff rates, within reasonable ranges, to enable developing countries to raise or lower tariff rates in line with shifting priorities to develop specific sectors, as opposed to permanently bound tariff ceilings; no specific goal in the SDGs.

5 Creating effective arrangements to reduce the probability and size of international financial crises; no specific goal, but some hints in Subgoal 17.13: 'enhance global macroeconomic stability including through policy coordination and policy coherence'.

6 Establishing orderly and equitable international financial and debt crisis resolution mechanisms; Subgoal 17.4: 'assist developing countries in attaining long-term debt sustainability through coordinated policies aimed at fostering debt financing, debt relief and debt restructuring, as appropriate, and address the external debt of highly indebted poor countries (HIPC) to reduce debt distress'.

Subgoal 17.5 calls for 'respect [for] each country's policy space and leadership to establish and implement policies for poverty eradication and sustainable development'. In protecting and enhancing space for national policies in developing countries, this paper presented a few proposals, including:

1 Revising the structure of international commitments so that, based on equity and common but differentiated responsibilities (see paragraph 5 of the OWG (2014) preamble), developed countries bear a greater burden than at present in international obligations and restrictions in the area of domestic subsidies, aid conditionalities and macroeconomic adjustments; the most problematic of these are developed countries' agricultural subsidies.

2 Reforming current approaches to bilateral BITs and FTAs that limit the ability of developing countries to undertake changes in policies and regulations which might alter the profit expectations of foreign investors.

3 Restoring the capacity of developing countries to regulate their capital accounts.

Efforts to reform international economic architecture are impeded by the constraint that the highest decision-making bodies in key institutions, such as the IMF, do not provide sufficient voting weight and policy influence to countries most affected by their actions. One effort under way but under capricious political obstruction is that of updating voting weights in the IMF in line with the changed economic structure. Even the G20, where important developing countries sit, has been unable to advance progress. Even though they are non-specific, the proposed SDGs (OWG 2014) have three items that could possibly be a basis for future efforts in this regard: Subgoal 16.6: 'develop effective, accountable and transparent institutions at all levels'; Subgoal 16.7: 'ensure responsive, inclusive, participatory and representative decision-making at all levels'; and Subgoal 16.8: 'broaden and strengthen the participation of developing countries in the institutions of global governance'.

The coming struggle therefore is one of achieving greater specificity in designing and implementing needed reforms. A historical precedent was the redesign of the international economic system through the Bretton Woods agreements in 1944, drawing on the lessons of the humanitarian catastrophes in the first half of the twentieth century. The political discussions in the UN on post-2015 development and the approval of the SDGs should be the occasion to build a development-enabling international economic environment, or at least to set in motion a process that can eventually eliminate the obstacles to development in the existing system.

Notes

1 The formulation of MDG8 Target 8.A is 'Develop further an open, rule-based, predictable, non-discriminatory trading and financial system' and Target 8.B is 'Deal comprehensively with the debt problems of developing countries'. There are also targets on the needs of LDCs and landlocked countries, and on the international governance of technology sharing. See UN (2013) and the series of previous reports from this annual series, which have attempted to interpret targets and monitor progress on MDG8.

2 China's exports destined for developed countries are heavily dependent on imported inputs from other developing countries (Akyüz 2012a). China's domestic demand is less dependent on imports and could have an impact on the export performance of other developing countries.

3 The original use of the phrase 'policy space' in an official document was in paragraph 16 of the Accra Accord of UNCTAD XII (UNCTAD 2008). In that formulation, policy space is defined in terms of the impact of international rules and arrangements. Policy space is essential to have the scope for introducing 'a range of policies for building domestic productive capacities and local technologies, and to establish

the institutions and support measures to spread the resulting gains' (UNCTAD 2011: 41).

4 Here 'practice' refers to the degree to which states adhere to international obligations, including to the extent that they can be effectively sanctioned when they do not fulfil their obligations.

References

Akyüz, Y. (2008) 'Global rules and markets: constraints over policy autonomy in developing countries', Working Paper no. 87, Geneva: Policy Integration and Statistics Department, International Labour Office, June.

— (2009a) 'Policy response to the global financial crisis: key issues for developing countries', Geneva: South Centre, May.

— (2009b) 'Industrial tariffs, international trade, and development', in M. Cimoli, G. Dosi and J. Stiglitz (eds), *Industrial Policy and Development*, Oxford and New York: Oxford University Press.

— (2012a) 'The boom in capital flows to developing countries: will it go bust again?', *Ekonomi-tek*, 1(1): 63–95.

— (2012b) 'The staggering rise of the South?', Research Paper no. 44, Geneva: South Centre.

— (2013) 'Waving or drowning: developing countries after the financial crisis', Research Paper no. 48, Geneva: South Centre, June, www.southcentre.org/index.php?option=com_content&view=article&id=1968 per cent3Awaving-or-drowning-developing-countries-after-the-financial-crisis&catid=142 per cent3Aglobal-financial-and-economic-crisis&Itemid=67&lang=en, accessed 28 November 2013.

Bulíř, A. and A. J. Hamann (2003) 'Aid volatility: an empirical assessment', *IMF Staff Paper* 50 (1).

Bulíř, A. and T. Lane (2004) 'Aid and fiscal management', in S. Gupta, B. Clements and G. Inchauste (eds), *Helping Countries Develop: The Role of Fiscal Policy*, Washington, DC: IMF, pp. 422–51.

Chang, H.-J. (2003) *Kicking Away the Ladder – Development Strategy in Historical Perspective*, London: Anthem Press.

Economist (2013) 'The missing $20 trillion', 16 February.

Erten, B. and J. A. Ocampo (2012) 'Supercycles of commodity prices since the mid-nineteenth century', DESA Working Paper no. 110, ST/ESA/2006/DWP/24, United Nations Department of Economic and Social Affairs, February.

FAO (Food and Agricultural Organization) (2010) 'The state of food insecurity in the world: addressing food insecurity in protracted crises', Rome: FAO.

Gallagher, K. (2011) 'The IMF, capital controls and developing countries', *Economic and Political Weekly*, xlvi(19), 7 May.

Hill, R. V. (2005) 'Assessing rhetoric and reality in the predictability of aid', Human Development Report Occasional Paper 2005/25, New York: UNDP.

IMF (International Monetary Fund) (2012) 'The liberalization and management of capital flows: an institutional view', Washington, DC: IMF, 14 November, www.imf.org/external/np/pp/eng/2012/111412.pdf, accessed 28 November 2012.

Izquierdo, A., R. Romero and E. Talvi (2007) 'Booms and busts in Latin America: the role of external factors', Working Paper 631, IADB Research Department.

Kharas, H. (2008) 'Measuring the cost of aid volatility', Wolfensohn Center for Development Working Paper

no. 3, Washington, DC: Brookings
Institution.

Khor, M. (2012) 'Food issues in the Rio+20
spotlight. SouthViews', Geneva:
South Centre, July, www.southcentre.
org/index.php?option=com_content&
view=article&id=1796 per cent3Afood-
issues-in-the-rio20-spotlight-19-july-
2012&catid=150 per cent3Asouthview
s&Itemid=358&lang=en, accessed 25
November 2012.

Kumar, M. (1988) 'The stabilizing role of
the Compensatory Financing Facility:
empirical evidence and welfare
implications', IMF Working Paper no.
88/108, Washington, DC, 21 December.

Lewis, A. (1979) 'The slowing down of
the engine of growth', Nobel Prize
Lecture, www.nobelprize.org/
nobel_prizes/economic-sciences/
laureates/1979/lewis-lecture.html,
accessed 20 September 2014.

Montes, M. F. (2012) 'Capital controls,
investment chapters and Asian
development objectives', Paper
presented at the conference
'Compatibility review of the
trade regime and capital account
regulations', CEDES, Buenos Aires,
28/29 June.

— (2013) 'Obstacles to development
in the international economic
architecture', Background paper for
the *European Report on Development
2013*, Brussels: European Commission,
www.erd-report.eu/erd/report_
2012/documents/bp/bgpapers/
Montesfinal.pdf, accessed 20
September 2013.

Nayyar, D. (2011) 'The MDGs beyond 2015',
Research Paper no. 38, Geneva: South
Centre.

Ocampo, J. A. (2011) 'A development-
friendly reform of the international
financial architecture', *Politics &
Society*, 39: 315–30.

Ocampo, J. A. and M. A. Parra (2006) 'The
dual divergence: growth successes

and collapses in the developing world
since 1980', DESA Working Paper no.
24, ST/ESA/2006/DWP/24, United
Nations Department of Economic and
Social Affairs, June.

OWG (2014) 'Open Working Group
proposal for Sustainable
Development Goals',
sustainabledevelopment.un.org/
sdgsproposal, accessed 28 November
2014.

Robe, M. A. and S. Pallage (2001) 'Foreign
aid and the business cycle', *Review
of International Economics*, 9(4),
November.

Ros, J. (2005) 'Divergence and growth
collapses: theory and empirical
evidence', in J. A. Ocampo (ed.), *Beyond
Reforms: Structural Dynamics and
Macroeconomic Theory*, Stanford, CA:
Stanford University Press, pp. 211–32.

South Centre (2007) 'The development
dimension agricultural negotiations',
Policy Brief no.7, Geneva: South
Centre, www.southcentre.org/
index.php?option=com_content&v
iew=article&id=185 per cent3Athe-
development-dimension-of-the-
agriculture-negotiations&catid=51
per cent3Atrade-in-agricultural-
goods&Itemid=67&lang=en, accessed
28 November 2012.

South Centre (2010) 'EPAs: the wrong
development model for Africa and
options for the future', Analytical
Note SC/TDP/AN/EPA/23, Geneva:
South Centre, March.

Tax Justice Network (2014) 'GFI: illicit
financial flows drained $991bn from
developing economies in 2012',
www.taxjustice.net/2014/12/16/
gfi-illicit-financial-flows-drained-
991bn-developing-economies-2012/,
accessed 30 December 2014.

UN (United Nations) (2000) 'United
Nations Millennium Declaration',
General Assembly A/RES/2, New
York, 18 September 2000.

— (2003) *The Monterrey Consensus*, Final text of agreements and commitments adopted at the International Conference on Financing for Development, Monterrey, Mexico, 18–22 March 2002, www.un.org/esa/ffd/monterrey/MonterreyConsensus.pdf, accessed 5 June 2013.

— (2005) *World Economic and Social Survey 2005: Financing for Development*, Sales no. E.05.II.C.1.

— (2008) *World Economic and Social Survey 2008: Overcoming Economic Insecurity*, Sales no. E.08.II.C.1.

— (2009) 'Report of the Commission of Experts of the President of the United Nations General Assembly on reforms of the international monetary and financial system', 21 September, www.un.org/ga/econcrisissummit/docs/FinalReport_CoE.pdf, accessed 25 November 2012.

— (2010) *World Economic and Social Survey 2010: Retooling Global Development*, Sales no. E.10.II.C.1.

— (2011a) *World Economic and Social Survey: The Great Green Technological Transformation*, New York: United Nations.

— (2011b) 'Programme of action for the Least Developed Countries for the decade 2011–2020', A/CONF.219/3/Rev.1, Istanbul.

— (2012) *The Millennium Development Goals Report*, New York: United Nations.

— (2013) *MDG Gap Task Force Report 2011: The Global Partnership for Development – the Challenge We Face*, Sales no. E.13.I.5ISBN 978-92-1-101278-1.

UNCTAD (United Nations Conference on Trade and Development) (2008) 'Accra Declaration', UNCTAD XII, Geneva: UNCTAD.

— (2009) *The Least Developed Countries Report 2009: The State and Development Governance*, New York and Geneva: UNCTAD.

— (2010) *The Least Developed Countries Report 2010: Toward a New International Development Architecture for LDCs*, Sales no. E.10.II.D.5, Geneva.

— (2011) 'Development-led globalization: toward sustainable and inclusive development paths', Report of the Secretary-General of UNCTAD to UNCTAD XIII, Geneva: UNCTAD.

UNECLAC (United Nations Economic Commission for Latin America and the Caribbean) (2010) 'Latin America and the Caribbean in the world economy 2009–2010', file:///C:/Users/montes/Downloads/7677.pdf, accessed 20 September 2012.

World Bank (2004) 'The Poverty Reduction Strategy Initiative: an independent evaluation of the World Bank's support through 2003', Washington, DC: Operations Evaluation Department, World Bank, ieg.worldbank.org/Data/reports/prsp_evaluation.pdf, accessed 20 September 2014.

WTO (World Trade Organization) (2001) 'Ministerial declaration', Doha Ministerial 2001, Geneva: WTO, www.wto.org/english/thewto_e/minist_e/min01_e/mindecl_e.htm, accessed 28 November 2014.

— (2005) 'Doha work program: ministerial declaration', Adopted 18 December, Hong Kong, www.wto.org/english/thewto_e/minist_e/min05_e/final_text_e.htm, accessed 20 September 2013.

7 | MDG2 IN BRAZIL: MISGUIDED EDUCATIONAL POLICIES

Thana Campos, Clarice Duarte and Inês Virginia Soares[1]

Introduction

Millennium Development Goal 2 aims to achieve universal primary education, to 'ensure that, by 2015, children[2] everywhere, boys and girls alike, will be able to complete a full course of primary schooling'. In Brazil, this has focused on the expansion of compulsory education for children aged seven to fourteen. In spite of the great progress the Brazilian government has achieved in relation to the primary education of young children, the same cannot be said in relation to those aged fifteen and over who did not receive a primary education at the appropriate age.

In a country like Brazil, where there is a great age discrepancy among students in the same grade, there are still a significant number of students over fourteen who have not yet completed primary school. According to the UNDP's *2013 Atlas of Human Development in Brazil*, in the period 1991–2010 the percentage of Brazilians aged fifteen to seventeen who completed primary school increased from 20 to 57.2 per cent. This means that, in Brazil, over 40 per cent of those aged fifteen to seventeen still do not have a full primary education.

This chapter will argue that, in spite of the impressive progress achieved in relation to MDG2's indicators in Brazil, educational policies aimed at children between the ages of seven and fourteen have had the unintended consequence of further marginalizing those primary students over fourteen. The chapter will argue that, indeed, those over fourteen now suffer a double exclusion. First, people over fourteen who have not completed primary education are more likely to be unemployed and thereby more likely to remain marginalized and in extreme poverty. They are therefore *socially* excluded. Secondly, they have been neglected by the current educational policies aimed exclusively at younger children. They are therefore *institutionally* excluded.

This chapter seeks to explain the double burden that the current educational policy imposes on uneducated Brazilian students over the age of fourteen. It argues that, if the purpose of MDG2 is 'universal primary education', then the age criterion, which fails to take into consideration other social factors, needs to be complemented by other criteria. It is often claimed that the age criterion was adopted with the purpose of helping to achieve the numerical targets set by MDG2's indicators more quickly. We argue that this purpose does not justify the perpetuation and exacerbation of the social exclusion and poverty of the population over fourteen who did not receive a full primary education. This is not to say that the current educational policies are without merit: the fact that in Brazil almost 100 per cent of children aged seven to fourteen now have a primary education is very good indeed; the pursuit of that good provided a sound reason in favour of said educational policies. Nevertheless, there is still great marginalization, some of which has been exacerbated by current policies, and this also provides sound reasons for policy reform. As is common after a policy achieves some success in bettering the conditions of a certain group, there is a change in the composition of the group of the more vulnerable people. This suggests that there should be a change in priority. As we will argue, the priority of educational policies should now be to rectify the fact that students over the age of fourteen are finding it significantly more difficult to get their basic primary school education. Additional measures are urgently needed, without prejudicing the progress already achieved for younger children.

The chapter is structured thus: Section 1 will discuss the purpose of MDG2 and will address the ways in which policies in Brazil have been successful in advancing this goal. Section 2 will expose some of the adverse effects of these policies on the double-burdened students, already referred to. Building on the argument that one should give priority to those more vulnerable, Section 3 will then argue that the structural injustice aggravated by current educational policies calls for reforms in existing Brazilian legislation, so as to prioritize the now more vulnerable over-fourteen age group.

MDG2 in Brazil: successful primary education policies

MDG2 encompasses three indicators:

1 Net enrolment ratio in primary education.
2 Proportion of pupils starting grade 1 who reach the last grade of primary school.
3 Literacy rate of fifteen- to twenty-four-year-olds, women and men.[3]

In its implementations of MDG2, Brazil has achieved almost 100 per cent of its targets as they relate to indicators (i) and (iii). As reported by the Brazilian government, 97.7 per cent of children aged seven to fourteen are enrolled in primary school and 98.7 per cent of people aged fifteen to twenty-four are considered literate. As the government declares, the success has resulted mainly from direct financial investment in the primary education of the seven-to-fourteen age group, which rose from 3.9 per cent of GDP in 2000 to 5.5 per cent in 2012 (see Neri and Osório 2014). The increase in public funding for primary education of children aged seven to fourteen has been a flagship success in terms of MDG2, reinforcing the understanding of education as a basic human right, fundamental to the dignity and development of the human person, as posited in the Brazilian Constitution:

Art. 214. Legislation shall establish the national education system, which will last for the period of ten years, and will have the objectives of articulating the national education system in a collaborative way, setting and implementing the guidelines, goals and strategies to ensure the maintenance and development of education at its various levels, stages and modalities through coordinated actions among the public branches and their separated powers, within the various federal spheres, towards:

I – illiteracy eradication;
II – universal school attendance;
III – improved quality of education;
IV – formation conducive to employment;
V – humanistic, scientific and technological developments of the country;
VI – settlement of the goal to use public resources for education in proportion to Brazil's GDP.

Brazil has made progress on all three MDG2 indicators. When it comes to indicator 1 – net enrolment ratio in primary education – huge progress has been made: in 1990, 81.2 per cent of children aged seven to fourteen were attending primary school, and in 2012 the percentage had risen to 97.7 per cent (Neri and Osório 2014). Therefore, nearly *all* children aged seven to fourteen are now enrolled in primary school. This includes children of colour from poor socio-economic backgrounds as well as white children from rich socio-economic backgrounds. It is worth mentioning that in 1990 only 67.6 per cent of coloured children in poor families had completed primary education, so, by 2012 the school enrolment disparity between the two groups had become virtually non-existent (IPEA 2014: 39). This drive towards the inclusion of the most marginalized (i.e. children of colour in poor families) can also be seen in relation to indicator 2.

Indicator 2 – proportion of pupils starting grade 1 who reach the last grade of primary school – focuses on the appropriate correlation between age and school grade. This indicator measures not only how many of those commencing primary school get to the last grade level, but also how long they take to complete primary schooling. This is still the greatest challenge in Brazil. The age-grade gap is particularly problematic among coloured families and those living in rural and remote areas. Children from poorer households are more likely to delay the start, progress and completion of their education for a number of reasons, including poor health and nutrition, the risks associated with travelling long distances to school, and the need to take up work instead of attending school.[4] This problem particularly affects the delayed primary school students above the age of fifteen, in the poorest families. Eventually, when these students return to school and resume studies at their original school grade, they lack the necessary incentives to persevere: they fail repeatedly, and then the age-grade gap is increased ever further. Students whose education is either interrupted or delayed are more likely to drop out, without mastering basic literacy and numeracy. Without these basic skills, they are unable to enter the job market, and are more likely to be permanently unemployed and socially marginalized. Some progress in the age-grade gap has, however, been made over the last few decades. While in 1990 50 per cent of primary school children aged nine to seventeen were enrolled at the appropriate school grade, by 2012 this percentage had risen to 60 per cent (IPEA 2014: 40–41).

Finally, when it comes to indicator 3 – literacy rate of fifteen- to twenty-four-year-olds, women and men, Brazil has achieved considerable success: in 1990, this literacy rate was 90.3 per cent, and in 2012 it was 98.7 per cent (Neri and Osório 2014). Therefore, nearly all fifteen- to twenty-four-year-olds are considered literate. This includes people of colour from poor socio-economic backgrounds, whose parents are likely to be illiterate. Although in families with illiterate parents the literacy rate is actually lower (93.5 per cent), it is worth mentioning here that the literacy rate in families with illiterate parents rose significantly, from 72.8 per cent in 1990 to 93.5 per cent in 2012 (IPEA 2014: 43).

As was noted earlier, Brazil's great achievements regarding MDG2 are linked to the government's decision to increase public investment in primary education, particularly through the *Bolsa Escola* programme, introduced in 1996, and then replaced in 2003 by the more wide-ranging *Bolsa Família* programme.[5] As discussed by Paes-Sousa and Jannuzzi in Chapter 5 of this book, these are conditional cash transfer programmes that provide financial incentives for school enrolment and attendance. Depending on the number of children in the family and on the family's level of poverty, the government pays between R$22 and R$200 (US$9–78) directly to the mother (rather than to the father), so long as all their children aged six to seventeen are enrolled in school and have a monthly attendance rate of at least 85 per cent. This money transfer is meant to alleviate poverty.

As of May 2014, 14 million families have received cash transfers under the *Bolsa Família* programme. The Brazilian Ministry of Education collects and analyses data on school attendance in order to monitor compliance with *Bolsa Família*'s requirements. Non-compliance triggers first a warning to the family; if it persists, the cash transfer is blocked; after that, if the families do not send their children back to school, the government suspends and eventually cancels the money transfer. This procedure was put in place as a tool to help local authorities identify when a family becomes at greater risk of poverty and in need of additional help. This is because when parents stop sending their children to school, it is often because they have started sending them to work to increase family income. It is precisely at this point that the family needs greater governmental attention and help to counter extreme poverty. Typically, the government sends a public servant to visit the family and tries to ascertain the reasons why they have not been able to fulfil their commitments regarding school attendance (Veras 2013).

This procedure has proved to be highly effective in helping government officials recognize families at risk of poverty so that they can intervene before too much damage has been done. According to the Brazilian president, Dilma Rousseff, 'Undoubtedly, the foundation of the Brazilian MDG's success is the *Bolsa Família* programme' (IPEA 2014: 7). The government also highlights:

the main point to be noted relates to the reduction of inequalities. The improvements of MDG-2 indicators do not relate exclusively to a greater number of children and young people attending schools; they also indicate that primary school is increasingly starting at the appropriate age, and that *children and young people have better chances of continuing their studies towards the secondary level and university, in an ever more inclusive way*. ... The percentage of young people between 15 and 24 who completed at least six years of primary education increased from 59.9% in 1990 to 84% in 2012. That is, the percentage of young people between 15 and 24 who failed to complete primary education fell two-fifths [sic!], from 41.1% [sic!] in 1990 to 16% in 2012. (IPEA 2014: 44, emphasis added)

Two crucial points are made in this quoted statement, and these points will be relevant for the critical analysis of MDG2 in Brazil in the next section of this chapter. The first is that the educational policy in Brazil clearly has as its ultimate goal *inclusion*, so that people will have 'better chances of continuing their studies towards the secondary level and university'. The second point is the Brazilian government's firm commitment to *all* primary school students, comprising therefore not only those below the age of fifteen, but also those above, 'in an ever more inclusive way'.

MDG2 in Brazil: the adverse effects of the 1996 and 2006 primary education policies

Brazil's successful achievements regarding MDG2's target and indicators are a result of a myriad of political initiatives that have been carried out since 1996.[6] In that year the government made a firm commitment to prioritize the so-called 'regular' primary education at the corresponding school grade. To this end, it amended Article 294 of its Constitution, introducing a comprehensive reform of the Brazilian educational system, under the umbrella of the *Bolsa Escola* programme. First, Brazil enacted the 1996 'Law on Directives and Foundations of the Educational System' (LDB – *Lei de Diretrizes e Bases*), as a result of an inclusive and participatory process whereby educators and other stakeholders in civil society were given a voice. LDB is the cornerstone of the current Brazilian educational system; it clarifies the different roles of municipalities, states and the federal government regarding the Brazilian educational system. Secondly, also in 1996, the constitutional amendment n.14 created the 'Fund for the Administration and Development of Education and Teaching' (FUNDEF – *Fundo de Manutenção e Desenvolvimento da Educação e de Valorização do Magisterio*).

FUNDEF regulated the allocation of funding for education in a more efficient and equitable way: not only did FUNDEF raise the public budget for education from R$35.2 billion to R$50.7 billion annually, it also required a minimal resource allocation per pupil for all primary schools. FUNDEF also increased primary school teachers' salaries: in general salaries rose by 13 per cent. In extremely poor and rural areas (see UN 2013: 15), where parents were more prone to putting their children to work at the expense of their studies, there was an additional increase of 60 per cent in salaries, to give teachers an additional incentive to fulfil their teaching responsibilities more diligently, which includes monitoring and reporting on their students' attendance.

However, FUNDEF's most controversial issue was that it diverted public resources originally destined for the 'Primary Education of Youth and Adults' – the so-called EJA (*Educação de Jovens e Adultos*) students above the age of fourteen who had not attended primary school at the proper age – towards the primary education of children aged seven to fourteen – the so-called 'regular' primary school students. The situation for primary school students above the age of fourteen worsened in 2006 when FUNDEF was replaced by FUNDEB (*Fundo de Manutenção e Desenvolvimento da Educação Básica e de Valorização dos Profissionais da Educação*), which explicitly and exclusively focused on the 'regular' primary school students.

It is true that the new fund raised the public budget for primary education (R$55 billion, 5.2 per cent of GDP) (OECD 2011: 182). It is also true that the new fund has covered a greater number of students (FUNDEB covers 61 per cent more students than its predecessor FUNDEF). Yet the most controversial point regarding FUNDEB is that it has not only continued its predecessor's strategy of focusing on 'regular' primary school students, by diverting public resources from EJA to 'regular' students, it has also established an upper limit of 15 per cent of public expenditure on EJA students.[7] To be precise, FUNDEB establishes different limits in public investments for primary school students based on the criterion of age alone, with the outcome that primary school students below the age of fifteen receive greater public investment than primary school students above the age of fourteen. In other words, FUNDEB's institutional scheme explicitly prioritizes primary school students below the age of fifteen and neglects primary school students above the age of fourteen. As mentioned earlier, it is often claimed that the reason for this priority is to achieve the numerical targets of MDG2's indicators – particularly indicator 2, which focuses on how many students commencing primary school complete it in an adequate time frame (i.e. by the age of fourteen). This is therefore a twofold social and institutional, mutually reinforcing marginalization.

Marginalization and poverty are multifaceted problems, which cannot be addressed simultaneously, making all poor people better off in exactly the same way, at the same time. This would not be feasible. It is thus sound policy that the government prioritizes certain groups in greater need. But the reasons for such a priority should be morally justifiable. As we will discuss in the next section, the moral problem with Brazil's current educational policies (FUNDEB in particular) is that the sole criterion of age is not a reasonable one. We will also discuss why this situation justifies further reforms in the Brazilian primary education system.

MDG2 in Brazil: the double burden imposed by current primary education policies

Generally speaking, there are good prima facie reasons to prioritize the primary education of young children over the primary education of older children and adults.

The most obvious reason is that young children are more vulnerable than older children and young adults. However, recent Brazilian education policies have neglected primary students over the age of fourteen, and as a consequence have increased their vulnerability as compared to before. Since this population of older primary school students now has special needs, it requires priority, especially in terms of allocating a greater portion of public investment to help address their needs.

As argued above, in the multifaceted reality of poverty, other variables need to be taken into account. We will argue here that when other social factors concerning primary students above the age of fourteen are brought into view, age alone becomes a morally unacceptable criterion.

Why is this differentiation of primary school students based *exclusively* on the criterion of age morally unacceptable?

Generally speaking, the practical reasons for giving some good (e.g. resources) to one particular vulnerable group are either the same as the practical reasons for giving it to any other vulnerable group, or they are different. If the practical reasons for giving to each vulnerable group are the same, then these groups are owed the same treatment, and it would be arbitrary and unreasonable to treat the parties unequally. If the reasons for giving to each vulnerable group are different, then these groups are owed different kinds of treatment, and it would then be arbitrary and unreasonable to treat them equally (see Finnis 2011: ch. 1). In light of this general practical principle, what are the practical reasons for giving primary education to group 1 (i.e. children aged seven to fourteen) and to group 2 (i.e. primary school students above the age of fourteen)? Are these reasons the same or are they different?

The purpose of primary education for both groups is precisely the same: students must first and foremost complete primary education to develop their moral and intellectual capacities so that they gradually mature their sense of responsibility in striving to pursue their own good and the good of the community of which they are members. For the development of the human person, primary education seeks to ensure that students master, for example, basic literacy and numeracy, and acquire skills in preparation for the job market. The purpose of the basic human right to education thus applies equally to both groups: the right to education is fundamental to the dignity and development of the human person, independently of the person's age.

The fact that younger students are *ceteris paribus* more vulnerable than older students justifies a differentiated and preferential treatment in response to such greater vulnerability. But likewise, the fact that older students have now become more vulnerable than before also justifies a differentiated and preferential treatment. Let us call this 'the principle of primary school inclusion'.

Would this principle contradict the understandings of MDG2 or the Brazilian Constitution? MDG2 focuses on 'children' in general, without specifying their age – only indicator 3 explicitly addresses youth aged fifteen to twenty-four, but this does not mean that this group is necessarily excluded from indicators 1 and 2; it just means that this particular problem (i.e. illiteracy) afflicting this particular population group (i.e. students aged fifteen to twenty-four) in a particular way has to be eradicated by 2015. So, MDG2's understanding does not contradict the principle of primary school inclusion.

Likewise, the Brazilian Constitution seems to accommodate the principle of primary school inclusion. In fact, Article 294 of the Brazilian Constitution seems to go even further than accommodating it: it seems positively to promote the principle, when it requires that primary education should strive for 'universal school attendance' and 'formation conducive to employment'. By doing so, the Brazilian Constitution is endorsing not only the idea that primary education shall include *all* students, but also the idea that school attendance is necessary for obtaining skills conducive to employment. The latter also applies to *all* students in an inclusive way – and even more so to the primary students above the age of fourteen, who are more likely to be unemployed. President Rousseff has very recently reinforced these ideas, when she emphasized the importance of primary education for the development and formation of 'children *and* young people ... in a ever more inclusive way' (IPEA 2014: 44).

So, if both MDG2 and the Brazilian Constitution promote the principle of primary school inclusion, why did the recent educational policies in Brazil (FUNDEB in particular) contradict this principle by not treating primary school students with like needs in the same way, and instead differentiating them according to the criterion of age alone, when other social factors are also applicable? Arguably, Brazil has opted to reach the numerical targets of MDG2's indicators at all costs because this would demonstrate Brazil's progress and success regarding MDG2. And this is particularly evident in the numerical targets of indicator 2, Brazil's most challenging indicator. Since Brazil arguably wanted to maximize the fulfilment of indicator 2 at all costs, it adopted certain policies to tackle primarily the age-grade gap.

It is true that Brazil has made progress on this particular matter, and the age-grade gap has been declining since 1996. However, such progress needs to be carefully assessed. The 1996 reform of the Brazilian educational system under the *Bolsa Escola* programme laid particular emphasis on the urgent need to correct late school entry and grade repetition as the way to more quickly reducing the age-grade gap. In this respect, the 1996 'Law on Directives and Foundations of Educational System' (LDB) has established a number of measures to ensure the start and the completion of primary education between the ages of seven and fourteen, including, for example, speedy primary schooling for delayed primary-school students, limitation on the school entry age, and the abolition of grade repetition. The latter aims at automatic progress from one school grade to the next in order to ensure that students leave school at the expected age of fourteen. But the great criticism is that it allows primary students to leave school without necessarily having mastered the basic skills required for employment. This suggests that there has been no real concern for students' actual learning and development (see Haddad 1998: 158): the only real concern has been the lowering of figures for the age-grade gap, so that improvements on MDG2 indicators could be made more quickly.

So, the real reason for the focus on the age criterion alone and for the priority given to primary school students aged seven to fourteen, with the concomitant neglect of primary school students above the age of fourteen, seems not to be the correction of the particular vulnerability of this group that would *ceteris paribus* justify granting priority to younger children over older children and adults. The real reason seems to be to more quickly achieve MDG2's numerical targets.

Is this option morally justifiable? If the main purpose of Brazilian educational policies was to exhibit victorious figures to the international community, showing the success of a more universal primary education for Brazilian children *on paper*, then the criterion of age alone may be justified. But if the main purpose of the Brazilian educational policies is to provide a universal, quality primary education in reality, age cannot be the sole or the most adequate criterion for distinguishing and defining investment priorities. That is not to say that the criterion of age has no relevance at all in the allocation of public investments; but other factors in the Brazilian context need to be taken into consideration.

Again, poverty is a complex problem, and a multiplicity of social factors need to be considered. The fact that primary school students over the age of fourteen have not completed primary education, and are overly burdened, both institutionally and socially, and are now more likely to be unemployed and to remain in a situation of marginalization and poverty, raises compelling reasons to question the reasonableness of using the age criterion alone. These are additional relevant social factors to which the post-2015 Sustainable Development Goals' (i.e. the Rio+20 outcome document; see Paes-Sousa and Jannuzzi this volume) agendas need to give priority, when determining and specifying the allocation of public investments for primary education in the future.

Conclusion

This chapter has discussed the double burden that Brazil's current educational policy imposes on primary school students above the age of fourteen. We have argued that the fact that older primary school students have now become more vulnerable than before justifies a differentiated and preferential treatment. The chapter argues that, if the purpose of MDG2 is 'universal primary education', then age alone is not a reasonable or morally justifiable criterion for identifying the priority group in the Brazilian context. Other factors must also be taken into account. The age criterion alone has served the purpose of achieving more quickly the numerical targets set by MDG2's indicators. But the complex social factors that led to the perpetuation and exacerbation of social exclusion and poverty for primary students over the age of fourteen with uncompleted primary education have been left out of account. The fact that almost 100 per cent of Brazilian children aged seven to fourteen now have full primary education is to be applauded. But, equally, the fact that uneducated students over the age of fourteen have now been made all the more vulnerable calls for them to be prioritized in the context of the post-2015 development agenda.

Notes

1 The authors are grateful to Dr Francisco Urbina, Fr Alban McCoy, Dr Alisha Gabriel and Professor Thomas Pogge for their comments on earlier versions of this chapter.

2 Note that MDG2 mentions 'children' in a general sense, without making specifications regarding age.

3 Available at www.undp.org/ content/undp/en/home/mdgoverview/ mdg_goals/mdg2/.

4 According to the UN: 'Household poverty is the single most important factor keeping children out of school ... Children and adolescents from the poorest households are at least three times as likely to be out of school as their richest counterparts. Location of residence also matters. Rural children are nearly twice as likely to be out of school as urban children' (UN 2013: 15).

5 Four existing cash transfer programmes, including *Bolsa Escola*, were integrated under the same umbrella – i.e the *Bolsa Família* programme. The idea was to increase the total amount of funding available and the number of poor/extremely poor families covered, as well as to increase the efficiency of the programme's administration. *Bolsa Escola* covered 5.7 million families; and this number has reached 14 million families under the *Bolsa Família* programme. See OECD (2011: 182).

6 There are a vast number of political programmes and initiatives, in partnership with local governments as well as civil society, that can be mentioned: a) *o Plano de Metas e Compromisso Todos pela Educação*; b) *o Plano de Desenvolvimento da Educação*; c) *o Fundo de Manutenção e Desenvolvimento*

da Educação Básica e de Valorização dos Profissionais da Educação (FUNDEB); d) *os Programas nacionais suplementares para educação, como o de transporte escolar;* e) *o Índice de Desenvolvimento da Educação Básica* (IDEB); f) *Prova Brasil;* g) *Programa Nacional de Reestruturação e Aquisição de Equipamentos para a Rede Escolar Pública de Educação Infantil* (PROINFÂNCIA); h) *Obrigatoriedade do ensino dos 4 aos 17 anos;* i) *Programa Mais Educação;* j) *Programa de Formação Continuada do Ensino Fundamental;* k) *Programa do Livro;* l) *Programa Nacional de Tecnologia Educacional;* m) *Programa Brasil Alfabetizado;* n) *Universidade Aberta do Brasil;* to name only a few. For a description of each programme and initiative, see IPEA (2014), particularly p. 45. See also OECD (2011: 180–92).

7 Public resources for EJA (i.e. primary school students above the age of fourteen) may not exceed 15 per cent of the FUNDEB total budget (Pinto 2007).

References

Finnis, J. (2011) *Reason in Action*, Oxford: OUP.

Haddad, S. (1998) 'Educação escolar no Brasil', in A. Toni (ed.), *As faces da pobreza no Brasil: programa de trabalho*, Rio de Janeiro: Ed Arte Maior.

IPEA (2014) 'Objetivos de desenvolvimento do milenio, relatorio nacional de acompanhamento', May, www.pnud.org.br/Docs/5_RelatorioNacionalAcompanhamento ODM.pdf.

Neri, M. and R. Osório (2014) 'V National Monitoring Report on the Millennium Development Goals – changes and challenges', www.sae.gov.br/site/wp-content/uploads/Release-ODM-English-Final.pdf.

OECD (2011) 'Encouraging lessons from a large federal system', in *Strong Performers and Successful Reformers in Education: Lessons from Pisa for the US*, ch. 8, www.oecd.org/pisa/46623978.pdf.

Pinto, J. M. R. (2007) 'A politica recente de fundos para o financiamento da educação e seus efeitos no Pacto Federativo', Educação *e Sociedade*, 28(100): 887–97, October, www.cedes.unicamp.br.

UN (2013) *The MDG Report 2013*, www.un.org/millenniumgoals/pdf/report-2013/mdg-report-2013-english.pdf.

Veras F. (2013) 'MDG-2 in Brazil', International Policy Centre for Inclusive Growth, UNDP, mdgpolicynet.undg.org/ext/MDG-Good-Practices/mdg2/MDG2A_Brazil_Bolsa_Familia.pdf.

PART THREE

POLICY AND SOCIETAL ALTERNATIVES

8 | IRRELEVANCE OF THE MDGS AND A REAL SOLUTION TO POVERTY: UNIVERSAL CITIZEN'S INCOME

Julio Boltvinik and Araceli Damián[1]

Introduction

In this chapter, we examine the relevance of Millennium Development Goal 1 (MDG1), Target 1 on halving from 1999 to 2015 the proportion of the population below the World Bank's extreme poverty lines, both in itself (methodologically) and against the background of two features of capitalism – periodic economic crises and the process of automation – which can be seen as the main forces determining global poverty trends.

The first section compares the central features of the Keynesian and neoliberal variants of capitalism, showing how the first mitigates capitalism's tendency to produce poverty and the second reinforces it. The tendency of global poverty to increase during the present neoliberal phase of capitalism is denied by the World Bank (WB), whose calculations imply the opposite trend. These calculations are shown to be biased. Moreover, the poverty threshold used by the WB is shown to be an Ultra Extreme Poverty Line (UEPL) arbitrarily detached from any conception of human need, implying that human beings can be treated as cattle.

Once the 'empirical evidence' from the WB has been shown to be false, we continue with our argument, looking, first, at MDG1 as a very limited initiative, as *it is completely disconnected from the main causes of poverty trends*. The second section discusses the conceptual limitations of MDG1, while the third looks at the Mexican experience, showing that, at least in this experience, this goal is completely irrelevant, both because the method for the identification of the poor is flawed and does not correspond to the methods which the Mexican federal government and the Mexico city government use to identify the poor, and because the fact that Mexico subscribed to the MDGs has not modified, in any sense, Mexican anti-poverty policies.

The fourth and fifth sections broach the two main causes of global poverty trends. Some Marxist and mainstream theories of capitalist crises are analysed in the fourth section. The fifth section starts by pointing out the nature and consequences of the Scientific and Technical Revolution (STR), which has made possible automation, and which is bringing to an end a form of a societal organization centred on paid work, i.e. the wage-based society. We look also at the (potentially) positive consequences of automation as it opens up the possibility of human emancipation from 'forced', repetitive and alienating work. The policy response of a Basic or Universal Citizen's Income – regarded as a promising alternative that saves capitalism and gradually, peacefully, transforms it into the basis for a more humane post-capitalist society – is addressed in the sixth and last section, together with other proposals. A very brief section of final reflections closes the chapter.

Capitalism and poverty in the Keynesian and neoliberal periods

Although capitalism per se has a tendency to produce poverty, this tendency was mitigated by Keynesian welfare states, while left unbridled by neoliberalism. Keynesian welfare states combined economic policies aimed at full employment and the institution of unemployment insurance so as to maintain positive rates of growth in effective demand, with very broad social policies. This variant of capitalism, prevalent for around forty years in many high-income countries, developed as a response to the 1929 Great Depression, which in turn was a crisis of overproduction and over-accumulation of capital, associated with low wages, as well as a response to the perceived successful establishment and economic performance in the USSR of what appeared as an alternative to capitalism.

Neoliberalism, on the other hand, was developed as a response to the 1970s crisis, which was generated by a declining rate of profit. In Keynesianism, employment and wages are regarded as factors of effective demand. However, the Keynesian model ceased to be functional for capital when the rates of profit became too low. At that point in time, capital had the power to replace Keynesianism with a variety of capitalism that regards employment not as a demand factor but merely as a production cost, which, as all costs, must be reduced. Capital's counter-revolution was launched and is still under way globally. Neoliberalism can be seen as a global drive to reorganize the entire social order so as to subordinate it to the logic of accumulation and profit. The restructuring of capitalism focused on an offensive against labour, which was devalued and fully recommodified. The result has been a massive redistribution of income from labour in favour of capital on a global scale. But in its sin, neoliberalism carried its own penance: in generating global production without global consumption, it raised to a planetary scale the unsolvable contradiction between global growth of production and global decline in real wages, the same contradiction which had caused the Great Depression of 1929.

The global devaluation of the workforce occurred in the context of two revolutions: one in information technologies that made deterritorialization of production possible, and the other in automation, which is making the direct use of labour less and less necessary in the production process. Under neoliberalism, the main instruments to expand demand are credit expansion, based on over-indebtedness of households, enterprises and governments, and financial bubbles or financialization.

Capitalism has gone back to the laissez-faire variant of capitalism that prevailed before 1929, and has globalized it further. The style of globalization fostered has been asymmetrical: commodities and capital move freely, but labour does not. The mobile factor of production (capital) imposes its conditions on the non-mobile factor (labour).

Capitalism is again in a crisis – the *Great Financial Crisis* – at least as severe as the 1929 Great Depression, and more global. Neoliberal capitalism increases poverty as it is based on the full commodification of labour, and on its devaluation. This is in stark contrast with Keynesian welfare state modalities of capitalism, which decreased poverty, at least in the developed countries, by revaluing the labour force.

Capitalism is coming to an end. It can be saved only in a radical way that would lead gradually to its transformation into the basis for a post-capitalist society. The main reason for this is the automation revolution, which is under way not only in industry, but also in agriculture and, crucially, in services. It is incompatible with the wage system as the main distributor of income that enables the sale of commodities and the very reproduction of life – in other words keeping the worker alive and allowing for intergenerational reproduction. Both automation and deterritorialization of production imply the devaluation of labour, massive unemployment combined with the growing presence of precarious employment and with them the globalization or generalization of poverty. Capitalism has to be radically transformed from within, or it will destroy the planet as it tries, desperately, to save itself from death.

The decline of global poverty in the neoliberal period according to the World Bank

This analysis of a generalization of poverty is negated by World Bank statistics. These present declining levels of poverty in the global South, where most of the world's poor live. These statistics are false and misleading. Thomas Pogge and Sanjay Reddy (2010: 42–54) have illustrated a number of problems and flaws in the World Bank's poverty measurement. They include *inter alia*:

1 The alleged evolution of world poverty between 1981 and 2005 depends highly on the poverty line (PL) used. If using the 'official' WB PL of $1.25 (at purchasing power parities: PPP) per person per day, poverty over those twenty-five years decreases by 27 per cent; but if using a $2.00 PL, poverty increases by 1 per cent. Using a $2.5 PL, it increases by 13 per cent. As can be seen, three totally different diagnoses: the lower the PL, the more optimistic and more favourable the outcome of neoliberal capitalism. The total population living in poverty in 2005 would be, respectively: 1.38 billion at $1.25 PL; 2.56 billion at $2 PL; and 3.08 billion at $ 2.50 PL.

2 The WB official PLs have been falling in real terms, while the institution attempted to give the impression of a rising PL. The reality is that in terms of 2009 purchasing power, the original PL of $1, which was used between 1990 and 1997, was $1.99 dollars; that of $1.08, used between 2000 and 2008, was $1.60; and that of $1.25, which is now being used, is equivalent to $1.37.

By lowering the PL in real terms, the WB calculations imply that poverty is falling, thereby adding a fallacy to an open and shameless cynicism implied in offering, to nearly half of the world's population, a perspective of bare animal-level survival – a standard of living attainable with $1.25. The PLs of $1.25 and $2.00 per person per day lack any conception of human needs. This can be illustrated with the example of Mexico, where the PL of $1.25 PPP results in very low poverty incidence levels (5.3 per cent in rural areas and 1.3 per cent in cities). Conversely, the two official poverty measures (one multidimensional, the other income poverty) applied by the federal government (Coneval) show poverty incidences of around 50 per cent of the national population. Two other measurement options (one of which is the official one for Mexico City) show a poverty incidence around 80 per cent.[2]

Moreover, in basing its PL on the extreme poverty line (EPL) of the poorest countries, the WB falls into circular reasoning, since it takes as a normative parameter the lowering of expectations by accepting a universal extreme poverty line (UEPL). The WB assumes food to be the sole human need, leaving all other needs fully unmet, and thus adopting a conception that reduces human beings to the status of animals.

The conceptual limitations of MDG1

The 2008 financial crisis has spread around the world, and its negative effects have combined with the food crisis, caused by increases in food prices. Consequently, the achievement of MDG1, Target 1 – halving extreme poverty in developing countries – is threatened (World Bank 2009: xi). The WB estimated in 2009 that between 55 and 90 million people would fall into extreme poverty as a result of the crisis.

Among the various factors behind the adoption of such a low UEPL is the dominance, since the early twentieth century, in social sciences, especially in economics, of logical positivism and the replacement of human needs by preferences. Putnam (2002: 33, emphasis in original) deconstructs the idea of the facts/value dichotomy as follows:

> What of the idea that the correct description of the world is
> the same as objectivity? This idea rests, pretty clearly, on the
> supposition that 'objectivity' means *correspondence to objects* …
> But it is not only normative truths such as 'murder is wrong' that
> pose counterexamples to this idea; … *mathematical and logic truths*
> are likewise examples of *objectivity without objects* … it is time we
> stopped equating *objectivity* with *description*.

For Putnam, acceptance since the 1930s of the fact/value dichotomy destroyed the capacity of welfare economics to undertake an evaluation of economic well-being. The logical consequence of accepting the fact/value dichotomy in economics should have been that economists reject altogether the existence of the discipline of welfare economics. Instead, economists sought an optimal economic performance criterion that was neutral in terms of values, and found one in the notion of the 'Pareto optimal' – or at least so they thought. Putnam highlights the weakness of the Pareto optimality criterion using the defeat of Nazi Germany in 1945 as an event that, according to this criterion, did not improve the world's well-being because at least one agent, Adolf Hitler, was worse off. Taking this example, Putnam argues that if there should be a discipline of welfare economics, and particularly if it is to deal with problems of poverty and other deprivations, then welfare economics cannot avoid substantive ethical issues.

Economists who defend the fact/value dichotomy have, paradoxically, invaded the study area of *poverty*. Poverty is an entangled term, where statements of facts cannot be separated from value judgements. As economists assume that in terms of values there can be nothing rational, they have not taken seriously the definition of the poverty threshold, which is a heavily value-laden task, thus facilitating the task for the World Bank and others of its ilk, which seeks to reduce measured poverty to a minimum. Opponents of value judgements, orthodox economists have impoverished poverty studies in the same way they impoverished welfare economics.

Let us look at how the WB defines its UEPL. In its first report on poverty (World Bank 1990: 26–7), the Bank defines it as 'the inability to reach a minimum standard of living', a standard which the WB defines as a level of consumption which must include 'two elements: the expenditure necessary to achieve a minimum level of nutrition and other basic needs, and an additional amount that varies from one country to another and reflects the cost of participating in daily life of society' (ibid.: 26). The first of the above elements is regarded by the WB as being 'relatively simple' to calculate, because it can be done 'by finding out the prices of the foodstuffs that comprise *the diet of the poor*'. Ignoring the circular reasoning involved in this last phrase, the WB then argues that the second element is 'by far *more subjective* as in some countries piped water inside the dwelling *is a luxury*, but in others it is *a "necessity"*' (ibid.: 27, emphasis added). The Bank regards the decision to consider piped water necessary *a subjective exercise* and tries to induce the belief that it is impossible to reach agreement on what human needs are, by qualifying piped water as both a 'luxury' and a 'need'.

Several authors have criticized the denial, in different disciplines, of the *existence of universal human needs* (see Doyal and Gough 1991;

Wiggins 1987; Boltvinik 2005). Wiggins (1987) states that the irreplaceable character of the term 'need' in the political-administrative process forces one to capture the special content from which it derives its strength. If in the phrases formulating *claims of need* we try to replace 'needing' by 'wanting', 'desiring' or 'preferring' the result lacks not only the rhetorical force of the original, but even its particular meaning, its consistency and its logical argument. Wiggins defines necessities (the objects needed) as follows: 'a person needs X [absolutely] if and only if, whatever the moral and socially acceptable changes that can be envisaged (economic, technological, political, historical ...) occurring in the relevant period, *he/she will be damaged if she/he lacks X*' (ibid.: 10). Avoiding harm to human beings is what gives strength to the claims of needs.

The WB decides, in its definition, to take food as the sole need, leaving all other needs fully unmet and thus showing its conception of human beings. It implicitly reduces us to the level of animals since the UEPL suffices only to – inadequately – provide for nutritional requirements. Arguing that there is no consensus on what other needs are, the second element in the poverty definition of the World Bank (1990) is sidestepped. This is a crucial controversy. If norms regarding needs are seen not to have an objective social existence, then the concept of poverty would not be appropriate for scientific research, and the measurement of poverty would be a subjective exercise. As Sen has put it, it would be 'unleashing one's personal morals on the statistics of deprivation' (Sen 1981: 17). Sen has assumed the position that what researchers do is to describe existing social prescriptions, which constitutes 'an act of description and not of prescription'. For Sen (ibid.:17–18) there is a considerable degree of social consensus on minimum well-being standards. He quotes Adam Smith, who, speaking about how much an individual needs, says that a worker would be ashamed if he/she had to appear in public without a linen shirt and leather shoes. In the same line of argument, Boltvinik (2005) quotes Marx to show that there is an agreement in every society on the requirements of workers' consumption, which is expressed in real wage levels, the only price that includes, according to Marx, a historical and a moral element.

The irrelevance of MDG1 in the Mexican experience

According to the Mexican presidency, in 1989, adopted as base year, 9.3 per cent of Mexico's population was ultra-poor, using the $1.25

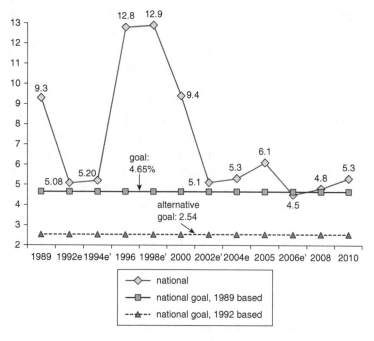

8.1 Evolution of Ultra Extreme Poverty incidence (per cent) in Mexico and MDG1 ($1.25 PPP)

dollar PPP threshold. UEP incidence has evolved as shown in Figure 8.1.[3] This is a skewed selection of a base year, since the debt crisis started in 1982 and poverty was at a historical peak in 1989. Thus, MDG1 would require Mexico to reduce its UEP population to 4.65 per cent by 2015. As can be seen in Figure 8.1, if the year 1992 had been selected as a base year, the goal would have been set much more ambitiously, at 2.54 per cent, since UEP incidence in 1992 was lower than in 1989 – at 5.08 per cent. In 2010, UEP was 5.3 per cent, which is close to the minimalist goal of 4.65 per cent. But if 1992 had been the base year, the figure for 2010 (5.3 per cent) would be farther away from the alternative goal (2.54 per cent) than the base-year figure, which was 5.08 per cent. It also shows that the selection of 1989 as base year was a manipulation to ensure that Mexico would 'accomplish' MDG1.

Figure 8.2 shows UEP incidence evolution for the years 1992 to 2006 at the national, urban and rural levels using the $1.08 PPP threshold. Here we can appreciate that these minimalist thresholds would imply

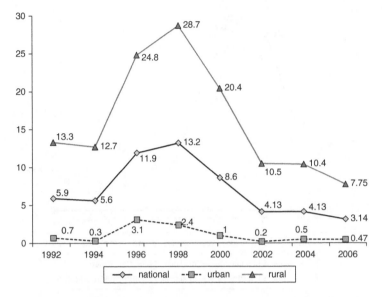

8.2 Evolution of UEP (per cent) in Mexico (national, urban and rural)
(UEPL = $1.08 PPP)

that there is almost no poverty in the urban areas of Mexico: the urban
graph starts at 0.7 per cent and ends at 0.47 per cent, providing a
paradisiacal view of Mexico as a country that has no poverty in the
urban areas and where less than 10 per cent of the rural population is
poor. But these series end in 2006; after that year poverty incidence
started to increase again, as shown in Figures 8.3 and 8.4. In both,
the respective goals using 1992 as base year[4] have been added. The
first compares the evolution of UEP incidence in rural settlements in a
longer series: 1992 to 2010,[5] showing that the evolution of rural poverty
is quite similar using the two thresholds of $1.25 PPP and $1.08 PPP,
and adds information about the evolution from 2006 to 2010 using
the $1.25 UEPL. The $1.25 series shows that Mexico had, by 2010,
merely reduced UEP incidence by less than three percentage points in
rural settlements, while the goal would have required reducing it by 7.5
points. In 2006, the outcome is better for the $1.08 UEPL: it lies only
1.1 percentage points above the goal, whereas with the $1.25 UEPL,
the outcome was 2.25 points worse than the goal.

Figure 8.4 presents the evolution of UEP in urban settlements and
contrasts it with the two non-official goals. These goals had already

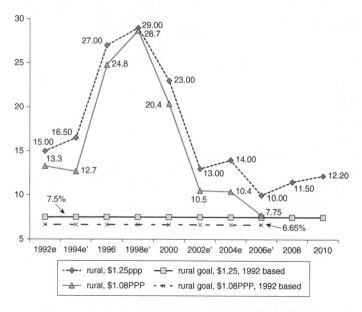

8.3 Evolution of UEP (per cent) in rural settlements with $1.08 and $1.25 PPP UEP lines (goals with 1992 as base year)

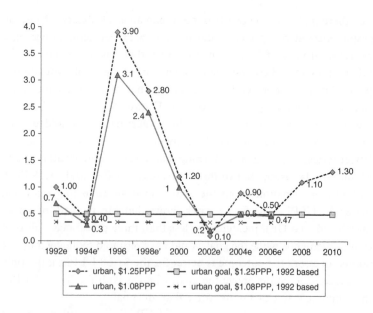

8.4 Evolution of UEP (per cent) in urban settlements with $1.08 and $1.25 PPP UEP lines (goals with 1992 as base year)

been achieved in 1994, and again in 2002. In 2006, one of them had been reached and the other was quite close to attainment. The reader might conclude that whereas MDG1 is set too low for urban areas of Mexico, it might be adequate for rural areas. However, this is not so.

Figure 8.5 shows the acute contrast between poverty incidence levels, using the $1.25 PPP threshold and Mexican government thresholds. In Mexico, there are currently two official poverty measurement methods: one adopted by the federal government and the other by the government of Mexico City. The current federal method (identified in Figure 8.5 as FED, MD and intersection) shows multidimensional poverty, and replaced the previous income poverty method, which the federal government had introduced in 2002 (identified in the figure as Previous FED Income). The method adopted by the Mexico city government (identified in Figure 8.5 as MexCityGov, IPMM) is the Integrated Poverty Measurement Method, developed by Boltvinik in 1990–92. The figure also includes the reinterpretation of the current official federal-level method, using a union criterion of poverty instead of the official intersection criterion. The responsible agency, Coneval, has interpreted the larger population identified as poor in the union approach, arguing that it identifies the sum of the poor plus the vulnerable. The figure compares poverty incidence by these five methodological options at the national, urban and rural levels.

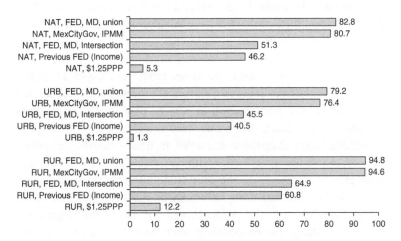

8.5 The $1.25 PPP incidence compared with three official poverty measurements and one reinterpretation prevailing in Mexico (per cent)

The contrasts are stark. At the national and urban levels, the $1.25 PPP line renders one-digit poverty incidence levels (5.3 and 1.3 per cent respectively) whereas the other options show poverty incidences in the range 40–95 per cent. The four alternative indices result in very high multiples of the incidences obtained with the MDG1 lines.

It is obvious that these huge discrepancies in MDG1 estimates of poverty incidence in Mexico vis-à-vis the official estimates make them and the MDG1 goal for 2015 absolutely irrelevant. The issues at hand are what is the purchasing power in Mexico of $1.25 PPP, what does the UEP mean, and to what did the Mexican government commit itself by committing itself to attain MDG1?

As mentioned, to calculate poverty in 2005, the WB updated the values of the PPP dollars, relative to the currencies of most countries. In May of that year, a dollar PPP was equivalent to 7.13 pesos when the nominal exchange rate was 10.96 pesos per dollar (World Bank 2008: 25). Therefore, the poverty line defined by the WB ($1.25) was 8.91 pesos per person per day (81 per cent of a current dollar value at that time). The very frugal 'food' line of the federal government recognizes that to acquire the raw food basket to cover nutritional requirements, an income of 19.50 and 26.36 pesos was needed in rural and urban areas, respectively. This means that people who have income equal to the WB's UEPL would be able to acquire only 46 and 34 per cent of the minimum requirements for not being extremely (or food) poor according to federal criteria, in rural and urban areas respectively. This shows that the UEPL of the WB is meaningless for Mexico, as it is well below what even the federal government considered its most extreme poverty threshold.

Two further points need to be made. First, from a methodological point of view, the measurement is statistically meaningless. To measure the incidence of a phenomenon as rare as UEP incidence in urban Mexico (1.3 per cent), one would need sample surveys of orders of magnitude larger than those employed in most countries, including Mexico, to capture its incidence with reasonable confidence intervals. With present sample sizes, the confidence intervals are so large that the results become statistically meaningless. For example, some of the abrupt fluctuations in the incidence of UEP observed in Figure 8.4 might be partially due to sampling errors and the observed changes between observations might be statistically non-significant (confidence intervals may overlap).

Secondly, from a policy point of view too, MDG1 had no relevance. The fact that Mexico committed to the Millennium Development Goals had no influence on its policy to combat extreme poverty. In the year 2000, when the Millennium Declaration was issued, Mexico had already been running the *Progresa* programme for three years. The programme title was changed in 2001 to *Oportunidades*. It has continued to grow, and has had a large influence (via the World Bank) on many other countries. It is a CCT (Conditional Cash Transfer) programme consisting of monetary transfers to the extremely poor only, conditional on certain behaviour requirements the beneficiaries have to follow

An impressionistic panorama of theories of capitalist crises

Marxian theory of capitalist crises[6] is based, essentially, on the law of the declining rate of profit. This law establishes that labour is the only creator of value (and thus of surplus value). To the extent that the process of production is mechanized and automated – *which is something capitalism cannot stop doing* – the work process will be provided with more and better means of production. As a consequence, the 'organic composition of capital' – the proportion of constant capital invested in means of production and inputs in total capital – will increase. The rate of profit diminishes accordingly. Hence, the above-mentioned law is a consequence of mechanization and automation. Additionally, Marxist theory of capitalist crises is based on the Law of the Two Faces, which establishes that as a reaction to the first law, capital will do everything necessary (despite the falling rate of profit) to increase the mass of surplus value (which requires the employed workforce to increase), which in turn forces capital to search for the maximum rate of accumulation and to expand geographically. So, both the decrease in the rate of profit and the increase in the absolute amount of surplus value are necessary conditions for the functioning of capitalism. From this, John Strachey (1935) derived the Basic Dilemma of Capitalism, which makes capitalist crises inevitable; it is the dilemma by which wages are both too low and cause an excess supply (as in 1929 and 2007) and too high to diminish the rhythm of accumulation, as was the case in the 1970s.

Keynes' theory of capitalist crises refutes Say's Law ('supply creates its own demand'), contesting two myths of neoclassical theory: the myth of the rate of interest as the price that equates savings and investment, and the myth of wages as the price that equates supply and demand of labour. Keynes replaced these two myths by the thesis that the level of employment depends on effective demand (investment plus consumption) and that investment is determined by profit expectations (the expected rate of profit, which he called the marginal efficiency of capital, should be above the rate of interest so that new investment may proceed). Full employment ceases to be automatic and any level of employment becomes possible. Capitalism is not self-regulated; state intervention is hence indispensable.

Neo-Marxists Foster and Magdoff, in *The Great Financial Crisis* (2009), characterize the present phase of capitalism as financial monopoly capitalism. They postulate the need of current capitalism for financial bubbles (financialization). Their departure point is the tendency of monopolist capitalism to stagnate, as formulated by Baran and Sweezy (1966). Minsky (1986) had observed the tendency of capitalism to create financial bubbles, which pile debt on debt and will inevitably burst. Financialization has become the main mechanism (displacing military expenditures) to temporarily absorb the gigantic surplus generated and thus keep afloat financial monopoly capitalism. This is a phenomenon which they call the symbiotic embrace between stagnation and financialization, and which we characterize as *spontaneous private Keynesianism*. There is no possibility for the capitalist system to absorb the enormous surplus through productive investment. As, additionally, the financialization process itself is in crisis, Foster and Magdoff foresee a profound and prolonged stagnation.

Krugman (2008), winner of the Nobel Prize in economics, thinks that the fact that 'the shadow banking system' is unregulated is the cause of the bubble, which will burst inevitably. He argues that when the housing bubble burst, the lack of a replacement bubble led to the widespread crisis, thus *acknowledging the need capitalism has of financial bubbles*. Krugman stated clearly, even before the current crisis, the impotence of conventional economic theory to face a crisis. The stagnation of Japan in the 1990s would confirm the neo-Marxist thesis of the tendency to stagnation of financial monopoly capitalism.

The biggest difference between Krugman and Foster/Magdoff lies in the policy recommendations. While Krugman sees regulation of the shadow banking system as the solution, Foster and Magdoff think regulation would lead capitalism to chronic stagnation because of their analysis of the need for capitalism to create financial bubbles. In our view, this regulation would be equivalent to suppressing spontaneous private Keynesianism. Capitalist crises magnify the tendency of capitalism to create poverty.

The preceding argument requires an additional perspective to explain the current situation. This additional perspective is the Scientific and Technical Revolution (STR), a long-term process that began after the Second World War, goes beyond cyclical crises, and transforms the character of production as it creates the conditions for full automation. Full automation ushers in the inevitable end of capitalism and anticipates an era of upheaval. This is discussed in the next section. Meanwhile, let's recall Marx's (2000 [1859]: 425) famous Preface: 'At a certain stage of their development, the material productive forces of society come in conflict with the existing relations of production ... From forms of development of the productive forces these relations turn into their fetters. Then begins an epoch of social revolution.'

Automation and the end of the wage-work society

Capitalism, in its relentless search for higher profits, constantly revolutionizes the techniques of production. It has generated at least two industrial revolutions: the eighteenth-century First Industrial Revolution centred on coal and the steam engine and its multiple applications in factories, and in railway and maritime transport; and the twentieth-century Second Industrial Revolution centred on oil, the internal combustion engine, electricity and the telephone. In both revolutions, production in industry, agriculture and mining was greatly transformed. Machines replaced an important proportion of direct human labour. In many branches of industry, workers increasingly became supervisors of automatic machinery. But this machinery was based exclusively on mechanical principles, which have limits.

In contrast, the Scientific and Technical Revolution (STR), starting towards the end of the Second World War, introduced cybernetics, information technology, artificial intelligence and robotics. It unleashed a spiral of technological development that can be termed the Third 'Industrial' Revolution (TIR), covering all human productive activities. These revolutions have led to a gigantic replacement of human labour, first by mechanical machinery, and now by what

Richta et al. (1968) called autonomous production complexes. The stability of capitalism is very easily shaken by decreases in wages and/or employment, which diminish effective demand and lead the system to crises, as output cannot be sold. For the USA, Heilbroner (1995: xii–xiii) reminds us that technological change reduced the proportion of the agricultural labour force from 75 per cent in 1850 to just 3 per cent in 1990, and then reduced employment in industry: between 1960 and 1990, manufacturing output continued to grow while the number of jobs was reduced by half. These reductions were offset by an increase in employment in services, which rose from 3 to 90 million persons between 1870 and 1990. But as in industry, in services too technology creates jobs with one hand and destroys them with the other. 'We are pushing the relationship between machines and work beyond the difficult adjustments of the last two hundred years,' concludes Heilbroner, 'towards a new relationship about whose configuration we can only say it will be very different from the past' (ibid.: xiii). He refers to an anecdote from the history of economic thought:

> In 1817 the famous economist David Ricardo wrote that the amount of employment in an economy was of no consequence as long as rent and profits, out of which flowed its new investment, were undiminished. 'Indeed?' replied Simonde de Sismondi … 'In truth then, there is nothing more to wish for than the king, remaining alone on the island, by constantly turning a crank, might produce, through automata, all the output of England'. Jeremy Rifkin's mind-opening book *is about a world in which corporations have taken the place of kings, turning cranks that set into motion the mechanical, electrical, and electronic automata that provide the goods and services of the nation.* (Ibid.: xi)

There are not enough new commodified, profit-driven, labour-intensive activities to create enough new waged jobs to compensate for those that are being lost owing to automation. Although this transformation might take decades to bring about its full consequences, it has been silently contributing to crisis, stagnation, unemployment, underemployment, generalization of precarious employment (the 'precariat', as aptly dubbed by Guy Standing in 2011), poverty and hunger. But the full consequences might come earlier than the moment when a high percentage of the working-age population has been displaced by automation. As Martin Ford (2009: 108–9) has stated, replicating the type of analysis of expectations Keynes did so well:

> As automation begins to eliminate jobs in an increasingly wide range of industries and occupations, its impacts are clearly not going to be kept a secret ... As a growing percentage of the population is exposed to direct evidence of ongoing job losses, many people will begin to experience a greatly heightened level of stress and worry. Facing this, individuals will take the obvious action: they will cut back on consumption, perhaps quite dramatically, and try to save more in anticipation of a very uncertain future ... But what if, at some point in the coming decades, there is a general coalescence of belief that suggests the basic character of the economy has changed to such an extent that jobs may *not* be available – or at least will be very hard to obtain – in the future? If this were to occur in a critical mass of the consumers ... we could clearly be thrust into a very dark scenario ... a dramatic economic downward spiral would almost certainly be precipitated.

As a result of unstoppable automation progress, capitalism will fall into increasingly severe crises until it becomes completely non-viable. This is what a very distinguished group of scientist led by Robert Oppenheimer, constituted as the Ad Hoc Committee on the Triple Revolution, were pointing at, more than fifty years ago, when they published an open letter to the president of the United States in the *New York Times* which argued that cyber-technologies were forcing a change in the relationship between income and work and urged president and Congress 'to consider guaranteeing to every citizen, as a matter of law, adequate income'. Their text says (at www.marxists.org/history/etol/newspape/isr/vol25/noo3/adhoc.html): 'The continuity of the link between income and employment as the only major distribution system of effective demand – to grant the right to consume – *now acts as the main brake of the almost limitless capacity of the cybernetic system of production*'.

Compare the phrase in italics with Marx's words (cited above) in the 1859 Preface: 'At a certain stage of development, the material productive forces of society come in conflict with the existing relations of production ... From forms of development of the productive forces these relations turn into their fetters.'

In response to the Oppenheimer Committee request, President Kennedy decided to establish a National Commission on Automation, which was created by President Johnson. It published its report in 1965. The Commission argued that technology reduces the number of jobs, not work. Rifkin (1995: 83) comments that this is also the view of the Oppenheimer Committee: if the economy produces work without workers, as both sides suggest, then some form of government intervention would be necessary to provide a source of income, of purchasing power, to the growing number of workers displaced by technology. But ultimately, the presidential commission concluded that the technological displacement of workers was a necessary and temporary condition engendered by progress.

Rifkin (2003: 27) predicted that the twenty-first century would be faced with the end of mass work. 'This is the anthropological point where we are. We have a technological revolution that can create a renaissance or a great social upheaval. We can take a leap forward for the generation of your children or we can have years, decades and generations of instability and unrest.'

The renaissance option relates to texts by Marx and by Richta et al. Marx (1976 [1876]: 532) quotes Aristotle and then Antipater:

'If every tool, when summoned, or even by intelligent anticipation, could do the work that befits it, just as the creations of Daedalus moved of themselves, or the tripods of Hephaestus went of their own accord to their sacred work, if the shuttles were to weave of themselves, then there would be no need either of apprentices for the master craftsmen, or of slaves for the Lords'. Antipater, a Greek poet of the time of Cicero, hailed the water-wheel for grinding corn, that most basic form of all productive machinery, as the liberator of female slaves and the restorer of the golden age!

In *Civilisation at Its Crossroads* (1968: 35–6, 133–7), Richta et al. argue:

Over the past decades, the impetuous development of science and technology has begun to escape the limits of the industrial revolution ... The work instruments exceed the limits of mechanical machines and assume functions which, in principle, transform them into *autonomous production complexes ... the*

subjective aspect of production, unchanged for centuries, is amended: the
direct production functions performed by simple labour force disappear
gradually ... New social productive forces enter the process of production,
the main being science and its technical applications ... The originality
of the yet incipient development, which ... defines it as scientific
and technological revolution, lies in its shaking of the entire
elemental structure of production to *radically alter the place occupied*
by man. It ensures the triumph of the automatic principle in the
widest sense of the term ... (Ibid.: 35–6)

[While the] predominant type of worker in mechanised industrial
production is the worker-operator handling machinery or caught
in the mechanism of the assembly line ... [p. 133], *complex*
automation goes increasingly further, *freeing man from his direct*
involvement in the process of production, the role of simple 'gear' in the
system of machines and offers him, in return, the role of promoter, creator
and director of the technical system of production ... (Ibid.: 135)

We can expect the process of the STR to absorb traditional simple
industrial work, which *is not an internal need for man, but is imposed*
by an external necessity. On the other hand, *once man ceases to*
produce the things that things themselves can produce in his place, the
possibility to devote himself to a creative activity that mobilizes all
his forces, that tend to research new pathways, that expands his
capacities, opens up before him ... (Ibid.: 136)

The general diffusion of this type of human activity will in fact
mark the *overcoming of work.* Indeed, once the material forms of
human activity give to it the character of active manifestations of
self, the external necessity, determined by the need of subsistence,
gives way to the inner necessity of man; at that moment, human activity
becomes a human need that exists for itself and enriches him; then the
abstract contradictions between work and pleasure, between work
and leisure wither away: human activity becomes entangled with
life. (Ibid.: 136–7)

Rifkin (1995: 84–9), quoting David Noble (1984), posits that with
respect to automation, most trade unions capitulated to companies,
and this contributed to extinguishing a debate on the effects of

automation. Fearful of being labelled modern Luddites and considered obstacles to progress, labour leaders were on the defensive and many embraced labour-saving technology, causing the labour movement to lose the strength it had acquired in the early post-war years. In collective bargaining, the workers relinquished control over technology in exchange for job retraining. Workers could have negotiated collective agreements to ensure a share in productivity gains derived from automation. However, unions grossly overestimated the number of skilled jobs that would be created by the new technologies. As a consequence, they lost members and influence. Eventually, automation destroyed their most powerful weapon: the strike. The new technology allowed management to operate plants with very few staff.

Rifkin (2003) recognized the clothing and electronics industries as the last cheap labour markets responsible for growth in the developing world, but added 'German engineers have automated the seam' and 'we are quickly going to the automated production of electronic components'. He wondered what would happen in the global South when these branches too become automated.

One year before Rifkin published *The End of Work*, Aronowitz and DiFazio published *The Jobless Future* in which they make the following point (1994: xi–xii):

> As experts, politicians, and the public become acutely aware of new problems associated with the critical changes in the economy – crime, poverty, homelessness, hunger, education downsizing, loss of tax revenues to pay for public services, and many other social issues – the solution is always the same: jobs, jobs, jobs. The central contention of this book is that *if jobs are the solution, we are in big trouble*. We argue that *the tendency of contemporary global economic life is toward the underpaid and unpaid worker* ... Scientifically based technological change in the midst of sharpened internationalization of production means that there are *too many workers for too few jobs*, and even fewer of them are well paid ... The aim of this work is to suggest political and social solutions that take us in a direction in which it is clear that *jobs are no longer the solution, that we must find another way to ensure a just standard of living for all.*

They observed (ibid.: 3–4) that, contrary to expectations that the service sector would absorb the unemployment generated in manufacturing, the new information technologies were also displacing workers. Rifkin (1995: 141–57), recognizing that computers can understand speech, read text and perform tasks previously performed by human beings, forecast a new era in which the services would be increasingly automated. Not only routine personal services, but also more complex services are being taken on by intelligent machines. Retail trade is also being automated. The use of bar codes, by increasing the efficiency of cashiers – the third-largest job in services in the USA (1.5 million) – will eliminate many jobs. Self-service checkouts are appearing in supermarkets, menacing the jobs of cashiers, as has already happened in car parks. Retail trade was the sponge that absorbed unemployment (Rifkin 1995) – this no longer holds true. The exceptions are the education and health sectors, where available data show for the USA that these continue to create jobs.

Rifkin (ibid.: 121) returns to the end of work theme:

> Big data, advanced analytics, algorithms, Artificial Intelligence
> (AI), and robotics are replacing human labor across the
> manufacturing industries, service industries, and knowledge
> and entertainment sectors, leading to the very real prospect of
> liberating hundreds of millions of people from work in the market
> economy in the first half of the twenty-first century.

He quotes the 4 November 2011 issue of *The Economist*, which cites Rifkin (1995), who had 'argued prophetically that society was entering a new phase – one in which fewer and fewer workers would be needed to produce all the goods and services consumed … *the process has clearly begun*'. Rifkin reacts to this text:

> It wasn't that I was clairvoyant. The signs were everywhere,
> but in the growth years, most economists were so attached to
> conventional economic theory – that supply creates demand and
> that new technologies, while disruptive, reduce costs, stimulate
> consumption, spur more production, increase innovation, and
> open up opportunities for new kinds of jobs – that my message fell
> largely on deaf ears. Now economists are taking notice. (Rifkin
> 2014: 122)

He adds:

Today, near workless factories run by computer programs are
increasingly the norm, both in highly industrialized countries
and developing nations ... [Many] blame blue-collar job losses
on the relocation of manufacturing to cheap labor markets like
China. The fact is that something more consequential has taken
place. Between 1995 and 2002, 22 million manufacturing jobs
were eliminated in the global economy while global production
increased by more than 30 percent worldwide ... Manufacturers
that have long relied on cheap labor in their Chinese production
facilities are bringing production back home with advanced
robotics that are cheaper and more efficient than their Chinese
workforces ... (Ibid.:123)

As Rifkin acknowledges (ibid.: 128), after the Great Financial Crisis
there has been a boom in publications 'warning about automation's
impact on jobs ... and their message of a coming *workerless world*
began to gain attention in social media outlets, even attracting some
comments from policy makers, think tank researchers, economists, and
President Barack Obama'.

Martin Ford links the advancing technology with the current
crisis (2009: 6), and is concerned that economists reject the idea that
technology displaces human labour and dismiss those raising concerns
regarding technological unemployment as 'neo-Luddites', coining the
term *Luddite-fallacy* (ibid.: 47–8). He is very clear on the role of the
labour market in capitalism:

The reality is that the free market economy, as we understand it
today, simply cannot work without available labor market. Jobs
are the primary mechanism through which income – and therefore
purchasing power – is distributed to the people who consume
everything the economy produces. If at some point machines
are likely to permanently take over a great deal of the work now
performed by human beings, then that *will be a threat to the very
foundation of our economic system*. This is not something that will
just work itself out. (Ibid.: 5)

He perceives, correctly in our opinion, that 'off-shoring is a prelude
to automation' (ibid.: 56–7): '... many jobs that are currently being off-
shored will, in the future, end up being fully automated'; 'Off-shoring

is the small wave that distracts you. Automation is the big one further
out that you don't see coming.'

Brynjolfsson and McAfee (2012, 2014) provide further evidence on
the impact of automation on job displacement. For instance, they show
clearly that job growth has been de-accelerating constantly since the
1940s.

> The population of the United States grew by 30 million in the
> past decade, so *we would need to create 18 million jobs just to keep
> the same share of the population working as in the year 2000. Instead,
> we've created virtually none*, reducing the employment to population
> ratio from over 64% to barely 58%. The lack of jobs is not simply
> a matter of massive layoffs due to the Great Recession. Instead,
> it reflects deep structural issues that have been worsening for a
> decade or more. (Ibid.: 35)

In a more radical vein, André Gorz, the great Marxist thinker,
begins *Reclaiming Work. Beyond the Wage-Based Society* (1999: 1) by
saying: 'We must dare to break with this society that is dying and will
not reborn. We must dare to Exodus. There is nothing to be gained
from symptomatic treatment of the "crisis" because there no longer is
any crisis. A new system has been installed which is abolishing "work"
on a massive scale.'

There is a partial diagnostic agreement between Gorz, Rifkin,
Brynjolfsson and McAfee, and Aronowitz and DiFazio. Gorz main-
tains that 'It is not this abolition we should object to, but its claiming
to perpetuate that same work, the norms, dignity and availability of
which it is abolishing, as an obligation, as a norm, and as the irreplaceable foundation of the rights and dignity of all' (1999: 1). He
concludes:

> We must dare to prepare ourselves for the Exodus from 'work-
> based society': it no longer exists and will not return. We
> must want this society, which is in its dead-throes, to die, so
> that another may arise from its ruins. We must learn to make
> out the contours of that other society beneath the resistances,
> dysfunctions and impasses which make up the present. 'Work'
> must lose its centrality in the minds, thoughts and imagination
> of everyone. We must learn to see it differently: no longer as

something we have – or do not have – but as *what we do*. We must be bold enough to regain control of the work we do.
(Ibid.: 1, emphasis in original)

Gorz also discusses the nature of the work that is being eliminated: 'it is what everyone calls work, but not work in the philosophical or the anthropological sense, nor the work of giving birth to a child, nor the work of the sculptor or poet'.

It is not work as the 'autonomous activity of transforming matter', nor as the 'practico-sensory activity' by which the subject exteriorizes him/herself by producing an object which bears his/her imprint. It is unambiguously, the specific 'work' peculiar to industrial capitalism, the work we are referring when we say 'she doesn't work' of a woman who devotes her time to bringing up her own children, but 'she works' of one who gives even some small part of her time to bringing up other people's children ...
(Ibid.: 2)

From the above analyses, we conclude that the development of productive forces compatible with capitalism appears to be coming to an end. Globalization and industrial expansion to capture the very cheap and docile labour of the global South appear as temporary steps before the full automation of production.

What can be done within capitalism? Universal, Sufficient and Unconditional Citizen's Income

Earn your bread by the sweat of your brow, says the Bible, and we may add: 'and by the humiliation of your spirit'. Maslow (1987 [1954]: 27) wrote that the experience can reassess more pre-potent needs (the physiological): 'a man who has quit his job to keep self-respect, and lives hungry for six months, may be willing to return to work even at the price of losing his self-respect'. Heilbroner (1963) has shown that in the history of mankind there are three ways to solve the fundamental economic problem, defined as the mobilization of human energy to work: tradition, coercion or literal whip, and the *metaphorical whip of hunger*. Despite the monotonous nature of work and the humiliations imposed, the proletarian cannot quit her job because she is dominated by the whip of hunger.

The growing contradiction between automation and the wage-based society, which heralds the end of capitalism, has stimulated different proposals to solve a challenge, which could result in a global apocalypse. Rifkin (1995) offered a proposal: a reduction of the work week and the promotion of non-profit-oriented activities, in a third sector or social economy, beyond the market and the public sector, providing community and social services. This sector would be promoted through tax incentives and by the government paying a social wage to those 'holding a job' in it. This can be interpreted as an attempt to save capitalism, although Rifkin posits that capitalism will constitute a declining proportion of the future economy, while the third sector would increase. Rifkin's proposal is not in the line of a Basic Income approach, which he discusses but does not incorporate into his proposal.

Martin Ford has also offered solutions to this blind alley seeking to save capitalism. He acknowledges, 'in order to preserve the mass market in a largely automated economy, we need to provide an alternative to jobs. We need a mechanism that can get a reliable income stream into the hands of consumers. This, of course, is a proposition that will be very difficult for most of us to accept; the idea that we must work for a living is one of our most basic core values' (2009: 159). He adds (ibid.: 160), 'there is simply no way to envision how the private sector can solve this problem. There is simply no real alternative except for the government to provide some type of income mechanism for consumers.' To fund this income-providing mechanism, Ford (ibid.:162–79) proposes to recoup wages lost as a consequence of automation via taxation. Incomes would be *unequal* and would depend on three factors: level of education, participation in community and civic activities, and positive behaviour towards the environment. He sums up his proposal (ibid.: 195) as follows: 'By offering unequal incentive-based income to consumers, we not only sustain consumer demand, but also drive people to act in ways that benefit us all …' It could be called a *conditional basic income*, which apparently would not be universal but targeted at those directly affected by automation.

The great aspiration to overcome scarcity and alienation, achievable from the point of view of the productive forces for the past fifty years (Richta et al. 1968), is, in our assessment, unattainable within capitalism. The intensified contradiction between the forces of production and the rules of income distribution in capitalism was observed, from the 1960s, by persons who were more interested in saving capitalism than in overcoming it.

Oppenheimer and the group of scientists he led, which included Robert Theobald, proposed a Universal Citizen's Unconditional Income (UCUI). Theobald coordinated one of the first publications on a 'Guaranteed Income' (Theobald 1965). In his contribution to that volume, Fromm argued that the UCUI could, for the first time, free the individual from the threat of starvation, from economic threats. Nobody would have to accept conditions of work merely because he otherwise would be afraid of starving ... the woman could leave her husband, the teenager his family (Fromm 1965: 176).

In another approach, with a view to transcending rather than saving capitalism, André Gorz made the case that, with automation, the labour society, the wage society, was coming to an end. It was therefore time to distinguish between 'the imperative need for a sufficient, regular income' and 'the need to act, to strive, to test oneself against others, and be appreciated by them' (Gorz 1999: 72). The right to a sufficient, regular income will no longer have to depend on the permanent occupation of a steady job. The need to act, strive and be appreciated by others will no longer have to take the form of paid work done to order ... *'Working time would no longer be the dominant social time.'* These are the outlines of a new civilization 'which is struggling to be born beyond the wage-based society ... They correspond to the aspiration for a multi-active life ...' and personal autonomy (ibid.: 73, italics in original).

Discussing his proposal of a guaranteed income for life, Gorz argued that it must meet two conditions: it needs to be sufficient to avoid poverty, and it needs to be unconditional. One could therefore call it a *Universal, Sufficient and Unconditional Citizen's Income* (USUCI). A USUCI would allow people to refuse non-dignified working conditions (ibid.: 82–3). USUCI is intended to 'enable people to reject inhuman working conditions. It must be part of *a social environment which enables all citizens to decide on an ongoing basis between the use value of their time and its exchange value,* that is to say between the 'utilities' they can acquire by selling their working time and those they can 'self-provide' by using that time themselves' (ibid.: 83). The aim of USUCI is 'not to enable people not to work at all, but rather to give genuine effect to the right to work: not the right to that work you are "employed" to do, but to the concrete work you do without having to be paid for it'. In this sense, work represents a mastery of self and of the surrounding world which is necessary for the development of human capacities. 'As the need for "work" diminishes, fairness requires that it should diminish in everyone's life and that the burden of work should be equitably distributed' (ibid.: 84).

USUCI differs fundamentally from the guarantee of an income below the poverty line proposed by neoliberals, which seeks to force the unemployed to accept reduced pay and thus make profitable otherwise unprofitable jobs, creating a lumpen labour market (ibid.: 81).

According to Gorz, free time allows individuals to develop their capacities for invention, creation, conception. The consequence – but not the purpose – of this is unlimited productivity. It allows converting production into an ancillary activity and enables the maximization of available time to become the inherent meaning and purpose of economic reason. It replaces work – as the dominant form of activity – with personal activity.

To replace the society of work with the society of multi-activity, the USUCI must be accompanied by the redistribution of work, and new modes of cooperation and exchange (ibid.: 93–100). There is only one way to distribute a decreasing volume of work among a growing number of people: to work increasingly in a discontinuous way and allow people the choice between various forms of discontinuity, thereby transforming it into a new freedom: the right to work intermittently and lead a multi-active life.

Gorz finds one concrete example for this approach in Denmark. There, non-work is subsidized. Its principles give equal importance to the right to work and to the right not to work and the links between them: the right to work discontinuously with a continuous income. Payment when not working is 63 per cent of normal salary; thus someone who works half-time receives a salary equal to 81.5 per cent of a full-time salary. The limit of the Danish formula lies in the fact that it guarantees a conditional social income that not everyone can achieve. But as a transitional formula it is particularly interesting, Gorz concludes (ibid.: 96–8).

The issue of funding as an objection to USUCI 'comes to encapsulate the problem of the system as a whole': although working time is no longer the measure of created wealth, it still remains the basis for the distribution of incomes. Wassily Leontief (quoted by Gorz) puts it as follows: 'When wealth creation depends no longer on work, men will die of hunger at the gates of paradise, unless a new income policy is established as a response' (Gorz 1998: 100). As an important financial source for USUCI and decommodification, two lines of action should be gradually implemented. First, land rent should be appropriated by the state, by way of very high and progressive property taxes on commercial land use. A second source would come from a tax on financial transactions and on foreign currency transactions, and a capital gains tax.

A USUCI would eliminate poverty radically and at the same time solve the contradiction between gigantic levels of actual and potential production and shrinking consumer demand as a result of wage loss due to automation. It would save capitalism, but plant in it the seed of its transformation by eliminating the whip of hunger and thus liberating people.

Final reflections

If capitalist crises and automation are the two basic forces determining the trends of global poverty, then it is logical to conclude that the adoption of poverty reduction goals is a somewhat futile exercise, unless this exercise examines the causes of global poverty trends and establishes the changes required to modify those trends. The chapter has argued that capitalism is coming to an end because automation continuously decreases the jobs required to produce a potentially increasing amount of goods and services. When jobs decrease, the income in the hands of the vast majority of consumers also decreases, making the sale of goods produced impossible. This growing contradiction can bring to an end a society that distributes income mainly by wages.

The conclusion is straightforward: the global community must discuss how to design and implement a mechanism that could decouple income from paid jobs, if it wants to avoid the social chaos that could be coming soon, both in developed and in developing countries, if it continuous pretending that fixing poverty reduction goals is all it has to do.

USUCI, or something equivalent to it, prevents the coming social chaos as it decouples income from declining jobs and allows for the capitalist system to continue functioning. Not only extreme poverty – all poverty is eliminated completely and permanently. The barriers that social relations of production pose to the further development of productive forces are eliminated.

On the other hand, the adoption of ultra-extreme poverty reduction goals does not respond to the social chaos threat. These goals have led many countries to the adoption of CCTs (Conditional Cash Transfer) targeted at ultra-extreme poor households, following recommendations by the World Bank to achieve the goals. But CCTs result in a lumpen proletariat labour market, promoting the growth of the 'precariat' (Standing 2011), and do not reduce poverty significantly, as transfers are very low and the causes of poverty trends are not taken care of.

Notes

1 Unless otherwise stated, emphasis in quoted material is the authors'.

2 The official poverty measurement method used by the Government of Mexico City is the Integrated Poverty Measurement Method (IPMM), a multidimensional method developed by Boltvinik in the early 1990s. The other is a reinterpretation of Coneval's official poverty measurement method, conceiving as poor all households/ persons belonging to each of two sets: those below the poverty line and showing one or more 'social lacks' (i.e. deprivation in direct indicators), instead of using an intersection, as does Coneval.

3 In the figure the years that show an *e* have been estimated from a graph in on the Mexico presidency's web page and also using previous and more detailed information from INEGI which includes

all the years since 1989 where information is available and which separates rural and urban figures on UEP incidence.

4 The year 1989 cannot be used as baseline as there is no comparable information for that year to identify urban and rural settlements.

5 National poverty data for 1989 cannot be disaggregated by rural and urban areas because the corresponding 1989 survey used a very odd rural–urban definition.

6 Marx did not formulate systematically a theory of capitalist crises, but wrote a lot about them in dispersed passages of his main economic writings: *Capital*, *Grundrisse* and *Theories of Surplus Value*. John Strachey (1935) was one of the first to systematize his thought on this topic, together with Paul Sweezy (1970 [1942]).

References

Aronowitz, S. and W. DiFazio (1994) *The Jobless Future: Sci-Tech and the Dogma of Work*, Minneapolis and London: University of Minnesota Press.

Baran, P. A. and P. Sweezy (1966) *Monopoly Capital*, Monthly Review Press.

Boltvinik, J. (2005) 'Ampliar la Mirada. Un Nuevo enfoque de la pobreza y el florecimiento humano',

PhD dissertation, Centro de Investigación y Estudios Superiores en Antropología Social, Occidente, Guadalajara, Mexico.

Brynjolfsson, E. and A. McAfee (2012) *Race against the Machine*, New York: Norton.

— (2014) *The Second Machine Age: Work, Progress, and Prosperity in a Time of Brilliant Technologies*, New York; Norton.

Doyal, L. and I. Gough (1991) *A Theory of Human Need*, London: Macmillan.

Ford, M. (2009) *The Lights in the Tunnel. Automation, Accelerating Technology and the Economy of the Future*, San Bernardino, CA: Acculant Publishing.

Foster, J. B. and F. Magdoff (2009) *The Great Financial Crisis: Causes and Consequences*, New York: Monthly Review Press.

Fromm, E. (1965) 'The psychological aspects of the Guaranteed Income', in R. Theobald, *The Guaranteed Income. Next Step in Economic Evolution*, New York: Doubleday, pp. 175–84.

Gorz, A. (1998) *Miserias del presente: Riqueza de lo posible*, Buenos Aires: Paidós.

— (1999) *Reclaiming Work: Beyond the Wage-Based Society*, Cambridge: Polity Press.

Heilbroner, R. (1963) *The Making of Economic Society*, Prentice Hall.

— (1995) 'Foreword', in J. Rifkin, *The End of Work*, New York: Putnam, pp. xi–xiii.

Krugman, P. (2008) *The Return of Depression Economics and the Crisis of 2008*, New York: Norton.

Marx, K. (1976 [1867]) *Capital: A Critique of Political Economy*, vol. 1, London: Penguin.

— (2000 [1859]) *Preface to A Critique of Political Economy*, in D. McLellan (ed.), *Karl Marx: Selected Writings*, Oxford: Oxford University Press.

Maslow, A. (1987 [1954]) *Motivation and Personality*, 3rd edn, New York: Addison-Wesley Longman.

Minsky, H. (1986) *Stabilizing an Unstable Economy*, Yale University Press.

Noble, D. (1984) *Forces of Production: A Social History of Industrial Automation*, New York: Knopf.

Pogge, T. and S. Reddy (2010) 'How not to count the poor', in S. Anand, P. Segal and J. Stiglitz, *Debates on the Measurement of Global Poverty*, Oxford: Oxford University Press, pp. 42–85.

Putnam, H. (2002) *The Collapse of the Fact/Value Dichotomy and Other Essays*, Cambridge, MA: Harvard University Press.

Richta, R. et al. (1968) *La civilización en la encrucijada*, Madrid: Artiach.

Rifkin, J. (1995) *The End of Work*, New York: Putnam.

— (2003), 'Tiempo libre para disfrutarlo o hacer filas de desempleados', in L. J. Alvarez, *Un mundo sin trabajo*, Mexico City: Editorial Dríada, pp. 15–49.

— (2014) *The Zero Marginal Cost Society*, New York: Palgrave Macmillan.

Sen, A. K. (1981) *Poverty and Famines: An Essay on Entitlements and Deprivation*, Oxford: Clarendon Press.

Standing, G. (2009) *Work after Globalization: Building Occupational Citizenship*, Cheltenham: Edward Elgar.

— (2011) *The Precariat: The New Dangerous Class*, London: Bloomsbury.

Strachey, J. (1935) *The Nature of Capitalist Crisis*, New York: Covici Friede Publishers.

Sweezy, P. (1970 [1942]) *The Theory of Capitalist Development*, New York: Monthly Review Press.

Theobald, R. (1965) *The Guaranteed Income: Next Step in Economic Evolution*, New York: Doubleday.

Wiggins, D. (1987) *Needs, Values, Truth: Essays in the Philosophy of Value*, Oxford: Clarendon Press.

World Bank (1990) *World Development Report 1990: Poverty*, Washington, DC: World Bank.

— (2008) *Global Purchasing Power, Parities and Real Expenditures, 2005*, Washington, DC: International Comparison Program, World Bank.

— (2009) *Global Monitoring Report 2009, A Development Emergency*, Washington, DC: World Bank.

9 | SOCIAL SOLIDARITY MUST REPLACE POVERTY ERADICATION IN THE UN'S POST-2015 DEVELOPMENT AGENDA

Bob Deacon[1]

Introduction and overview

This chapter does the following. It

- reviews the beginnings of the discussion within and around the UN regarding what should be the UN development agenda after 2015. It suggests that while the initial outcomes of the review held out the possibility that the post-2015 agenda might shift from a targeted and technical residual approach to alleviating poverty to an approach which is more concerned with *policy and process focused in part upon overcoming social structural inequity both within and between countries*, this agenda a) became complicated by the injection of sustainability concerns into it and moreover b) by the time of the publication in late 2014 of the Open Working Group's outcome document the focus on social policies that might address structural inequality was lost.
- argues, and presents support for the case, that the continuing global politics of poverty alleviation and eradication should indeed shift towards *a new global politics of building social solidarity* and include a focus as much on the welfare needs of middle-class state builders as on the poor in order to create those solidarities.
- reviews several global policy responses that have been concerned with poverty issues consequent upon the global economic crisis of 2008. These include a) affording more resources to the IMF, b) the development of the UN-wide Social Protection Floor initiative, c) the increased attention given to the concept of freedom from poverty as a human right and d) a renewed focus on state-lead development.
- asks which if any of these approaches might both address the issue of building solidarities and of being likely to be embedded in the post-2015 agenda.

The UN discusses the post-MDG agenda

To initiate the process of thinking through the post-2015 development agenda within the UN system the first step was given to the internal UN Task Force made up of spokespersons from over fifty UN agencies. It began its work in January 2012 with a Zero Draft[2] prepared by UNDESA and UNDP staff drawing on a number of critical papers such as those of Gore (2010) and Fukuda-Parr (2010). In its balanced review of the perceived positive and negative aspects of the MDG goals it noted among the shortcomings of the MDG agenda that it was 'not explicit as to what are to be seen as the *structural causes of poverty and social exclusion* [my emphasis], nor regarding the strategies and policy actions to be taken to address the structural causes to facilitate the achievement of the MDGs' (UN 2012a: 4). It went on to suggest that 'critics have suggested that the MDGs have introduced an undue and mechanistic association of poverty reduction with economic growth with no reference to the structural causes of poverty and deprivation' (ibid.: 7). The think piece asked 'How to bring into the development framework questions of inequality, peace and security, global and national governance, human rights, sustainable development without overloading the agenda to the point of losing its operational value?' (ibid.: 8).

After several video conferences and other forms of communication the Task Force reported in May 2012 (UN 2012b). Its Executive Summary was predictably bland but did suggest a future development agenda centred on 'four key dimensions of a more holistic approach: (1) *inclusive social development* [my emphasis]; (2) inclusive economic development; (3) environmental sustainability; and (4) peace and security' (ibid.: 2). It suggested a high degree of policy coherence was needed to achieve this. The baton then passed to the High Level Panel (HLP) on the Post-2015 Development Agenda whose membership and terms of reference were announced on 15 July 2012. In setting out the terms of reference the UN Secretary-General reordered the items in the Task Force report which had suggested inclusive social development as number one by now putting economic growth as the number-one priority. It commanded the Panel to make 'Recommendations on how to build and sustain broad political consensus on an ambitious yet achievable Post-2015 development agenda around the three dimensions of economic growth, social equality and environmental sustainability; taking into account the particular challenges of countries in conflict and post-conflict situations' (UN 2012c: 5). UK prime minister David Cameron, Liberian president Ellen Johnson Sirleaf and President Susilo Bambang Yudhoyono, of Indonesia, are co-chairs. Cameron has been rewarded for keeping the UK commitment to reach the 0.7 per cent of gross national income spent on development aid. Unfortunately his pre-occupation is what he calls the 'golden thread' of development. Owen Barder, Europe director of the Centre for Global Development think tank, says the golden thread stresses free markets, jobs and growth, but not other ways to encourage positive social and economic change, such as reducing inequality, tackling the power of elites, providing social protection, and ensuring a strong voice for civil society.[3]

Initial reaction from the Beyond 2000 Civil Society Campaign Group (Beyond 2000 2012) was critical of the terms of reference. It was 'surprised and disappointed that the ToRs do not include a single reference to **human rights**'. It did, however, 'welcome the HLP plans to set out key principles to **reshape global partnership**. One lesson learnt from the MDGs is the need to better deliver **equity and equality**, within but also between countries'.

In the event the final report of the High Level Panel included the concept of human rights but avoided a focus on equity by continuing to address in the spirit of the MDGs the issue of extreme poverty. Thus it concluded: 'After 2015 we should move from reducing to ending extreme poverty, in all its forms. We should ensure that no person – regardless of ethnicity, gender, geography, disability, race or other status – is denied universal human rights and basic economic opportunities' (UN 2013: 8).

In parallel to setting up the HLP the UN Secretary-General took the step of establishing the Sustainable Development Solutions Network (SDSN) on 9 August 2012, which

> will provide global, open and inclusive support to sustainable-development problem solving at local, national, and global scales. The SDSN will work together with United Nations agencies, other international organizations, and the multilateral funding institutions including the World Bank and regional development banks, to mobilize scientific and technical expertise to scale up the magnitude and quality of local, national and global problem solving, helping to identify solutions and highlighting best practices in the design of long-term development pathways.

Professor Jeffrey D. Sachs, Special Advisor to the UN Secretary-General on the MDGs, will direct the project with the core aim of creating an open, inclusive and world-class global network of expertise and problem-solving. The network will comprise mainly universities and scientific research institutes, but will also tap technical expertise within technology companies, science foundations and academies of sciences and engineering. Columbia University's Earth Institute will serve as the secretariat for the network. However, an examination of its website suggests a lower profile in the process than might have been expected.

The other context for this crafting of the UN development agenda beyond 2015 is, of course, the widely criticized outcome of the Rio+20 conference, which produced a broad thesis on sustainable development with little specific policy guidance. George Monbiot (blog, 21 June 2012) was particularly scathing about the outcome:

> In 1992, world leaders signed up to something called 'sustainability'. Few of them were clear about what it meant; I suspect that many of them had no idea. Perhaps as a result, it did not take long for this concept to mutate into something subtly different: 'sustainable development'. Then it made a short jump to another term: 'sustainable growth'. And now, in the 2012 Rio+20 text that world leaders are about to adopt, it has subtly mutated once more: into 'sustained growth'. This term crops up 16 times in the document, where it is used interchangeably with sustainability and sustainable development. But if sustainability means anything, it is surely the opposite of sustained growth. Sustained growth on a finite planet is the essence of un-sustainability.

In relation to our concern with poverty, equity and inclusive social development the recent significant International Labour Conference recommendation that countries should develop a Social Protection Floor (see later) ended up relegated to one sub-paragraph (n) of paragraph 58 of the Rio+20 document concerned with the green economy, which should, among sixteen concerns, 'address the concern about inequalities and promote social inclusion, including social protection floors'.

The Open Working Group on Sustainable Development Goals was set up following Rio+20 to work on sustainable development goals.[4]

The OWG (UN 2014) reported in late 2014, listing seventeen goals, each with a number of targets. In terms of the concerns of this chapter it is notable that goal one remains couched in the language of the global politics of poverty alleviation and eradication, calling for the end of poverty in all its forms everywhere. The nearest the specific targets get to addressing social policies that might ensure that this happens is the vacuous target that urges the creation of 'sound policy frameworks, at national, regional and international levels, based on pro-poor and gender-sensitive development strategies to support accelerated investments in poverty eradication actions'.

Inequality is addressed in goal 10, which calls for the reduction of inequality within and between countries and suggests in one associated target that countries should 'adopt policies especially fiscal, wage, and social protection policies and progressively achieve greater equality'.

In relation to the vexed question of sustainability, the Open Working Group's report, like the Rio+20 outcome document, is littered with the undefined 'sustainable' adjective. It is applied to water, energy, economic growth, industrialization, cities, consumption, oceans, forests and development in goals 6, 7, 8, 9, 11, 12, 13, 14, 15, 16 and 17. Lurking in goal 8, however, is the problematic sustained per capita economic growth of at least 7 per cent in developing countries. To repeat Monbiot, 'sustained growth on a finite planet is the essence of un-sustainability'.

So there have been parallel tracks in the work on the post-2015 development agenda; the trick for the UN will be to combine them into one. The UN appointed a new special adviser on post-2015 development planning, Amina Mohammed, who has said that both the High Level Panel and the Working Group on Sustainability share one secretariat, meaning that the end result will be 'one development agenda'. We await this in 2015. The synthesis report of the Secretary-General, the first draft of which was published in December 2014, entitled *The Road to Dignity by 2030: Ending Poverty, Transforming All Lives and Protecting the Planet*, might give some clues as to where the UN process will have reached by September 2015. The document (UN Secretary-General 2014) argues for 'six essential elements that would help frame and reinforce the universal, integrated and transformative nature of a sustainable development agenda and ensure that the ambition expressed by Member States in the outcome of the

Open Working Group translates, communicates and is delivered at the country level'. These are

- Dignity: to end poverty and fight inequalities.
- People: to ensure healthy lives, knowledge, and the inclusion of women and children.
- Prosperity: to grow a strong, inclusive, and transformative economy.
- Planet: to protect our ecosystems for all societies and our children.
- Justice: to promote safe and peaceful societies, and strong institutions.
- Partnership: to catalyse global solidarity for sustainable development.

The beginnings of the post-2015 discussions reviewed above therefore:

- Do open up for debate the issue of *inequality and equity* rather than just poverty.
- Do open up a space for engaging in *social policy recommendations* and not just targets.
- Do permit a *reordering of priorities* other than a simple focus on economic growth.

But also:

- Muddy the waters with more intangible, ill-defined, albeit important, concerns with *sustainability*.

This chapter now turns to argue how this opportunity for rethinking could be used during the final discussions in 2015 if policy recommendations for equity and social solidarity are to be advanced.

Welfare states, solidarity and social inclusion

The UN post-2015 development agenda must leave behind the *global politics of poverty alleviation, now poverty eradication*, and focus instead on shaping a new *global politics of social solidarity*. For the past thirty years the dominant discourse in international development has been the 'global politics of poverty alleviation', which focuses on the poor and seeks policies that lift populations out of poverty or protect others from falling into it. Subsequently, global policies have pursued the elimination of indirect causes of poverty, such as disease and poor education and compensation for lack of income, whether through cash transfers, microcredit or low-wage employment.

It is suggested here that the difficulties with this approach not only point to the general need for a new direction but also call for the more specific engagement of other social groups normally excluded from global policy interest. This would mean replacing the strategy of targeting the most vulnerable populations with support for a 'global politics of solidarity' based on inclusion of the 'middle class' in development policy. The new strategy would promote alliances between the poor and non-poor, especially the middle class, while making services and opportunities more available and more effective for all. Middle class here signifies educated men and women working in professions, small and medium-sized enterprises, management, public sector administration and skilled vocations. Based on the development of welfare states in the twentieth century, *social policy and social development science* tell us that the better way to reduce poverty is fairly consistent and involves middle-class buy-in to inclusive state welfare provision. In developed countries, Goodin et al.'s (1999) comparative research on liberal, conservative and social democratic welfare states concludes that whether the objective of policy is poverty alleviation, social inclusion or the facilitation of personal autonomy, social democratic welfare states are best at doing the job. This remains largely unchallenged by social policy analysts. For developing countries, Mehrotra and Jolly's (1997) comparative review of those countries with higher than expected human development indicators concluded too that a common feature of such human development leaders was the universal provisioning of social services. At the same time there is clear evidence that in both rich and poor countries more equity is good for growth, for poverty alleviation and well-being (Wilkinson and Pickett 2009).

Given this, who played the major role in helping to forge the best and most socially cohesive welfare states in Europe? A casual reading of the social policy literature and certainly of the development studies literature would suggest that either the poor struggled for their own interests or that a fraction of national and international reforming elites did so on their behalf. Sometimes a role is ascribed to organized trade union and working-class struggle, which has taken a variety of forms in a development context. Some have, however, drawn attention to the trade-off between targeting the poor (which might save money) and including the middle class (which ensures greater tax revenue). Korpi and Palme (1998) concluded that excluding the middle class from pension programmes may remove broad-based support for such programmes and make them unsustainable. There is a higher budget available for redistribution where targeting is *reduced*.

Twenty years ago, Peter Baldwin's (1990) *Politics of Social Solidarity: Class Bases of the European Welfare State* argued the case that middle-class expectations/demands fuelled service provision for all. As he put it, 'The simplest, and most frequently answered, questions posed to the welfare state concern the nature and extent of the benefits now won by the disadvantaged. A much more intriguing problem deals with the stake developed by the comfortably upholstered middle class in such reform' (ibid.: 9). For Baldwin, 'Although far from all social policies were implemented [in Sweden] with the bourgeoisie in mind, it did not take long for fortunate groups to recognise their interests in the right sort of measures. In Scandinavia, the middle classes have rarely shunned state intervention on their own behalf. From the start, they lobbied successfully for advantageous welfare policies' (ibid.: 28).

Baldwin's analysis was based on case studies of several European welfare state developments where universal social security acted as the mechanism for implementing the ideals of universalism and fulfilling the self-interest of all social groups to eliminate risk and uncertainty. Consistent with Goodin's conclusions, the social democratic welfare states of Scandinavia were successful in part because they provided high-quality public health and education services of all kinds, which ensured middle-class usage and a willingness to pay taxes. In terms of the conservative corporatist (or Bismarckian) welfare states of Germany and France and the Benelux countries, which did not fare too badly, the middle class had their welfare needs met through a wage- or salary-related social security system. The liberal 'welfare state' of the USA failed in part because the middle class were in general cast out on to the marketplace to have their needs met, except for social security, which was uncharacteristically a public commitment to insured workers. Where there are now moves to reduce the core universalism combined with status-differentiating aspects of European welfare states, there are signs of disquiet among middle classes, who begin to argue that the remaining basic level of social security should be linked to inducements to encourage responsible behavioural changes among the poor (Mau and Sachweh 2010).

It was not only in Europe that meeting the welfare needs of the middle class was seen as an important element of economic development. Those in charge of the state-led development project in East Asia and Latin America understood this logic. A recent paper describes the central role of welfare provisioning for the middle class in Korea's development in the 1960s: 'The social welfare benefits that white-collar workers received included housing loans, retirement benefits, subsidies for tuition fees as well as health insurance' and 'new apartments (built with city-state money and accessed with benefits to the better off) became the symbol of modernity and a new culture of the middle class' (Yang 2010: 10–12). In this way such states created a satisfied middle class committed to modernization.

The assault on universal welfare states in a development context

Whereas *social policy and social development science* explained the central role of the middle class in welfare state development in Europe, unfortunately the *economic scientific community* framed the analysis of emerging welfare states in a development context and therefore the policy response to their development in different terms. The story of structural adjustment is well known. A recent summary of the period captures the essence (Voipio 2011: 104): the structural adjustment drive was motivated not only by World Bank and IMF economists' objective analysis about what would be best for the poor countries and their poor people, but also by a deliberate ideologically motivated effort to reframe the idea of 'aid-for-poverty-reduction' as an instrument for promoting the paradigm of pro-market and anti-government neoliberalism. For us what is central is the direct assault on the embryonic welfare states carried out during this period by economists who knew nothing of the political economy of inclusive welfare state building within which the middle class were central.

The World Bank's econometric and technocratic approach was based on the use of a *beneficiary index* to assess which social groups benefited from public expenditure in Africa, Latin America and Asia. Armed with this tool the Bank's missions to country after country in the 1970s and 1980s concluded that the middle class benefited most from public expenditures and that this was a *bad* thing. They got better state pensions in Brazil, which was true. They got better state housing in Senegal, which was true.

Cost-cutting economists argued that this was unjust from the point of view of the poor. It was this line of thinking which led to the Bank's and the IMF's assault on the embryonic universal welfare states in those countries. It is worth recalling a key text of the time that argued for safety nets for the poor rather than services that met the needs of other social groups. Carol Graham (1994: 9–10), then a visiting fellow at the World Bank, argued:

> Safety net programs that give them [the poor] a political voice provide new channels of access to the state. By inviting new actors to help implement the programs, such as NGOs, the government can create a new political space for the poor, garner their political support, and therefore increase their chances of sustaining the *redirection* [my emphasis] of public resources [away from exiting better-off beneficiaries].

An alliance between the Bank, the poor and development NGOs (which have an interest in meeting the needs of the poor) was constructed that challenged fundamentally the universalism of the European social policy experience (Deacon 2007; Deacon et al. 1997). This gave rise to the UK-influenced[5] OECD–DAC (Organisation for Economic Co-operation and Development–Development Assistance Committee) poverty targets focused upon the poor, which in turn resulted in the MDGs, themselves a retreat from the more universalist formulations of the 1995 Copenhagen World Summit for Social Development. Those who constructed the global politics of poverty alleviation between the 1980s and 2000 were ignorant of the political economy of welfare state building, which teaches us that the latter depends on the construction of cross-class alliances and middle-class buy-in to reform.

One final twist in the global politics of poverty alleviation centred on an aid business powered by a global NGO community was the absorption of the neglected and impoverished poor middle class into its project. Finnish scholar Jeremy Gould demonstrated that the aid business has played a major part in seducing the professional and middle class of developing countries away from the developmental role they used to occupy. Writing about Tanzania and other African countries, Gould blames the decline of the nationally engaged middle class on the actions of international aid agencies: 'Seduced by access to the dollar economy, they prioritize acquiring skills for ... the requirements of the aid cartel ... at the expense of contributing to the development of domestic manufacturing and processing industries that would generate actual wealth within the national economy' (Gould 2005: 148–9).

This rupture between the middle class and the state in Tanzania was also evident in Morocco; here due to increasing economic insecurity among younger, educated men and women. Moroccans look to the globe to fulfil the ideal of individual potential they cling to as the consequence of education, family pressure and political discourse. In shifting their gaze beyond national borders, they detach themselves from national politics and social development, preferring either to work on local causes close to home or to engage in global cultural production and consumption. Cohen writes:

> ... the political goal of the global middle class would be to obtain access to services formerly subsumed within the province of the state, that now increasingly comes from the non-located, heterogeneous social relations that signify and support globalisation ... [as a result] the social and political bond between elite and non-elite falls apart globally and locally leaving only economic benefit and exploitation. (Cohen 2004: 114)

Interestingly, Graham conceded (1994: 10): 'this does not imply that hard hit middle sectors of society do not merit some form of compensation or that they will not be the focus of government attention in the future'. That future is here. The hope has to be that their seduction into the global dollar economy has not lost them for good from the state-led development projects of the future.

Is the social policy in development discourse bringing the middle class back in?

Despite the deliberate neglect of, or even attack on, the idea of public policy meeting middle-class welfare needs in international policy discourses in the last century, a small shift seems to have occurred in development discourse since then. The World Bank's (2003) *World Development Report 2004*, which focused on making services work for poor people, hinted at some movement towards considering the middle class. Within the text (and probably among the authors) there was a tension between those who stayed with the line that much public spending by developing countries benefits the rich and is therefore to be refocused on the poor (e.g. ibid.: 4, Figure 2) and those who appeared now to argue that 'cross class alliances' between the poor and non-poor are needed to pressure governments to 'strengthen public sector foundations for service delivery' (ibid.: 180, Figure 10.1) (Deacon 2005). Most striking was the assertion that 'In most instances making services work for poor people means making services work for everybody – while ensuring poor people have access to those services. Required is a coalition that includes poor people and significant elements of the non-poor. There is unlikely to be progress without substantial "middle class buy-in" to proposed reforms' (World Bank 2003: 60). This section of the report goes on to quote Wilbur Cohen, US Secretary of Health, Education and Welfare under President Lyndon Johnson in the 1960s: 'Programmes for Poor People are Poor Programmes'.

More recently, policy analysts like Nancy Birdsall, using income-based definitions of class, have associated political stability with a large middle class (2007). Like modernization theorists before her, Birdsall makes the assumption that the middle class, educated and dependent on modern institutions and technologies, will engage in civic activism and support political liberalization. Analysing the failure of relatively successful African economies to undergo political transformation, she remarks,

> The implicit assumption of the donor community is that Africa is trapped by its poverty, and that aid is necessary if Africa is to escape the trap. In this note I suggest an alternative assumption: that Africa is caught in an institutional trap, signalled and reinforced by the small share of income of its independent middle-income population. Theory and historical experience elsewhere suggest that a robust middle-income group contributes critically to the creation and sustenance of healthy institutions, particularly healthy institutions of the state. I propose that if external aid is to be helpful for institution-building in Africa's weak and fragile states, donors need to emphasize not providing more aid but minimizing the risks more aid poses for this group in Africa. (Birsdall 2007: 4)

Developing her arguments, which have a lot of synergy with mine, in a later paper she argues:

> A focus on the middle class does not imply a lack of concern for the poor. To the contrary; in the advanced economies the poor

have probably benefited from the rule of law, legal protections, and in general the greater accountability of government that a large and politically independent middle class demands, and from the universal and adequately funded education, health and social insurance programs a middle class wants and finances through the tax system. (Birdsall 2010: 159)

These arguments have been reproduced recently in a research report of the African Development Bank:

The middle class is also helping to improve accountability in public services through more vocal demands for better services. The middle class is better educated, better informed and has greater awareness of human rights. It is the main source of the leadership and activism that create and operate many of the nongovernmental organizations that push for greater accountability and better governance in public affairs ... policies that include the promotion of middle class growth are more cost-effective and generate more long-term poverty reducing benefits than policies that focus solely on addressing problems of the poor. (AfDB 2011: 15)

Despite the marginalization of the middle class in global policy, there are immediate practical, political, social and economic reasons for policy-makers at a global level to address directly the welfare of the 'middle class'. On the most material level, public and NGO services depend on the presence, motivation and skills of local staff. The World Bank, the UN, national aid agencies and NGOs have long noted the shortage of teachers and health workers (DfID 2009) as a consequence of emigration and low education rates as well as conflict and poor facilities. The World Bank has also investigated the reasons for health worker and teacher absenteeism in the public sector and its consequences for care and learning (Chaudhury et al. 2006). Lastly, the focus on corruption among aid agencies reflects salary conditions and morale within the public sector in developing countries (Hellsten and Larbi 2006).

More particular to development, agencies like DfID and academics have criticized the migration of competent public sector staff to international organizations attractive for their salaries and career options

(DfID 2006). As we noted earlier, Jeremy Gould analysed how aid agencies in Tanzania and other parts of Africa had lured professionals away from the developmental role they used to occupy. He further argues: 'the intellectual and entrepreneurial class must choose between a self-referential and parasitic post-developmentalism, and national(ist) development projects – enhancing domestic savings and productive investment, improving the productivity of land and labour, building the revenue base of the public economy' (Gould 2005: 149).

His comments point to possibly more urgent and profound reasons for considering the role of the middle class in global social policy. Promoting demand and productivity, which Gould cites as a function of the middle class, necessarily means addressing the economic insecurity among middle-income groups provoked by the global recession or more long-standing trends in unemployment among educated younger generations. The relative decline in revenue of middle-income groups, forced into focus by the global recession, has arguably blurred the segregation of need characteristic of 'target-based' policies. Furthermore, trends in unemployment and declining income coupled with the failure of national policy-makers to incorporate the middle class into a vision of social and political progress have engendered profound alienation and, in areas like the Arab world, resistance aimed at regime change. As mentioned earlier, researching the global aspirations of the middle class in Morocco, Cohen (2004) argued that increasing economic insecurity among younger, educated men and women has ruptured the relationship between the middle class and the state in the region. This rupture has pushed younger generations away from conventional political participation associated with the modern nation-state.

Global social policy responses to the economic crisis

But what of the most recent developments in the global social policy discourse in the wake of the global economic crisis? Reviewing the impact of the global economic crisis on the shifting global discourse, Deacon (2010) suggested that the crisis has highlighted three strands of thinking about social policy in a development context. The first, derived from the large sums agreed by the G20 with the IMF in 2009, still leaves the IMF's parsimonious approach targeted towards the most vulnerable poor in a dominant position. No focus on the middle class here. At the other extreme, the second raises anew the case for a kind of state-led development within which state capacity is central. Thus the UNCTAD *Least Developed Countries Report 2009* argued that 'the developmentally orientated elite ... should establish a social compact through which broad sections of society support the developmental project' (UNCTAD 2009: 51). Here support for middle-class state-builders is central. The third is the idea of a global social floor, or more precisely the ILO Recommendation on Social Protection Floors (ILO 2012), which the global economic crisis has propelled to centre stage. Though evoking universal access to a minimum standard of welfare or social security guarantees, it can be argued that the concept does not go far enough in recognizing the role of a middle class in engineering improved collective well-being. If attention is focused, however, on the twin-track approach for extending social security not only horizontally but also vertically the policy might be more amenable to our concern (Deacon 2013: 159. Finally there is the increased attention being given to the argument that poverty is an abuse of human rights. The UN Special Rapporteur on extreme poverty has put this case strongly[6] and has argued (Sepulvda and Nyst 2012) for the importance of the human rights approach to poverty alleviation and social protection, as indeed has Thomas Pogge (2010). The question arises, as with the Social Protection Floor, as to whether such an approach leads only to a policy approach targeted on the poor. Each of these global responses is now considered in more detail: a) IMF support, b) Social Protection Floor, c) the human rights approach, and d) State-led developmentalism.

IMF support The task of providing the first coordinated world response to the global economic crisis fell to the first ever meeting of the G20 at heads-of-state level at the 2 April 2009 G20 summit. It fashioned a global policy on the hoof. It committed US$1.1 trillion to support countries in crisis, as follows: US$750 billion to be used under the guidance of an unreformed IMF, US$250 billion for trade facilitation, and only US$100 billion for development purposes (including social development), through unreformed multilateral development banks. The UN was given only a marginal role, to monitor the crisis, with no additional resources. So in April 2009 we were faced with an interesting paradox. The world's rich countries were embarking, albeit briefly with the exception of the USA, on huge fiscal stimulus packages involving often large social spending guided by long-forgotten Keynesian principles, while for the poorer countries, the equivalent task was being given to the IMF without a word of comment about the fact that the IMF historically was focused upon forcing countries into neoliberal short-term procyclical budget-balancing macroeconomic policies, which were the total opposite of what was being (briefly) prescribed for rich countries. The key question was whether the IMF was about to change its spots and policies and embark on a policy of encouraging poorer countries to invest in social expenditures to spend their way out of their crisis and moreover to spend on the middle class as well.

Dominique Strauss-Kahn, who was then the new IMF boss, insisted it was a new IMF and its website insisted

> The IMF tries to ensure that economic adjustments taken to combat the impact of the crisis also take account of the needs of the most vulnerable by developing or enhancing social safety nets. Social spending is being preserved or increased wherever possible. For instance, in Pakistan expenditure will be increased to protect the poor through both cash transfers and targeted electricity subsidies. About a third of programs in low-income countries include floors on social and other priority spending. Structural reforms are designed in a way to protect the most vulnerable. For instance in Hungary, low-income pensioners were excluded from benefit reduction.

Even if we take this at face value, the drift of the argument is *not* for social expenditures as social investments to support a renewed state-led development project. It is not even for a global Social Protection Floor. At best it is for a targeted approach to poverty alleviation and a residual means-tested approach to social policy. The Centre for Economic Policy Research (CEPR) finds that nine agreements that the Fund has negotiated since September 2008, including with eastern European countries, El Salvador and Pakistan – contained some elements of contractionary policies. These include fiscal (budget) tightening, interest rate increases, wage freezes for public employees, and other measures that will reduce aggregate demand or prevent economic stimulus programmes in the current downturn. Similarly, Eurodad's analysis (Molina-Gallart 2009) of ten IMF agreements signed in 2009 shows that the IMF is still advising stringent fiscal and monetary policies to low-income countries, as well as controversial structural reforms. The paper comments that 'If the Fund is to provide funding to poor countries to meet the financial gaps created by the crisis it has to change and it has to do it soon. Reacting poorly and reacting late may mean death and starvation for millions of people in poor countries.' Other research on loans to El Salvador, Latvia and Ethiopia come to the same conclusions (ibid.). Work by Lendvai and Stubbs in central and eastern Europe confirms that in that region the message of the IMF, now in alliance with the EU, which is faced with its own crisis in Greece, is uncompromisingly for public sector restraint and a targeted welfare approach (Lendvai and Stubbs 2015). Isabel Ortiz and her colleagues at UNICEF urgently addressed this failure of the IMF to change its approach, insisting there was an alternative. The UNICEF paper on *Prioritizing Expenditures for a Recovery for All: A Rapid Review of Public Expenditures in 126 Developing Countries'* (UNICEF 2010) showed that in 2011 fiscal consolidation/ austerity swept across developing countries and the risks of worsened social outcomes increased. The paper has become an important source of information with which to challenge the IMF procyclical economic policy advice, but the IMF does not seem to be listening. Isabel Ortiz, now Social Protection Director at the ILO, continues to report this gloomy story, noting in a recent (26 November 2014) contribution to the recovery-human-face e-discussion board:

> Since 2010 many governments embarked on fiscal consolidation (or austerity policies) and premature contraction of expenditures, despite an urgent need of public support among vulnerable populations. In 2015, the scope of public expenditure adjustment is expected to intensify significantly. According to the latest IMF fiscal projections contained in the World Economic Outlook (October 2014 http://www.imf.org/external/pubs/ft/weo/2014/02/), 120 countries, of which 86 are developing, will be contracting expenditures in terms of GDP. The scope of adjustments is expected to affect 131 countries in 2016.

In other words, put simply, we cannot look to the IMF's contribution to the post-2015 debate for any support for the need to spend not only on the most vulnerable but also the middle class. There are no social contracts being built within this framework.

Social Protection Floor This forefronting of the G20 and the IMF as the global agencies to address the crisis annoyed many in the UN system and concretely led to a meeting of the UN Chief Executive Board in Paris later in April 2009, which generated the UN CEB Issue Paper 'The global financial crisis and its impact on the work of the UN system'. The meeting was able to draw upon an earlier draft report considered on 26/27 February 2009 by the CEB's High-Level Committee on Programmes. The report called for coordinated action across the UN system in eight key policy fields: i) finance, ii) trade, iii) employment and production, iv) environment, v) food security, vi) social services, empowerment and protection of people, vii) humanitarian, security and social stability and viii) international cooperation for development. In terms of specific policies the ILO would lead on a Global Jobs Pact and 'to help developing countries cope with the crisis, a counter-cyclical global jobs fund could be established'.

Most important from this chapter's point of view was initiative six, which was to work towards a global 'Social Protection Floor which ensures access to basic social services, shelter, and empowerment and protection of the poor and vulnerable'. This was subsequently elaborated in the June 2009 UNCEB document (UNCEB 2009) as a 'floor [that] could consist of two main elements: (a) public services: geographical and financial access to essential public services (water, sanitation, health, education); and (b) transfers: a basic set of essential social transfers ... to provide a minimum income security'. The ILO and the WHO would lead on this policy, supported by a host of other agencies such as UNICEF and UNDESA. The Global Social Floor had become UN policy at least in terms of the UNCEB.

The Social Protection Floor became a formal new ILO standard in June 2012, when the International Labour Conference agreed the wording of its Recommendation on Social Protection Floors (SPFs) for countries. The SPFs should comprise at least the following basic social security guarantees: '(a) access to a nationally defined set of goods and services, constituting *essential health care*, including maternity care that meets the criteria of availability, accessibility, acceptability and quality; (b) *basic income security for children*, at least at a nationally defined minimum level, providing access to nutrition, education, care and any other necessary goods and services; (c) *basic income security*, at least at a nationally defined minimum level, for persons *in active age* who are unable to earn sufficient income, including in particular in cases of sickness, unemployment, maternity and disability; and (d) *basic income security*, at least at a nationally defined minimum level, *for older persons'*.

There are two very different assessments that can be made of this new ILO Recommendation. For its supporters the Recommendation is historic because, in the words of its main protagonist inside the ILO, it asserts that the ILO has a role in formulating social protection policy for *residents, not just workers*, it challenges the growth-first economists with the priority of *social protection whatever the level of the economy*, and it argues for *redistribution nationally and internationally*.

For those who would want to detract from its significance it is easy to point to the compromises and changes of definition that have been necessary to ensure that by the time of the 2012 ILC most controversial issues had already been dealt with. My study (Deacon 2013) of the history of the SPF demonstrates the changing formulations from when the concept was first mooted inside the ILO to the final 2012 text. These changes involved (a) a shift from a set of specific *benefits* such as universal pensions or child benefits to a set of *outcomes*, met by governments in whatever way they saw fit, (b) a shift from a *global social floor* under the global economy to *nationally defined floors* with each country defining its own minimum guarantee level, and (c) a retreat from an emphasis on *international financial support* for such a floor to mainly *national responsibility* for revenue-raising to fund the floors. Furthermore the issue of social protection of migrants was ducked by leaving the definition of 'resident' to countries.

An earlier assessment of mine (Deacon and Cohen 2011) regarding the development of this SPF policy was sharply critical in terms of whether such a new policy would encourage a renewed focus on the social security needs of the middle class. A focus on the poor, I argued, distracts from cross-class solidarity-building and a focus on the poor undermines the middle-class commitment to pay taxes. This assessment is echoed by Francine Mestrum (2012: 14–15). She argues:

> A[n] SPF is meant for the poor or '*all in need*', it does not go beyond poverty reduction, even if the ILO stresses its link with the social security extension campaign. But the divergent references to 'universalism' leave some doubts. It is not always clear whether 'universalism' refers to the whole population, to all the poor or to all the deserving poor.

... In short, however positively the plans for a Social Protection Floor can be assessed ... if the SPF is limited to its minimal requirements, it will be compatible with Washington Consensus policies. And that means the impoverishment processes will not be stopped.

The counter-argument made by the ILO's authors of the SPF Recommendation stresses, to the contrary the fact that the Recommendation, largely to ensure it got support from the Workers' Group of the ILO, is focused as much on the *vertical extension of social security*, which involves encouraging more countries to establish formal wage-related social security systems. Thus they acknowledged the possible criticism of an SPF focused only on the poor by saying that 'a social protection system that does not support higher benefit levels to a significant proportion of its population can lose the support of its own beneficiaries and contributors' (Cichon and Wodsak 2011: 8).

Debate about this will continue. However, it has to be pointed out that while the ILO seemed initially to miss the chance to inject the SPF as a post-2015 policy priority in the first discussions between UN agencies between January and May 2012 and in the Rio+20 outcome document, it has been more influential in shaping the more recent developments of the Open Working Group. In March 2014 the New York office of the ILO organized a technical workshop at the UN in New York to discuss possible indicators and means of implementation associated with the proposal to include Social Protection Floor targets as part of the SDGs. It is pleasing that Target 3 of the first goal reads. '[countries should] implement nationally appropriate social protection systems and measures for all, including floors, and by 2030 achieve substantial coverage of the poor and the vulnerable'.

The human rights approach Much of what has been said above about the SPF might apply to the issue of whether a focus on the human rights approach to poverty reduction can also accommodate the welfare needs of middle classes and help build solidarities within and between countries. The case for the SPF is predicated on a human rights agenda. Sepulveda and Nyst assert (2012: 18):

The added value of the human rights approach to poverty reduction can be conceptualised in at least three different ways. Of critical importance is that the human rights approach provides a *normative framework for practical action to reduce poverty*. Human rights can provide practical guidance to the design, implementation, evaluation and monitoring of poverty reduction efforts ... From a human rights perspective, individuals are *rights-holders* that can make legitimate claims, and States and other actors are *duty-bearers* that are responsible and can be held accountable for their acts or omissions. ... Human rights also provide the *legal imperative for poverty reduction policies*.

Even if these arguments are accepted, the assertion by the poor as rights-holders that the state has a legal obligation to support them and adhere to a global set of policy principles does not ensure that the non-poor on whose taxes the state depends will finance their being met. A legal contract between the poor and the state is not a social contract between the better-off and the poor. Indeed, controversially it can be argued that the reference by the poor to a set of internationally formulated rights might undermine such a contract within a polity where the dominant discourse might be about the perceived 'abuse' by claim-holders (particularly outsiders and migrants) of the international human rights agenda. The concept of poverty as an abuse of human rights may give anti-poverty protesters one more bit of discursive armoury. It does not, however, address the social policies that are needed to build cross-class solidarities within one country or how the post-2015 UN Development agenda can contribute to that.

State-led developmentalism The approach to the post-2015 agenda which focuses on state-led economic and social investment within countries might be more fruitful in creating the required cross-class solidarities. Such an approach would address the needs of the middle class who otherwise may turn (if relatively well off) to have their needs met from a global private marketplace (hence undermining their commitment to a national social contract), or (if impoverished) turn to non-modernist political agendas. The involvement of the otherwise marginalized agency UNCTAD as a potential supporter of this approach, together with the ILO, would be important. Although it has to be added that UNCTAD is not monolithic – it is mainly the LDC report that has argued in this direction, and one or two statements by the Secretary-General prior to UNCTAD XIII on the developmental state.

International policy could address economic insecurity among low- and middle-income populations and promote social solidarity through a number of strategies. The first concentrates on framing the discourse and substance of policy around the aim of elevating collective welfare. Conceptually, this path would imply relating the expansion and security of the middle class to meeting the needs of more vulnerable groups. Substantively, the strategy would first revitalize the notion of universal access and common quality of services for all, particularly through supporting public institutions as service providers or partners in services provided by other sectors offering equal quality and access. The strategy would also explicitly link job creation and sustainable income to improvements in services and the manufacture of products used in confronting the conditions of poverty, from housing to safe appliances. Emphasizing social solidarity would enhance the job creation strategy of the ILO.

International organizations and national government supporting this strategy would likewise need to reverse the brain drain of professionals and convince diaspora communities, international NGOs and other sources of funding to look for reinvigorated public institutions and other signs of social solidarity when making decisions about investment. Practically speaking, *revitalizing or building public services in education and health would be important for both the middle class and low-income groups for a number of reasons.* Regarding health, reinforcing public services could mean the adequate treatment of pervasive conditions and health issues that private doctors and insurance companies can reject because of their expense, such as diabetes, and supporting the education of younger medical staff through supporting public teaching hospitals. In education, reinforcing public education could offer similar shared benefits for the middle class and the poor, namely by giving the state more power to coordinate education with labour market possibilities, and improving working conditions and the status of public school teachers removes incentives to work privately. Investing in public institutions would, as was the logic with welfare states, theoretically succeed because they should benefit both administrators and recipients. This statement has several implications. The first is that the institutions responsible for social mobility, such as education, would now be charged openly with ensuring the quality of future practitioners and increasing the opportunities and well-being of current users. The second is that effective management of public institutions would refer at least partially to the quality of relations between practitioners and service users, with service evaluation assessing the impact of social relations and any activities aimed at integrating the institution into the larger community.

Conclusions

This chapter has argued that the opportunity should be taken by the discussions surrounding the post-2015 MDG agenda to ensure that the current *global politics of poverty eradication* should shift towards *a new global politics of building social solidarity* and include a focus as much on the welfare needs of middle-class state builders as on the poor in order to create those solidarities. It has reviewed the several global policy responses that have been concerned with poverty issues consequent upon the global economic crisis of 2008. These were the affording of more resources to the IMF, the development of the ILO Social Protection Floor policy, the increased attention given by the Office of the High Commissioner for Human Rights (OHCHR) to the concept of poverty as a human right, and a renewed focus on state-led development by parts of UNCTAD. The only one of these approaches which might address the issue of building the cross-class solidarities I have argued for is that of UNCTAD. Also, so long as the twin-track approach of the vertical and horizontal dimensions of the ILO SPF policy is taken seriously, this might help too. The IMF is irrelevant unless it can be persuaded to create more fiscal capacity in a country to permit social investments. Human rights is a rallying cry but does not get to the heart of the social structural issues. Whether the UNCTAD–ILO approach becomes embedded within the post-2015 agenda remains the issue.

In terms of the vexed question of how the world might follow this social solidarity path as well as addressing at the same time the important issue of sustainability, it is clear that the continued uncritical endorsement of economic growth in both the Open Working Group's report and the Secretary-General's attempted Synthesis Report has to be confronted. These issues are discussed in the useful volume by Kaasch and Stubbs (2014) on *Transformations in Global and Regional Social Policies*, in which, referring to a contribution by Ian Gough, they suggest 'that nothing short of a transformative paradigm is needed, moving ... towards an "eco-social policy" capable of achieving ecologically beneficial and socially just impacts "by promoting new patterns of production, consumption and investment, changing producer and consumer behaviour while improving wellbeing, and ensuring a fairer distribution of power and resources"'(ibid.: 12).

Notes

1 The third, fourth and fifth sections of this chapter draw upon Deacon and Cohen (2011).

2 The technical term for the very first draft of any UN document written by civil servants before it has even been discussed by a first meeting of those who have the responsibility for drafting the document.

3 www.guardian.co.uk/global-development/2012/oct/31/post-2015-development-agenda-explained.

4 Ibid.

5 The role of Clare Short, then minister for development in UK DfID, was significant here, although Sakiko Fukuda-Parr suggests that Fukuda herself was influential in shaping similar Japanese policy on this point.

6 The Special Rapporteur has produced reports to the United Nations Human Rights Council and General Assembly on human rights and cash transfer programmes (A/HRC/11/9), the role of social protection in the face of the global financial crisis (A/64/279), a human rights framework for non-contributory pensions (A/HRC/13/31), the importance of social protection measures in achieving the MDGs, with a particular focus on gender-related concerns (A/65/259), and the human rights approach to recovery from the global economic and financial crises (A/HRC/17/34), which included an analysis of the important role played by social protection programmes during times of crisis and recovery. She also undertook an analysis of social protection programmes in her visits to Ecuador (A/HRC/11/9/Add.1), Zambia (A/HRC/14/31/Add.1), Bangladesh (A/HRC/15/55), Vietnam (A/HRC/17/34/Add.1), Ireland (A/HRC/17/34/Add.2), Timor-Leste (A/HRC/20/25/Add.1) and Paraguay (A/HRC/20/25/Add.2).

References

AfDB (African Development Bank) (2011) 'The middle of the pyramid: dynamics of the middle class in Africa', Market Brief, 12 April.

Baldwin, P. (1990) *The Politics of Social Solidarity: Class Bases of the European Welfare State 1875–1975*, Cambridge: Cambridge University Press.

Beyond 2000 (2012) 'Beyond 2015 and GCAP comments on the set up and Terms of References of the High-Level Panel of Eminent Persons on the Post-2015 Development Agenda', www.beyond2015.org/sites/default/files/Beyond%202015%20GCAP%20HLP%20ToRs%20analysis_0.pdf.

Birdsall, N. (2007) 'Reflections on the macro foundations of the middle class in developing countries', Centre for Global Development Working Paper 130.

— (2010) 'The (indispensable) middle class in developing countries; or the rich and the rest, not the poor and the rest', in R. Kanbur and M. Spence (eds), *Equity and Growth in a Globalizing World*, Washington, DC: World Bank, pp. 157–88.

Chaudhury, N. et al. (2006) 'Missing in action: teacher and health worker

absence in developing countries',
Journal of Economic Perspectives,
20(1): 91–116.

Cichon, B. and V. Wodsak (2011)
*The UN Social Protection Floor
Initiative: Turning the Tide at the ILO
Conference*, Germany: Friedrich Ebert
Stiftung.

Cohen, S. (2004) *Searching for a Different
Future: The Rise of the Global Middle
Class*, Durham, NC: Duke University
Press.

— (2009) 'Journée d'étude sur la class
moyenne', Paper presented at the
Moroccan Policy Conference, Rabat,
April.

Deacon, B. (2005) 'From safety nets back
to universal social provision: is the
global tide turning?', *Global Social
Policy*, 5(1): 19–28.

— (2007) *Global Social Policy and
Governance*, London: Sage.

— (2010) 'Shifting global social policy
discourse and governance in times
of crisis', Paper presented at the
UNRISD conference on the Social
Implications of the Global Economic
Crisis, Geneva, November.

— (2012) 'Shifting global social policy
discourses and governance in times
of crisis', in P. Utting et al., *The Global
Crisis and Transformative Social
Change*, Basingstoke: Palgrave.

— (2013) *Global Social Policy in the
Making: the Foundations of the Social
Protection Floor*, Bristol: Policy Press.

Deacon, B. and S. Cohen (2011) 'From the
global politics of poverty alleviation
to the global politics of social
solidarity', *Global Social Policy*, 11(2/3):
233–49.

Deacon, B., P. Stubbs and M. Hulse (2007)
*International Organisations and the
Future of Welfare*, London: Sage.

DfID (Department for International
Development) (2006) 'Making
governance work for the poor', White
Paper, London: DfID.

— (2009) 'Eliminating world poverty',
White Paper, London: DfID.

Fukuda-Parr, S. (2010) 'Reducing
inequalities – the missing MDG: a
content review of PRSPs and bilateral
donor policy statements', *IDS Bulletin*,
41(1): 26–35.

Goodin, R. et al. (1999) *The Real World
of Welfare*, Cambridge: Cambridge
University Press.

Gore, C. (2010) 'The MDG paradigm,
productive capacities and the future
of poverty reduction', *IDS Bulletin*,
41(1): 71–9.

Gould, J. (2005) *The New Conditionality:
The Politics of Poverty Reduction
Strategies*, London: Zed Books.

Graham, C. (1994) *Safety Nets, Politics and
the Poor*, Washington, DC: Brookings
Institution.

Hellsten, S. and G. A. Larbi (2006)
'Public good or private good? The
paradox of public and private
ethics in the context of developing
countries', *Public Administration and
Development*, 26(2): 135–45.

ILO (International Labour Organization)
(2010) *Global Employment Trends*,
Geneva: ILO.

— (2012) *Recommendation on Social
Protection Floors*, Geneva: ILO.

Kaasch, A. and P. Stubbs (eds) (2014)
*Transformations in Global and
Regional Social Policies*, Basingstoke:
Palgrave Macmillan.

Kabbani, N. and E. Kothari (2005) 'Youth
employment in the MENA region:
a situational assessment', Social
Protection Discussion Paper no. 0534,
Washington, DC: World Bank.

Korpi, W. and J. Palme (1998) 'The paradox
of redistribution and strategies
of equality: welfare institutions,
inequality, poverty in the western
countries', *American Sociological
Review*, 63(5): 661–87.

Lendvai, N. and P. Stubbs (2015)
'Europeanization, welfare and

variegated austerity capitalisms – Hungary and Croatia', *Social Policy & Administration Regional Issue: Europeanization of Welfare*, 49(4): 445–65.

Mau, S. and P. Sachweh (2010) 'The middle class in the German welfare state: beneficial involvement at stake?', Paper presented at the International Sociological Association Conference, Sweden, July.

Mehrotra, S. and R. Jolly (1997) *Development with a Human Face*, Oxford: Clarendon Press.

Mestrum, F. (2012) 'Social Protection Floor: beyond poverty reduction?', www.globalsocialjustice.eu.

Pogge, T. (2010) *Politics as Usual: What Lies behind the Pro-Poor Rhetoric*, Cambridge: Polity Press.

Sepuleva, M. and C. Nyst (2012) *The Human Right Approach to Social Protection*, Helsinki: Ministry of Foreign Affairs of Finland.

UN (United Nations) (2012a) 'Post-2015 United Nations Development Agenda: Preliminary Review of the Contribution of the MDG agenda', Zero Draft, 6 January.

— (2012b) 'UN System Task Team: Report: Realizing the future we want for all', www.un.org/en/development/desa/policy/untaskteam_undf/unttreport_summary.pdf.

— (2012c) 'UN Secretary-General appoints High-Level Panel on Post-2015 Development Agenda', Press release, www.un.org/millenniumgoals/Press%20release_post-2015panel.pdf.

— (2012e) 'The future we want', Rio+20 outcome document, www.uncsd2012.org/content/documents/727THE%20FUTURE%20WE%20WANT%20-%20FINAL%20DOCUMENT.pdf.

— (2013) *High Level Panel: The Post 2015 Development Agenda*, www.post2015hlp.org/the-report/.

— (2014) *Open Working Group on Sustainable Development Goals*, sustainabledevelopment.un.org/focussdgs.html.

UN Secretary-General (2014) *The Road to Dignity by 2030: Ending Poverty, Transforming All Lives and Protecting the Planet*.

UNCEB (2009) 'The global financial crisis and its impact on the work of the UN system', UNCEB Issue Paper.

UNCTAD (United Nations Conference on Trade and Development) (2009) *The Least Developed Countries Report 2009*, Geneva: UNCTAD.

UNICEF (2010) *Prioritizing Expenditures for a Recovery for All: A Rapid Review of Public Expenditures in 126 Developing Countries*, New York: UNICEF, www.unicef.org/socialpolicy/index_56435.html.

Voipio, T. (2011) 'From poverty economics to global social policy: a sociology of aid for poverty reduction', Doctoral thesis, University of Eastern Finland, Kuopio.

Wilkinson, R. and K. Pickett (2009) *The Spirit Level: Why More Equal Societies Almost Always Do Better*, London: Allen Lane.

World Bank (2003) *World Development Report 2004: Making Services Work for Poor People*, Washington, DC: World Bank.

Yang, M. (2010) 'The making of the urban middle class in South Korea: discipline, nation building and the creation of the ideal subject', Paper presented at the International Sociological Association, RC 19 Session, Gothenburg, Sweden, 11–17 July.

10 | LOOKING BACK AND LOOKING FORWARD: THE CASE FOR A DEVELOPMENTAL WELFARE STATE

Gabriele Koehler

The challenge[1]

Seventy years ago, with the historic creation of the United Nations, human rights and dignity, freedom from fear and freedom from want became universal normative principles. Fifteen years ago, the stirring Millennium Declaration promised human development and a considerable reduction in poverty and hunger. However, despite decades of development effort, these goals remain elusive.

This chapter looks back at the history of development agendas, and forward towards the emerging next development agenda. It places the MDGs in the context of development decades, pursued by the UN and the international community since the 1960s, which, over time, moved from a primary orientation towards development in the sense of economic growth, to a broader attention to poverty and a focus on social or human development. It posits that the MDGs were a success in terms of raising the visibility of poverty and social development as global political concerns. They were nonetheless a failure in that the majority of the targets were not met; this was a result of conceptual shortcomings, and most importantly due to the lack of an explicit policy design and vision.

Building on this assessment, the objective of the chapter is to revisit, and revive attention to, policy-making and hence the role of the state. The state is the only political institution at least notionally accountable to citizens, and therefore carries the primary responsibility for enabling and ensuring sustainable human development, and guaranteeing human rights. Ideally, a democratic state is oriented to both economic development – and hence developmentalist – and to social development and human rights – and hence a welfare state. This case is presented with an eye on the emerging, next development agenda – the globally applicable Sustainable Development Goals (SDGs).

Looking back

The MDG agenda The Millennium Declaration and the MDGs were introduced at the turn to the twenty-first century. It was a time when North–South power dynamics were in flux. In 1989, with the end of the Cold War, there was a renaissance of – at least rhetorical – concern for social justice, human rights and development in global policy thinking, and in public awareness. The 1990s had seen a series of UN-initiated social-policy-oriented summits – most significantly the UN Social Summit (Copenhagen, 1995), which formulated an ambitious agenda for employment, social inclusion and participation. Social democratic governments were in place in several European countries, with a fortuitous constellation of social democratic gender-aware development ministers in power in the Netherlands, Germany and Sweden. Fiscal resources were available. As a result, a certain degree of policy space was emerging. The UN seized the momentum and launched the Millennium Declaration and its ensuing developing goals.

There were good and bad reasons for the international community to develop a new goal set. There was disillusionment with the four UN development decades which had up until then been a guide for development – the UN General Assembly had declared each of them in turn unsuccessful, not reaching their goals. Conceptually, the development decades' remit was too narrow because they presented quantified goals primarily directed at economic growth and restructuring, so that the social goals they also contained appeared less crucial. So there was a case for correcting the economistic bias (Koehler 1996). However, an equal driver for the move to a new agenda in the year 2000 was the fact that the international development decades had a strongly Keynesian flavour, and ascribed poor development outcomes to disadvantageous international conditions. This was out of tune with the neoliberal policy framework, which had become the predominant economic policy orientation since the rise of the structural adjustment regime of the international financial institutions, reinforced by the collapse of the Soviet Union and its planned and centralized economies.

Thus, at the cusp of the new millennium, political pressure for a change to the international development regime was issuing from many sources. It converged towards formulating a new and somewhat different development agenda.

In 2015, this Millennium Development Agenda and its set of goals, the MDGs, have arrived at a built-in juncture. However, the current international political situation is very different from the one that prevailed in the late 1990s when the MDGs were formulated and launched (Hulme and Wilkinson 2014: 186). On the positive side, government constellations are shifting. Many of the Group of 77 (G77) developing countries are economically strong, having experienced sound GDP growth rates and an increase in sovereign wealth funds, partly as a result of high commodity prices during the past decade. A number of non-OECD countries have emerged as development cooperation players. Leftist governments hold office in several Latin American countries, and one observes the advance of an at least notionally rights-based social policy agenda in South Asia (Koehler and Chopra 2014). In the multilateral arena, owing to public pressure and enhanced lobbying, civil society representation in multilateral discussions has grown exponentially, from roughly one hundred NGOs in the 1970s to 4,000 in 2013 (Bissio 2014: 195f.). The nine 'major groups' representing NGOs, local authorities, indigenous peoples, women, youth and children, trade unions, agriculture and business have become acknowledged partners in the negotiating process on the post-2015 agenda (Sustainable Development Knowledge Platform 2015). This would suggest a multipolar dynamic with room for shifting the goalposts.

On the negative side, however, are the economic, social and political effects of unbridled financial capitalism and a persistent global recession. Income and wealth inequality are at unprecedented extremes (Milanovic 2011; ADB 2012; UNRISD 2012a; Cimadamore et al. 2013; Piketty 2014; Oxfam 2014). The share of capital and labour in global GNI has shifted over the past decades to the benefit of capital (Lübker 2007; Milanovic 2011; Ortiz and Cummins 2012). Malnutrition continues to affect almost one billion people, and despite advances in the mitigation of extreme income poverty, 1.2 billion people have to survive with less than $1.25 a day (UNDP 2014: 19; UN 2014). In a more meaningful statistic which shows poverty across an individual's life domains, more than 2.2 billion people are vulnerable to multidimensional poverty, including almost 1.5 billion who are multidimensionally poor (UNDP 2014: 19).[2] Registered unemployment is expected to rise to above 211 million over the next five years (ILO 2013), and more immediately palpable, massive youth unemployment affects most countries, whether high- or low-income. Austerity programmes are cutting down social expenditures in many countries (Ortiz and Cummins 2014). These trends have weakened labour movements, and they pit the working poor and those in the informal economy within each country and across countries against each other. Environmental catastrophes and global warming affect high- and low-income countries alike, and the poor in these countries the most. The poor situation of global public goods – security threats, the missing resources for health, most recently in the Ebola pandemic – have painfully raised awareness of the lack of government capacity (Mackie and Williams 2015). Not one of the LDCs – despite their relatively good growth performance in the early 2000s – has been able to achieve all the MDGs (UNCTAD 2014). The Southern countries among the BRICs, while functioning as new development policy leaders because of their progressive social protection policies, are falling short in the policy domain of governance, employment and environment management. The 'North' is, at the moment, predominantly in a politically conservative mode, as a result of constellations in the US Congress, and the homogenizing effect of a coordinated EU development policy which favours the lowest common denominator. The private sector has become an accepted partner in the UN system, pushing for its own commercial interests. The UN system – which could be a leader in the development agenda process – is fragmented and compartmentalized (see Hulme and Wilkinson 2014; Browne and Weiss 2014).

These factors have an influence on global economic and political dynamics. Democracy, good governance and tackling corruption and a rights-based approach, concern over inequities and anxieties over the environment and climate change have become accepted mainstream topics. The concerns have paved the way, in academic and development circles, for a new interest in a regulatory role for the state (see, for example, UNDP 2013). But the concentration of economic wealth and political power is unprecedentedly strong and may override the more progressive trends.

What, then, are the possibilities for formulating a new, progressive, egalitarian and rights-based development agenda, post-2015, which would engender a genuine approach to eradicating poverty and achieving inclusive and equitable human development in the foreseeable future? Will developmental welfare states be in place to carry these shifts? Will 'five big, transformative shifts' (High-Level Panel Report 2013: 7ff.)

materialize? That will depend, *inter alia*, on a critical re-evaluation of the MDGs, and of the history of earlier development efforts. The following sections look into this.

History of development agendas The MDG agenda derived directly from the seven development goals proposed by the OECD Development Assistance Committee (DAC) in 1996 (OECD DAC 1996; Fukuda-Parr 2012; Martens 2013; Hulme and Wilkinson 2014: 184; Ivanova and Escobar-Pemberthy this volume). These had quantified and time-oriented objectives, and all but one were carried over into the goals and targets introduced by the UN in 2002.[3]

However, there is another MDG precursor that is rarely mentioned: the UN development decades.[4] They, too, had quantified objectives. The first UN Development Decade (A/Res/1710 (XVI)) was adopted by the General Assembly in 1961, formally triggered by an address by the American president to the UN. This UN Development Decade laid out policy recommendations for low-income countries to achieve 'development'. It adopted a Keynesian approach, with an emphasis on economic growth, to catch up with the economically advanced countries in terms of incomes and productivity. The decade posited a minimum annual growth rate of 7 per cent in aggregate national income. It proposed interventions to transfer capital from developed to developing ('underdeveloped') countries, to maximize the mobilization of domestic resources, and to increase exports of manufactured and semi-manufactured goods. There was an emphasis on the function of development plans to address social as well as economic development; on administrative machinery and incentives for effective implementation; and on the redirection of science and technology to focus on national problems (UN GA 1960; UN Intellectual History Project 2010). But the Decade was also about achieving 'well-being and happiness not only of the present generation but also of the generations to come' (UN GA 1970: Article 4).

The goals of the first decade were not achieved, prompting the UN General Assembly to introduce the International Development Strategy for the Second United Nations Development Decade (1971–80). It reiterated the macroeconomic growth goals and objectives of the first, and again placed great emphasis on development planning (UN GA 1970). It also paid attention to social goals – employment, education, health, nutrition, participation – and noted that '[t]he ultimate objective of development must be to bring about sustained improvement in the well-being of the individual and bestow benefits on all' (ibid.: Article 7).

The subsequent Third United Nations Development Decade (1981–90) (UN GA 1980) proposed a new international economic order and called for institutional and structural changes in international economic relations (ibid.: Article 17).[5] It aimed for a reduction and elimination of poverty (sic) and a fair distribution of benefits (Article 43), the eradication of hunger (Article 93), and food security (Article 86). It featured a very extensive section on policy measures (Articles 52–168), covering international trade, industrialization, food and agriculture, energy, transport, financial resources for development, and the regulation of transnational corporations (TNCs). It referred to environmental and ecological soundness and the funding of environmental management (Article 156f.), picking up thinking from the first UN conference on the human environment, held in 1972.

The International Development Strategy (IDS) for the Fourth United Nations Development Decade (1991–2000) maintained a Keynesian policy orientation. Poverty eradication and environmental sustainability remained at the centre.[6] The Resolution incorporated commitments 'to speed up the pace of economic growth in the developing countries; devise a development process that meets social needs, reduces extreme poverty significantly, develops and uses people's capacity and skills, and is environmentally sound and sustainable; improve the international systems of money, finance, and trade; strengthen and stabilize the world economy and establish sound macroeconomic management' practices, nationally and internationally' (UN GA 1990).

The four Development Decades have much in common: the role ascribed to economic development, the attention paid to the international economic environment, and the commitment to poverty eradication. Their Keynesian approach is twinned with an explicit role ascribed to the role of the state and public policy. They also, unfortunately, have in common a lack of success: the high growth rates – conceived as a measure to close the GDP gap between high- and low-income countries – were not achieved, so that each decade in turn required an extension.

In fact, the four international development decades were followed by two new UN decades, explicitly devoted to poverty eradication. The first of these began in 1997, thus preceding the Millennium Declaration (UN General Assembly Resolution A/Res/50/107). The currently ongoing Second Poverty Eradication Decade (UN General Assembly Resolution A/Res/62/205) has as its main objective 'full employment and decent work for all' (UN GA 2009; UN DESA n.d. a and b) and commits to poverty eradication by 2017.[7]

Like their predecessors, the international development decades, they rely on public policy. They place employment at the centre of the argument and include active labour market policies and a call for social protection. A 2008 review of the first poverty eradication decade calls for '... effective institutions for the provision of public goods to the general population and the productive sector; pro-employment growth for decent work in a fair global economic environment; social protection and integration; and an effective international partnership' (UN General Assembly A/63/190, Section VI).

Curiously, the two Poverty Eradication Decades have gained only marginal attention in international development policy discussion, have so far not been mentioned in the academic literature, and do not reap any media attention, despite review sessions at the General Assembly. They have not been referenced in the MDG or SDG processes, nor in the UN Secretary-General's 2014 synthesis report, a fact that remains puzzling, all the more so as they are housed in the same UN department, the Department of Economic and Social Affairs (DESA), that also has been managing the MDGs and preparing the SDGs.

The MDGs' 'movement' versus their outcomes In one interpretation, the Millennium Agenda and the MDGs constituted the fifth development decade, if one builds on the tradition of development decades, and if one ignores the Poverty Eradication Decades. The MDGs too have goals, set timelines, and delineate areas of development that need to be addressed. They address both national goals and the international arena. Technically, they even go beyond the development decade approach, since they dissect goals into targets, and offer indicators to track and measure progress. However, the similarities end here.

As is well known, the seven country-level goals of the MDGs address poverty, employment, nutrition, education, gender equality, maternal health, child health, HIV/Aids and the environment. Thus, compared to the UN's development decades, and also compared to the Poverty Eradication Decades, the MDGs placed long-overdue emphasis on the social domains of development, but in the process downplayed the role of economic development aspirations.

The MDGs gained unprecedented visibility and traction. The UN Secretary-General's roadmap (UN SG 2001), listing the goals, arguably became one of the most widely referenced development agenda texts: they became a movement. In developing countries, the MDGs have had impact on goal formulation, and have informed five-year plans, visioning documents and poverty reduction strategies (Fukuda-Parr 2010; Ivanova and Pemberthy this volume). At the multilateral level, they have been influential in terms of awareness-raising, including for poverty and, more recently, for inequity.

They have also triggered a massive interest and activities in the field of impact evaluation (World Bank Group 2011, 2014; EADI 2014; Picciotto 2014), with national governments measuring progress on meeting the targets, and donors using them for evaluating official development aid (ODA) outcomes. The MDGs' twenty-one targets and sixty indicators, of which most relate to economic and social development at the national level, have influenced how governments and societies recognize and address development issues. In many countries, the indicators are disaggregated by sex, location, ethnicity, language or religion, and thus serve to illustrate the discrepancies in achievements caused by systematic economic and social exclusion (Kabeer 2010; UNDP National Human Development Reports various years; UNDP MDG Progress Reports various years).[8] The MDGs have functioned as a commonly agreed and measurable yardstick for developmental progress: in terms of 'branding' – awareness-raising and mobilization – they have been a success (Fukuda-Parr 2010; Ivanova and Escobar-Pemberthy 2015 this volume). However, it needs to be observed that much of this was due to effective marketing (Hulme and Wilkinson 2014: 188f.). As mentioned above, the international development decades also had time-bound goals – of specific GDP, per capita and sectoral growth rates, and an assessment process – albeit less stringent, during and at the end of each decade, but this is not acknowledged in the literature. The MDGs are often – erroneously – vaunted as the first development agenda with time-bound, measurable outcomes.

Conversely, the MDGs were not a success in terms of *results*. In people's everyday lives, the central criterion of success is how countries and societies have fared in terms of improving human well-being or human development. As several of the chapters in this volume illustrate (e.g. Boltvinik and Damian), both statistically, and on the ground, the targets have not been met satisfactorily. Recent reviews by the UN and by the World Bank Group reveal that key MDG objectives on hunger, poverty and mortality rates remain at intolerable levels. Many countries and regions are 'off track', and of those on track, many remain with high poverty levels, or large deficits in decent work (UN DESA 2012; World Bank Group 2011, 2014; UN 2014). Hunger – perhaps the most relevant development criterion – remains a scourge for one in eight people (UN 2014: 12).

There are misleading perceptions on MDG success. For example, while poverty reduction globally is presented as one of the positive outcomes, it is in essence attributable to three illusions: the 'per cent effect', an 'acute poverty effect' and the 'China effect'.

Looking at the 'per cent effect' requires disaggregating the statistics.[9] The proportion of the world population living below the $1.25 poverty line has been cut by half – from 36 per cent in 1990 to 18 per cent in 2010; in developing regions, $1.25 income poverty decreased from 47 to 22 per cent in the same period (ibid.: 8). Thus, as widely celebrated, the MDG income poverty goal was achieved ahead of schedule – in percentage and aggregated terms. However, sub-Saharan Africa was able to decrease $1.25 poverty only marginally, and is not expected to meet the target; in southern Asia, poverty was not halved – it fell from 51 to 30 per cent (ibid.: 8f.). In fact, in absolute numbers, for many countries and regions, poverty increased between 1999 and 2005, in India from 447 million to 456 million, in sub-Saharan Africa from 383 million to 388 million (World Bank Group 2011: 6; see also UN DESA 2008). As mentioned above, globally, 1.2 billion people – every fifth person – still live with an income of less than $1.25 per person per day. The number of people living below the $2-a-day poverty line is estimated at 2.5 billion; it has not changed since the early 1980s and has increased in all regions except East Asia and the Pacific (World Bank Group 2011: 5–6; see also UN 2014).

The hunger goal has been reached only in eastern and south-eastern Asia (UN 2014: 12). Overall, the proportion of undernourished people in developing regions decreased by less than projected – it fell from 24 per cent in 1990–92 to 14 per cent in 2011–13 (ibid.: 4). On a daily basis, approximately 870 million people were chronically undernourished in 2010–12, using a very restrictive hunger definition (FAO 2010, 2012; Pogge 2013);[10] 162 million children under five suffer chronic under-nutrition (UN 2014: 5). This means that the MDG goal on tackling hunger has also not been achieved. Moreover, progress has slowed down in the past decade (ibid.: 4).

Secondly, the MDGs are not substantively met. This is because of the 'acute poverty effect': the poverty line chosen, $1.25 per person per day, is unlivable, and unacceptably low in absolute and even more so in relative terms (see Boltvinik and Damian this volume). From a human development point of view, one should be using at the very least the $2 per person per day poverty line, or the $10 global median poverty line. It would moreover need to be supplemented by multidimensional poverty measurements as well as other social indicators to capture the extent of deprivation people are facing (Cimadomore et al. 2013; Koehler et al. 2014-).

Thirdly, regarding the 'China effect', the major share in poverty alleviation is attributable to a single country. In China, the extreme poverty rate declined from 36 per cent in 1999 to 16 per cent in 2005, which constitutes a decrease of 240 million people (World Bank Group 2011: 5). By 2010, $1.25 poverty in China decreased further to 13 per cent (UN 2014: 9). While it is remarkable for so many people to have moved out of extreme poverty, it needs to be flagged that 176 million people remain under this extreme poverty line, despite China's phenomenal rates of economic growth. Income inequality has gone as high as .4 to .6 on the Gini coefficient scale (Guo 2014). China, after all, had in 1948 set out to eliminate all poverty and inequality.

These MDG-related statistics are eye-openers. And one does not know the counterfactual (Hulme and Wilkinson 2014): whether the marginal improvements would also have materialized without the MDG efforts. In fact, some observers have argued that the MDG numerical targets merely followed the trend lines on improvement in social indicators observed in preceding decades (Vandemoortele 2012: 3), and thus, methodologically speaking, were not conceived to accelerate progress.

Accordingly, any critical assessment concerned with equitable and inclusive human development would conclude that, in terms of outcomes, the MDGs have not being achieved (Hulme and Wilkinson 2014; Pogge 2014). In the real world, for the majority of the world's population, the agenda has failed.

MDGs reconsidered: the shortcomings of a successful brand To understand the failure of the MDGs in terms of tangible, equitable human development outcomes, it is necessary to look for the inherent systemic shortcomings. One can discern at least three types of shortcomings.

The first shortcoming is in terms of the issues covered. Reproductive health, central to gender equality and women's health and well-being, and part and parcel of earlier development agendas – even in the OECD DAC's global development goals – was absent from the MDGs. The MDGs are weak also in their attention to environmental issues, climate change and sustainability: MDG 7 on ensuring environmental sustainability had only two explicit environment goals, namely on forest cover and biodiversity. Politically, the goals were silent. Participation, highlighted in the Social Summit outcome and the Poverty Eradication Decades, disappeared when the MDGs were formulated. To make them short and punchy, and palatable to all member states of the United Nations, cornerstone notions of development and dignity were dropped, although they had featured prominently in the Millennium Declaration (UN GA 2000; see Ivanova and Escobar-Pemberthy this volume).

Moreover, as mentioned earlier, the MDGs narrowed down the set of core development areas by concentrating on education, health, water and sanitation, or HIV/Aids. These are centred on the social as opposed to the economic domain. In that, the MDGs succeeded in drawing attention to social development – or human development – and thereby present an improvement compared to the overly economistic tendencies of the early UN development decades. But at the same time, the recognition of the centrality of economic development, of equitable international trade regulation, of value chains, of productivity, is completely absent. A core response to poverty – employment in decent work conditions – was missing altogether in the initial MDGs, and introduced only *post factum* in 2005.

By focusing on the 'social', the MDG agenda de facto handed the primary international responsibility for the economic agenda over to the World Bank and the IMF. It thereby permitted the discourse to remain in its neoliberal mode (Fukuda-Parr 2005, 2010; Hulme and Wilkinson 2014). This has, in many low-income and transition countries, come at the expense of strategic thinking regarding the larger development agenda, and led to policy omissions regarding employment, and economic investments in productive capacity, or economic infrastructure.[11]

Equity concerns were invisible in the MDGs as they looked at aggregates and global and country averages. Here, however, a consensus is emerging, even during the lifetime of the MDGs, that equity needs to be integrated into MDG assessment. This has led to introduction of an equity-adjusted human development index (Alkire and Foster 2010; UNDP 2010). Equity is prominent in the recent work of UNICEF, and is being integrated into MDG evaluations (World Bank Group 2014; UN 2014) and is integral to the SDG draft (UNDP 2012; UN Task Team on the Post 2015 UN Development Agenda 2012a and b; UNICEF 2010; Fukuda-Parr 2012; OWG 2014).

As a second major shortcoming, the MDGs eschewed any causal analysis. For example, the poverty and hunger goals did not reflect on the reasons for income and asset disparities and inequalities, or on power relations and institutional and systemic arrangements that create and recreate poverty and hunger (see Rogers and Balasz this volume). They did not look at functional income distribution. The MDGs, as cast in 2001, thus fell behind the analytical stances of earlier decades, such as the international development decades, where an analysis of root causes was integral to conceptualizing development strategies.

Thirdly, and most importantly, the MDGs were limited to spelling out objectives and targets, instead of taking a policy position, or at least linking the objectives to a set of policy options. This was a major departure from the international development decade culture, which had very specific policy recommendations. As a result, much MDG-initiated development discourse has been preoccupied with measurement issues, and there has been far less intense a discussion on which policies would be conducive to achieve each of the MDG goals and targets (Koehler and Stirbu 2007). Policy discussions have been eclipsed by this focus on measuring gaps and calculating investment to achieve the goals, without delving sufficiently into the policy choices and paths.

Those policy discussions that do take place tend to remain sectoralized within each domain, and siloed in the relevant line ministries. They rarely converge around MDG synergies, human development outcomes or 'well-being'. The outcome and policy discussions related to the education or health goals, for example, give insufficient consideration to cross-cutting synergies, such as the interplay among nutrition, health and education, or between maternal and child mortality, or each of these with employment and incomes and hence poverty reduction. Reasons include the fact that separate government ministries are responsible for discrete outcomes, and moreover compete for finite resources for their particular area of human development investment;[12] and that there is a lack of programme and policy coherence across the UN and donor agencies (Koehler 2011).

Many low-income countries adopted the MDGs in the sense of integrating the objectives into development plans, and using the indicators to track progress. However, at the policy level, countries were not harmonizing policies that would need to be more concerted if goals and targets regarding poverty and decent work were to be achieved. For example, most countries, even those organized in regional groupings, continued to compete with each other on labour laws, tax legislation, trade policy and environmental requirements. There were no initiatives to harmonize approaches to decent work provisions or minimum wages. Instead, there is often a race to the bottom in the form of neighbouring countries outcompeting each other on low wages or foreign direct investment (FDI) tax exemptions or environmental requirements, despite commitments at the national level. This too made it difficult to achieve the MDGs.

Looking forward

An agenda for development post-2015 The inherent shortcomings of the MDGs demonstrate the need for a complete and radical overhaul of the development agenda (see also Fukuda-Parr 2012; Nayyar 2011; Kozul-Wright and Ghosh 2013) as one rethinks developmental visions and goals for beyond 2015. Three processes are called for. First, it is important to build on the MDG momentum, but at the same time benefit from the critique of the agenda's shortcoming and failures. Secondly, one needs to search for and accept radical and comprehensive thinking on development policy and the role of the state. Thirdly, one would need to assess the political dynamics and power relations in which the SDG negotiations unfold (Dodds et al. 2014) – but that is an analysis beyond the reach of this chapter.

As an unofficial beginning of the post-2015 agenda,[13] the 2012 Rio Summit on Sustainable Development produced an outcome document called *The Future We Want* (UN Rio+20 Conference 2012). The catchy slogan triggers several issues: agreeing on what type of vision one would like to pursue and asking who is the *we*.[14] It is about imagining feasible alternatives and offering corresponding policies. From such questions derives a case for both returning to a normative mode and for offering explicit policy stances. It presented the notion of sustainable development, which was then successfully mainstreamed into the post-2015 discussions (Dodds et al. 2014).

In connection with the development of a next generation of development goals, discussion processes and proposals have spiralled since 2012 (see UN Rio+20 Conference 2012; Fukuda-Parr 2012; Martens 2013; Bissio 2014: 205ff.). The UN Task Team (UN Task Team on the Post 2015 UN Development Agenda 2012a: 24; see also UN Task Team on the Post 2015 UN Development Agenda 2012b; Ivanova and Escobar-Pemberthy 2015 this volume), for example, proposed four domains for the next development agenda:

• inclusive economic development;
• inclusive social development;
• environmental sustainability; and
• peace and security.

Each of these domains clustered areas of concern – eradicating income poverty and hunger, reducing inequalities and ensuring decent work and productive employment; adequate nutrition for all; quality education for all; reduced mortality and morbidity, gender equality and universal access to clean water and sanitation. This framework is useful in that it offers a systematic ordering of topical areas. It is also progressive in comparison to the MDGs in that it has returned to the universalist ethos of the 1990s UN summits. But this proposal retains many of the flaws of the original MDG roadmap and its 2005 revisions. The freedom from fear aspect, for example, is centred narrowly on peace and security, with human rights and democratic governance relegated to the level of 'enablers' – as opposed to functioning as objectives in their own right.

In his 2014 synthesis report (UN SG 2014), the UN Secretary-General identified six elements for the next agenda similar to the earlier UN Task Team classification. This is a well-taken attempt to structure the seventeen goal areas. They echo the Millennium Declaration, and have a normative edge to them.

1 Dignity: to end poverty and fight inequalities.
2 People: to ensure healthy lives, knowledge, and the inclusion of women and children.
3 Prosperity: to grow a strong, inclusive and transformative economy.

4 Planet: to protect our ecosystems for all societies and our children.
5 Justice: to promote safe and peaceful societies, and strong institutions.
6 Partnership: to catalyse global solidarity for sustainable development.

The proposal for the new development agenda issued by the Open Working Group on the SDGs is more specific, with seventeen goals and 169 targets (OWG 2014) (see Box 10.1). Several of these replicate the MDGs (see Ivanova and Escobar-Pemberthy this volume: comparator table) – those on poverty, hunger, health, education, gender, employment; several refer to, consolidate and highlight the sustainable development goals of the Rio+20 document – those on climate change, oceans and terrestrial systems and the call for sustainable production and consumption; and several indeed represent a departure from the MDGs' narrow focus on the social domain, by highlighting the need for industrialization, infrastructure, innovation and access to energy. In this, they refer back to the broader understanding of development as encapsulated in the UN development decades and the Poverty Eradication Decades. A reference, however, is not made.

In the OWG proposal, the last goal, headed 'means of implementation', is a weak reference to all the promises packed into international deliberations over the past decade – to international trade, investment and finance, and the call for more ODA.

At the target level, the proposal adopts the fifteen-year timeline of the MDGs; at the indicator level, it accepts the lowest possible denominator, for instance the $1.25 poverty line. But only two of the seventeen goals proposed represent a complete shift from the MDGs: the explicit call for tackling inequality in and among countries, and the goal around peaceful and inclusive societies with a commitment to human rights. In terms of vision, the SDG proposal is thus at best an incremental improvement compared to the MDGs – despite much rhetoric around transformational shifts (HLPR 2013).

The need for progressive policies The most jeopardizing flaw of the MDGs, in our analysis, was, however, that they lacked a policy dimension. Policies are necessary to effectively deal with the structural causes of poverty and 'underdevelopment'. The task at hand from a human development imperative is therefore not just to present a vision of social justice, or at least to imagine feasible alternatives, but also to

Box 10.1 SDGs as at January 2015 (OWG 2014)

1 End poverty in all its forms everywhere.

2 End hunger, achieve food security and improved nutrition and promote sustainable agriculture.

3 Ensure healthy lives and promote well-being for all at all ages.

4 Ensure inclusive and equitable quality education and promote lifelong learning opportunities for all.

5 Achieve gender equality and empower all women and girls.

6 Ensure availability and sustainable management of water and sanitation for all.

7 Ensure access to affordable, reliable, sustainable and modern energy for all.

8 Promote sustained, inclusive and sustainable economic growth, full and productive employment and decent work for all.

9 Build resilient infrastructure, promote inclusive and sustainable industrialization and foster innovation.

10 Reduce inequality within and among countries.

11 Make cities and human settlements inclusive, safe, resilient and sustainable.

12 Ensure sustainable consumption and production patterns.

13 Take urgent action to combat climate change and its impacts.

14 Conserve and sustainably use the oceans, seas and marine resources for sustainable development.

15 Protect, restore and promote sustainable use of terrestrial ecosystems, sustainably manage forests, combat desertification, and halt and reverse land degradation and halt biodiversity loss.

16 Promote peaceful and inclusive societies for sustainable development, provide access to justice for all and build effective, accountable and inclusive institutions at all levels.

17 Strengthen the means of implementation and revitalize the global partnership for sustainable development.

explore and promote radical policies – radical in the sense of addressing and tackling root causes.

There is an aversion in the multilateral arena to identifying with and recommending comprehensive, heterodox macroeconomic and structural policies. There are at least two reasons for this; both are political, and they are interrelated. One is a reluctance to propose policies that could be perceived as interventionist. The other is a disinclination to accord a positive role to the state.[15] Both of these stem from neoliberal ideology, which continues to cast its shadow on the development discourse. The role of policy space is acknowledged – a point which developing countries stress as a way to protect heterodox policy-making – but it avoids spelling out policy options. The role of governance is highlighted – but it takes on a micro-level meaning in the sense of having efficient government administration, it is not about the government having a responsibility to shape and deliver or regulate public goods, or about a social contract between citizens and the state.

But if, as the SDG proposal posits, poverty and hunger are to be eradicated, if economic growth is to become employment-rich and resource-neutral, if there is to be a redistribution between and within countries, one can only turn to 'progressive' policies, since none of these effects will evolve out of solely market-based economic processes. Even the building of infrastructure or 'industrialization', which can be co-financed by the private sector, requires government-level prioritization, coordination and design, and public subsidies so as to reach regions that are commercially not lucrative.

These requirements can underpin the case for an alternatively oriented development policy agenda, notably heterodox economic policies (Nayyar 2011). For the social sectors, this would mean reasserting health, education, water, sanitation and energy as public goods that are to be conceptualized as a right and require holistic policy-making. In the MDG era, there have been myriads of programmes on social policy, but they are locked in at the programme level, often siloed in disconnected ministries and international agencies, and have eschewed fundamental debate on their interdependence. They have had a defeatist policy orientation at best, advocating for primary health and primary education, but oblivious to the necessity of higher education levels, of sophisticated health services delivery in the interests of human development, and as a right of all.

For the economic sectors, the policy shifts would need to include some form of 'industrial' strategy – examining the government's role in regulating or possibly incentivizing productivity-enhancing, sustainable and equitable outcomes in agriculture, commodity production and trade, the manufacturing sector, all the way to services and creative industries (see, for example, UNCTAD 2009: 149ff., notably 155ff.).[16] It requires proactive labour market policy to move towards decent work and job and income security policies. It requires innovation strategies and public funding for foundation research and higher learning.

If one wanted to move beyond a reactive, palliative poverty alleviation approach, such a policy shift would also need to be radical and promote genuine structural reform, including some form of land reform and wealth and asset redistribution. It would require universalizing and upgrading social protection (UN GA 2010; Hanlon et al. 2010; Bachelet 2011; ILO 2012; World Bank 2012; UNICEF 2012; UN GA 2014).[17] There would need to be structured deficit spending to revitalize employment and investment or redress increasing hunger and poverty (Jolly et al. 2012; EuroMemo Group 2013; Ortiz and Cummins 2012). There would also need to be fundamental revisions to the governance of international finance, commodity trade and climate change.

Such policies would require a reversal of current trends. In many instances, they would go against the interests of powerful countries and of powerful elites in countries.[18]

Reinstating the role of the state Policies are the remit of governments. Making a case for a more systematic and open policy stance logically means addressing and reasserting the role of the state. There are two traditions on which this can draw. One derives from the theory of public finance and its concept of public goods (Musgrave and Musgrave 1989), later expanded into a theory of global public goods (Kaul et al. 2003; Kaul 2013). Its analysis is that services such as health, education, infrastructure, security or a clean environment are merit goods where it is in society's interest that they be consumed by all, and/ or are technically indivisible, and have unequal costs across different regions or for different communities. Such goods therefore cannot be provided equitably by the private sector. The second tradition is that of the social contract, which postulates that citizens and governments enter a relationship in which the state has obligations to deliver public goods and citizens have rights (Rousseau 2010 [1762]; Kabeer 2005).

Regardless of which framework is used, the complexity of policy domains and issues that need to be tackled to achieve human development makes it obvious that there is the need for a central institution tasked with overseeing, guiding, enabling and guaranteeing the delivery of the pertaining public goods and services. It is the role of the state to enable negotiations of a social contract or social pacts, and to ensure their realization; this is coupled with a role in ensuring the revenues necessary to reliably fund high-quality public goods and services, and with a view to economic equity, to ensure income and wealth redistribution (UNRISD 2010: 280f.; Deacon 2010). Hence there is a need to revisit the role of the state, and to integrate it into the post-2015 conceptualization. This discussion will be necessary in order for the new agenda to genuinely work towards eradicating poverty and hunger.

Apart from the UN development decades, there is another strand of development thinking that has accumulated considerable knowledge on systematic, strategic state interventions (UNCTAD 2009, 2011a and b, 2012; UNDP 2013; UNRISD 2010: 257ff.). A more encompassing notion of a 'developmental welfare state' comes from the academic literature (Kwon 1999, 2005a and b; Chang 2002; Gough 2004; Fritz and Rocha Menocal 2006; Ringen et al. 2011). Here, the state is seen to have responsibilities in terms of both economic development, and the delivery of public goods in the social domain – notably education, health and a habitable physical environment. This literature stresses that in low-income countries the state has a particular 'developmental' role: to promote economic growth as well as the structural transformation into higher-productivity sectors, and also to provide public goods and services that contribute to human development (Mkandawire 2004: 1).

Nevertheless, there are major reservations regarding the role of the state. Historically, states were part of both the problem and the solution to the question of (democratic) development. In both developed and developing countries, there are violations of basic human rights. Insecurities are rampant in all domains of life, at the individual, community, in-country and cross-border level, often perpetrated by authoritarian states. In many countries, the state tolerates systemic social exclusion of minorities, and political oppression issues directly from the state. It therefore seems naive to seek solutions from the state.

Secondly, there are numerous other entities with responsibility for their own and the community's human development, from individuals, households and families, through communities, trade unions, cooperative bodies representing the interests of the informal economy or the business sector, to organized civil society organizations, including regional and international political actors. Ideally, these actors can be democratically legitimized, and, if so, can be more representative of individual and community interests.

However, these entities cannot achieve sustained results for human development without coordinated public action through a reliable, functioning, accountable body – the state (UNRISD 2010: 257, 280). In making a case for the role of the state, it is therefore necessary in the same breath to insist that one is referring to a public sector that is controlled by and accountable to its citizens, democratic and rights-based. Thus, the argument remains that the new development agenda would need to integrate into its design the role of a rights-based, democratic developmental welfare state (ibid.: 257ff.; UNCTAD 2009: vii;[19] see also Koehler 2014),[20] even if this is an abstract or idealized notion. Its purpose would be to finance, deliver and/or regulate public goods and services that make human development progress.

To correspond to such expectations, 'the state' needs to be outfitted with a number of capacities (UNCTAD 2009: 42ff.; UNRISD 2010: 259ff.). These include the political capacity to formulate the development project, and to set and implement policies, and the capacity to protect civil rights, ensure legitimate mandates to govern and support social contracts, and channels for pressure on the public sector. They include technical capacity, meaning a politically, gender-wise and ethnically representative performant public administration[21] (adapted from UNCTAD 2009: 42ff., esp. 45, and UNRISD 2010: 263). Moreover, the state requires capacity to mobilize resources, notably savings and taxes, and to put them to effective use (UNRISD 2010: 264ff.; in a similar vein see UNCTAD 2012: 113ff.).

A transformative post-2015 development agenda? Closing reflections

The new post-2015 agenda must be a radical departure from the MDGs, if it wants to eradicate hunger and poverty, if it wants to redress local and global inequalities, if it wants to ensure sustainability – in other words, if it wants to be transformative in reality not just in rhetoric.

To do this, at the conceptual level, it could build on the conclusions and commitments generated by the UN development decades and the Poverty Eradication Decades, by the major UN conferences convened during the 1990s, as well as by the MDG experience itself.

There would also need to be a deeper process – a rededication at the normative level, to overarching principles such as the UN Charter, the Universal Declaration of Human Rights, the Covenants, and the UN Conventions. The global community needs to get back into a visioning mode and be 'ahead of the curve' (Emmerij et al. 2001), instead of merely reacting to changed conditions, if one is genuinely committed to creating a future everyone could want. From a development *policy* perspective, this means staking a claim for a rights-based developmental welfare state.

Is this a realistic proposition? Will the SDGs offer a 'transformative' development agenda, in the sense of attacking the root causes of poverty, inequality and climate change? At the level of the SDG negotiations, this will depend on the willingness and ability of progressive governments and civil society to coalesce, and their skills in driving bargains with governments and players who will defend the status quo and shy away from radical commitments. A post-2015 development agenda that formulates and notionally commits to transformation could then be a tool to, at long last, start genuine socio-economic restructuring. It could refer back to the impact of the UN Charter, in place for seventy years now, which helped to give normative power and analytical underpinning to decolonization and human rights movements across the globe, and which launched successive development decades. And it could move forward, building on but reaching beyond the positive momentum for poverty eradication and human development generated by the Millennium Declaration fifteen years ago.

Notes

1 An early version of this chapter was presented at the CROP workshop on the MDGs, Bergen, August 2012. The author sincerely thanks Alberto Cimadamore, Sakiko Fukuda-Parr and Mariana Stirbu for insightful comments on earlier versions. Sonja Keller provided technical support.

2 Based on available data from ninety-one countries. Also UNDP (2014: 72 and Table 6, 180f.).

3 They read as follows: to reduce by half the proportion of people living in extreme poverty between 1990 and 2015; enrol all children in primary school by 2015; make progress towards gender equality and empowering women by eliminating gender disparities in primary and secondary education by 2015; reduce infant and child mortality rates by two-thirds between 1990 and 2015; reduce maternal mortality ratios

by three-quarters; provide access for all who need reproductive health services by 2015; implement national strategies for sustainable development by 2005 so as to reverse the loss of environmental resources by 2015 (OECD DAC 1996).

4 For a complete overview of all the development decades, see UN (n.d.).

5 A declaration on the New International Economic Order had been adopted by the UN General Assembly in 1974 (UN GA 1974).

6 It 'singled out a number of areas of special priority: the eradication of poverty and hunger, human resources and institutional development, population, the environment and food and agriculture' (UN GA 1990: Article 15).

7 The poverty eradication decades derive from and draw on the UN Social Summit of 1995.

8 The Multi-Indicator Cluster Index assessments (MICs), led by UNICEF, have a similar effect. The MICs disaggregate key child-relevant outcomes such as infant, child and maternal mortality, school enrolment, birth registration, by sex, by income quintiles, and by regions within a country, giving a very clear picture of social injustices in a given country. See Minujin et al. (2005).

9 For a discussion on this see, for example, Reddy and Pogge (2003) and Pogge (2012).

10 The FAO has changed its methodology for measuring hunger and undernourishment at the request of the Committee on World Food Security (CFS). See www.fao.org/hunger/en. The most recent data estimates that 870 million people were chronically undernourished in 2010–12, but preceding estimates had calculated that figure at 925 million for earlier years (FAO 2012, 2010). That hunger would have decreased despite land-grabbing, intensifying eco-crises, the global recession and food price speculation is counter-intuitive.

11 This critique has been elaborated by UNCTAD in its *Least Developed Countries Report* (UNCTAD 2009). It has been partly addressed by the UN Millennium Project, which has spawned a process of MDG costing exercises across developing countries which have developed costing methodologies for economic infrastructure such as transport and energy as well as for the core MDGs – education, health, water and sanitation.

12 An interesting exception is the common minimum programme of the Indian government, where the large 'missions' – flagship policy campaigns, such as for education for all, global health and others – are cross-referenced in the five-year development plan to create a convergent, cross-sectoral policy approach.

13 As Dodds et al. (2014: 4) observed, government officials involved in the preparation of the Rio+20 summit in no way expected that conference to be a launching pad for a new development agenda.

14 Regarding the *we*: since the Rio+20 conference it has seemed evident that this is the global community, and the proposal for the SDGs as well as the UN SG synthesis report have adopted a universal approach – the goals, if indeed adopted, are to be applicable in all countries.

15 There is, of course, much discussion on good governance which, however, narrows the role of the state down to the realm of dysfunctions, or efficiency, and does not look into the larger picture of the responsibility a functioning and legitimate state has to bear in terms of providing public goods and services.

16 UNCTAD (2009: 155) lists the key features of a 'developmental industrial policy'.

17 For a history of the debates and negotiations leading to the Social Protection Floor, see Deacon (2013).

18 Hulme and Wilkinson (2014: 187) argue, for instance, that tackling the causes of poverty will not be possible 'because it is unlikely that the political economy of the current era will permit such a move', citing the strong US and private sector interests.

19 UNCTAD (2009: vii) speaks of a democratic developmental state, with continuing reflexive procedures calling on all actors, and (ibid.: vi) posits the case for 'developmental governance' geared to creating a better future for members of society through economic development and structural transformation.

20 UNRISD (2010: 261) also uses terms such as democratic developmental state, or developmental democracies, and UNCTAD (2011a: 86ff.) defines the role of a 'cohesive, strong, catalytic and effective state', the 'CDS' – catalytic developmental state for short – with a role in formulating a development vision and creating the policy space needed for structural transformation and dynamic comparative advantage (ibid.: 87–9).

21 UNRISD (2010: 281) makes the case for a 'Weberian' bureaucracy – professionals with a commitment to their job and a sense of service to their country, technical competence, a good work ethic, appropriately remunerated and recognized. On this, see UNCTAD (2009: 40, 45).

References

ADB (Asian Development Bank) (2012) *Asian Development Outlook 2012: Confronting Rising Inequality in Asia*, Manila: ADB.

Alkire, S. and J. Foster (2010) 'Designing the Inequality-Adjusted Human Development Index (IHDI)', Human Development Research Papers (2009 to present) HDRP-2010-28, New York: Human Development Report Office (HDRO), UNDP.

Bachelet, M. (2011) 'Social Protection Floor for a fair and inclusive globalization', Report of the Social Protection Floor Advisory Group, Geneva: International Labour Office.

Bissio, R. (2014) '"We the peoples" in the UN development system', in S. Browne and T. Weiss (eds), *Post-2015 UN Development: Making Change Happen?*, Abingdon and New York: Routledge, pp. 195–210.

Browne, S. and T. Weiss (2014) 'The UN we want for the world we want', in S. Browne and T. Weiss (eds), *Post-2015 UN Development: Making Change Happen?*, Abingdon and New York: Routledge, pp. 1–13.

Chang, H. (2002) *Globalization, Economic Development, and the Role of the State*, London: Zed Books.

Cimadamore, A. D. et al. (2013) 'Poverty and the Millennium Development Goals (MDGs): a critical assessment and a look forward', CROP Poverty Brief, January, Bergen: Comparative Research Programme on Poverty, www.crop.org/viewfile.aspx?id=423.

Deacon, B. (2010) 'From the global politics of poverty alleviation to the global politics of welfare state rebuilding', CROP Poverty Brief, June, Bergen: Comparative Research Programme on Poverty, www.crop.org/viewfile.aspx?id=210.

— (2013) *Global Social Policy in the Making: The Foundations of the Social Protection Floor*, Bristol: Policy Press.

Dodds, F., J. Laguna-Celis and L. Thompson (2014) *From Rio+20 to a New Development Agenda: Building a Bridge to a Sustainable Future*, London and New York: Routledge.

EADI (2014) Special Debate Section: 'Impact evaluation', *European Journal of Development Research*, 26(1),

www.palgrave-journals.com/ejdr/
past_special_issues.html - v26n1.

Emmerij, L. et al. (2001) *Ahead of the Curve? UN Ideas and Global Challenges*, Bloomington and Indianapolis: Indiana University Press.

EuroMemo Group (2013) 'The deepening crisis in the European Union: the need for a fundamental change', Berlin: EuroMemo Group, www. euromemorandum.eu/uploads/ euromemorandum_2013.pdf.

FAO (Food and Agriculture Organization of the United Nations) (2010) *The State of Food Insecurity in the World 2010: Addressing Food Insecurity in Protracted Crises*, Rome: FAO, www. fao.org/docrep/013/i1683e/i1683e.pdf.

— (2012) *The State of Food Insecurity in the World 2012*, Rome: FAO.

Fritz, V. and A. Rocha Menocal (2006) '(Re)building developmental states: from theory to practice', Working Paper 274, Overseas Development Institute, www.odi.org/sites/odi. org.uk/files/odi-assets/publications-opinion-files/2328.pdf.

Fukuda-Parr, S. (2005) 'Millennium Development Goals: why they matter', *Global Governance*, 10: 395–402.

— (2010) 'Reducing inequality – the missing MDG: a content review of PRSPs and bilateral donor policy statements', *IDS Bulletin*, 14(1): 26–35.

— (2012) 'Recapturing the narrative of international development', Gender and Development Paper 18, Geneva: UNRISD.

Gough, I. (2004) 'Human well-being and social structures: relating the universal and the local', *Global Social Policy*, 4(3): 289–311.

Guo, J. (2014) 'Social protection and economic development in times of crises – from inequality aspect', Mimeo, FES Social Protection Forum, Ulan Bator.

Hanlon, J., A. Barrientos and D. Hulme (2010) *Just Give Money to the Poor: The Development Revolution from the Global South*, Sterling, VA: Kumarian Press.

HLPR (High-Level Panel Report) (2013) 'A new global partnership: eradicate poverty and transform economies through sustainable development', Report of the High-Level Panel of Eminent Persons on the Post-2015 Development Agenda, New York: United Nations, www.un.org/sg/ management/pdf/HLP_P2015_Report. pdf.

Hulme, D. and R. Wilkinson (2014) 'The UN and the post 2015 development agenda', in S. Browne and T. Weiss (eds), *Post-2015 UN Development: Making Change Happen?*, Abingdon and New York: Routledge, pp. 181–94.

ILO (International Labour Organization) (2012) Text of the Recommendation Concerning National Floors of Social Protection, International Labour Conference, One Hundred and First Session, Geneva: ILO, www. ilo.org/wcmsp5/groups/public/-- -ed_norm/---relconf/documents/ meetingdocument/wcms_183326.pdf.

— (2013) *Global Employment Trends 2013*, Geneva: ILO, ilo.org/global/research/ global-reports/global-employment-trends/2013/WCMS_202326/lang-- en/index.htm.

Jolly, R. et al. (2012) *Be Outraged: There Are Alternatives*, Brighton: Oxfam.

Kabeer, N. (2005) *Inclusive Citizenship*, London: Zed Books.

— (2010) *Can the MDGs Provide a Pathway to Social Justice? The Challenges of Intersecting Inequality*, New York: IDS/MDG Achievement Fund, www.ids.ac.uk/files/dmfile/ MDGreportwebsiteu2WC.pdf.

Kaul, I. (2013) 'Global public goods. A concept for framing the Post-2015 Agenda?', German Development

Institute Discussion Paper 2/2013, www.die-gdi.de/en/discussion-paper/article/global-public-goods-a-concept-for-framing-the-post-2015-agenda/.

Kaul, I., I. Grunberg and M. Stern (2003) *Global Public Goods: International Cooperation in the 21st Century*, Oxford Scholarship Online, www.oxfordscholarship.com/view/10.1093/0195130529.001.0001/acprof-9780195130522.

Koehler, G. (1996) 'Development intervention: a parade of paradigms', in G. Koehler, C. Gore, U.-P. Reich and T. Ziesemer (eds), *Questioning Development: Essays in the Theory, Policies and Practice of Development Interventions*, Marburg: Metropolis, pp. 21–44.

— (2011) 'The challenges of delivering as one: overcoming fragmentation and moving towards policy coherence', ILO Working Paper no. 100, Geneva: Policy Integration Department, International Labour Office, www.ilo.org/wcmsp5/groups/public/---dgreports/---integration/documents/publication/wcms_153043.pdf.

— (2014) 'Preliminary reflections on the South Asian developmental welfare state', in G. Koehler and D. Chopra (eds), *Development and Welfare Policy in South Asia*, London: Routledge.

Koehler, G. and D. Chopra (eds) (2014) *Development and Welfare Policy in South Asia*, London: Routledge.

Koehler, G. and M. Stirbu (2007) 'MDG-based planning for development: policy interface and synergies of outcomes for South Asia', Report of the Millennium Development Goals Related Policy and Programme Review, Kathmandu: UNICEF ROSA, www.unicef.org/rosa/Rosa_Regional_interagency_MDGI_consultations_report_final_revision.pdf.

Koehler, G., T. Pogge and M. Sengupta (2014) 'Big holes in the SDG Draft', CROP Poverty Brief, August, Bergen: Comparative Research Programme on Poverty, www.crop.org/viewfile.aspx?id=561.

Kozul-Wright, R. and J. Ghosh (2013) 'Forget post-2015 development goals – a global new deal is what's needed', Poverty Matters blog, *Guardian*, www.guardian.co.uk/global-development/poverty-matters/2013/feb/05/post-2015-development-global-new-deal, accessed 2 April 2013.

Kwon, H. (1999) *The Welfare State in Korea: The Politics of Legitimation*, Basingstoke: Macmillan.

— (ed.) (2005a) *Transforming the Developmental Welfare State in East Asia*, UNRISD, Basingstoke: Palgrave Macmillan.

— (2005b) 'Transforming the developmental welfare state in East Asia', *Development and Change*, 36(3): 477–97.

Lübker, M. (2007) 'Labour shares', ILO Technical Brief no. 1, Geneva: International Labour Office.

Mackie, J. and R. Williams (2015) 'The dawn of the post-MDG era?', *Challenges for Africa–EU Relations in 2015*, 6, January, ECPDM Brussels, ecdpm.org/wp-content/uploads/Challenges_Africa_Eu_2015_final_ECDPM_Mackie_Williams.pdf.

Martens, J. (2013) 'Globale Nachhaltigkeitsziele für die Post-2015 Entwicklungsagenda', Global Policy Forum Europe, Terre des Hommes, January, www.globalpolicy.org/images/pdfs/GPFEurope/Report_Globale_Nachhaltigkeitsziele_Online.pdf.

Milanovic, B. (2011) *The Haves and the Have Nots: A Brief and Idiosyncratic History of Global Inequality*, New York: Basic Books.

Minujin, A., E. Delamonica, E. Gonzalez and A. Davidziuk (2005) 'Children living in poverty: a review of child poverty definitions, measurements and policies', tinyurl.com/yjqfxr.

Mkandawire, T. (2004) 'Social policy in a development context: introduction', in T. Mkandawire (ed.), *Social Policy in a Development Context*, Basingstoke: Palgrave Macmillan.

Musgrave, R. and P. Musgrave (1989) *Public Finance in Theory and Practice*, New York: McGraw-Hill.

Nayyar, D. (2011) 'The MDGs beyond 2015', South Centre Research Papers 38, Geneva: South Centre.

OECD DAC (Development Assistance Committee) (1996) *Shaping the 21st Century: The Contribution of Development Cooperation*, Paris: OECD.

OWG (Open Working Group) (2014) 'Proposal for Sustainable Development Goals', New York: United Nations Department of Economic and Social Affairs, Sustainable Development Knowledge Platform, sustainabledevelopment. un.org/sdgsproposal.

Ortiz, I. and M. Cummins (eds) (2012) *A Recovery for All: Rethinking Socio-Economic Policies for Children and Poor Households*, New York: UNICEF.

— (2014) 'The age of austerity: a review of public expenditures and adjustment measures in 181 countries', New York: Initiative for Policy Dialogue, policydialogue.org/publications/ working_papers/age_of_austerity/.

Oxfam (2014) *Even It Up: Time to End Extreme Inequality*, Oxford, www. oxfam.org/sites/www.oxfam.org/ files/file_attachments/cr-even-it-up-extreme-inequality-291014-en.pdf.

Picciotto, R. (2014) 'Evaluating the UN development system', in S. Browne and T. Weiss (eds), *Post-2015 UN Development: Making Change*

Happen?, Abingdon and New York: Routlege, pp. 112–26.

Piketty, T. (2014) *Capital in the Twenty-First Century*, Boston, MA: Harvard University Press.

Pogge, T. (2012) 'Poverty, human rights and the global order: framing the post-2015 agenda', Bergen: Comparative Research Programme on Poverty (CROP), www.crop. org/viewfile.aspx?id=401, accessed 4 August 2012.

— (2013) 'Poverty, hunger and cosmetic progress', in M. Langford, A. Sumner and A. Yamin (eds), *MDGs and Human Rights: Past, Present and Future*, Cambridge: Cambridge University Press.

— (2014) 'Die MDGs sind moralisch ein Skandal', *Zeitschrift für die Vereinten Nationen und ihre Sonderorganisationen*, 6: 248, Berlin: Deutsche Gesellschaft der Vereinten Nationen

Reddy, S. G. and T. Pogge (2003) *How Not to Count the Poor*, New York: Columbia University, www.columbia. edu/~sr793/Countshort.pdf, accessed 5 August 2012.

Ringen, S. et al. (2011) *The Korean State and Social Policy*, Oxford: Oxford University Press.

Rousseau, J.-J. (2010 [1762]) *Du contrat social ou Principes du droit politique*, Stuttgart: Reclam Verlag [Paris].

Sustainable Development Knowledge Platform (2015) Major Groups, sustainabledevelopment. un.org/majorgroups.

UN (n.d.) United Nations Observances. International Decades, www.un.org/ en/events/observances/decades. shtml.

— (2014) *The Millennium Development Goals Report 2014*, New York: UN, www.un.org/millenniumgoals/ 2014%20MDG%20report/MDG%202 014%20English%20web.pdf.

UN DESA (n.d. a) *First UN Decade for the Eradication of Poverty (1997–2006)*, New York: United Nations, social.un.org/index/Poverty/UNDecadefortheEradicationofPoverty/FirstUNDecadefortheEradicationofPoverty.aspx.

— (n.d. b) *System-wide Plan of Action on the Second United Nations Decade for the Eradication of Poverty (2008–2017)*, New York: United Nations, social.un.org/index/LinkClick.aspx?fileticket=DXNWg3yMF3s%3d&tabid=181).

— (2008) *World Economic and Social Survey 2008: Overcoming Economic Insecurity*, New York: United Nations.

— (2012) *Millennium Development Goals Progress Chart*, New York: United Nations, mdgs.un.org/unsd/mdg/Resources/Static/Products/Progress2012/Progress_E.pdf.

UN GA (General Assembly) (1960) 'United Nations Development Decade: a programme for international economic co-operation', GA 16th session, Res 1710, www.unpan.org/Portals/0/60yrhistory/documents/GA%20Resolution/GA%20Res%201710%28XVI%29.1961.pdf.

— (1970) 'International development strategy for the Second United Nations Development Decade', GA 25th session, Res 2626, www.un-documents.net/a25r2626.htm.

— (1974) Resolution adopted by the General Assembly 3201 (S-VI), Declaration on the Establishment of a New International Economic Order, www.un-documents.net/s6r3201.htm.

— (1980) *International Development Strategy for the Third United Nations Development Decade*, A/RES/35/56, www.un.org/en/ga/search/view_doc.asp?symbol=A/RES/35/56.

— (1990) *The International Development Strategy (IDS) for the Fourth United Nations Development Decade (1991–2000)*, A/Res/49 /99, www.un.org/documents/ga/res/45/a45r199.htm.

— (2000) Millennium Declaration, Resolution 55/2, www.un.org/millennium/declaration/ares552e.htm.

— (2009) Resolution on the Second Decade for the Eradication of Poverty (2008–2017), Resolution adopted by the GA, A/RES63/230, daccess-dds-ny.un.org/doc/UNDOC/GEN/N08/484/59/PDF/N0848459.pdf?OpenElement.

— (2010) 'Keeping the promise: united to achieve the Millennium Development Goals', Resolution adopted by the GA, A/RES/65/1, www.un.org/en/mdg/summit2010/pdf/outcome_documentN1051260.pdf.

— (2014) 'Extreme poverty and human rights', Note by the Secretary-General, A/69/297, daccess-dds-ny.un.org/doc/UNDOC/GEN/N14/501/65/PDF/N1450165.pdf?OpenElement.

UN Intellectual History Project (2010) 'The UN and development policies', Briefing Note no. 7, www.unhistory.org/briefing/7UNandDevStrategies.pdf, accessed 4 August 2012.

UN Rio+20 Conference (2012) *The Future We Want*, Outcome document, A/CONF.216/L.1, rio20.un.org/sites/rio20.un.org/files/a-conf.216l-1_english.pdf.pdf.

UN SG (Secretary-General) (2001) *Roadmap towards the Implementation of the United Nations Millennium Declaration*, Report of the Secretary-General, A/56/326, unpan1.un.org/intradoc/groups/public/documents/UN/UNPAN004152.pdf.

— (2014) *The Road to Dignity by 2030: Ending Poverty, Transforming All Lives and Protecting the Planet*, Synthesis Report of the Secretary-General on the post-2015 sustainable development agenda, UN GA, A/69/700, www. un.org/ga/search/view_doc. asp?symbol=A/69/700&Lang=E.

UN Task Team on the Post 2015 UN Development Agenda (2012a) *Realizing the Future We Want for All*, Report to the Secretary-General, New York: UN, www.un.org/ millenniumgoals/pdf/Post_2015_ UNTTreport.pdf.

— (2012b) 'Addressing inequalities: the heart of the 2015 agenda and the future we want for all', Thematic think piece, Mimeo, ECE, ESCAP, UN DESA, UNRISD, UN Women.

UNCTAD (2009) *The Least Developed Countries Report 2009, The State and Development Governance*, Geneva: United Nations.

— (2011a) *The Least Developed Countries Report 2011, The Potential Role of South–South Cooperation for Inclusive and Sustainable Development,* Geneva: United Nations.

— (2011b) 'Development-led globalization: towards sustainable and inclusive development paths', United Nations Report of the Secretary-General of UNCTAD to UNCTAD XIII, New York and Geneva: United Nations, unctad. org/en/docs/tdxiii_report_en.pdf.

— (2012) *Trade and Development Report 2012: Policies for Inclusive and Balanced Growth*, New York and Geneva: United Nations.

— (2014) *The Least Developed Countries Report 2014*, Geneva: United Nations.

UNDP (2010) *Human Development Report. The Real Wealth of Nations: Pathways to Human Development*, New York: Oxford University Press.

— (2012) *Keeping Humanity at the Heart of Development: How the Human Development Approach Can Help the Post 2015 Agenda*, Including a background paper on equity, inequality, and human development

in a post-2015 development framework, Jonathan Hall, Christina Hackmann, et al. Internal, June.

— (2013) *Human Development Report. The Rise of the South: Human Progress in a Diverse World*, New York: Oxford University Press, hdr.undp.org/sites/ default/files/reports/14/hdr2013_en_ complete.pdf.

— (2014) *Human Development Report. Sustaining Human Progress: Reducing Vulnerabilities and Building Resilience*, New York: Oxford University Press, hdr.undp.org/sites/default/files/ hdr14-report-en-1.pdf.

UNDP MDG Progress Reports (various years), www.undp.org/content/undp/ en/home/librarypage/mdg/mdg- reports.html.

UNDP National Human Development Reports (various years), hdr.undp. org/en/country-reports.

UNICEF (2010) *Narrowing the Gaps to Meet the Goals*, New York: UNICEF, www.equityforchildren.org/wp- content/uploads/2013/07/Doc1- Narrowing_the_Gaps_to_Meet_the_ Goals_090310_2a.pdf.

— (2012) *Integrated Social Protection Systems Enhancing Equity for Children*, UNICEF Social Protection Strategic Framework, New York: UNICEF.

UNRISD (2010) *Combating Poverty and Inequality: Structural Change, Social Policy and Politics*, Geneva: UNRISD.

— (2012) 'Inequalities and the Post-2015 Development Agenda', Research and Policy Brief 15, Geneva: UNRISD.

Vandemoortele, J. (2012) 'Advancing the UN Development Agenda post-2015: some practical suggestions', Report submitted to the UN Task Force regarding the post-2015 framework for development, Bruges, www. wssinfo.org/fileadmin/user_upload/ resources/DESA---post-2015-paper--- Vandemoortele.pdf.

World Bank (2012) *Resilience, Equity and Opportunity, the World Bank's Social Protection and Labor Strategy 2012–2022*, Washington, DC: World Bank.

World Bank Group (2011) *IEG Annual Report 2011: Results and Performance of the World Bank Group*, vol. I: Main Report, Washington, DC: Independent Evaluation Group, World Bank, IFC, MIGA, ieg.

worldbankgroup.org/Data/reports/rap2011_vol1.pdf.

— (2014) *IEG Annual Report 2013: Results and Performance of the World Bank Group*, vol. I: Main Report, Washington, DC: Independent Evaluation Group, World Bank, IFC, MIGA, ieg.worldbank.org/Data/reports/chapters/rap2013_vol1_updated2.pdf.

ABOUT THE EDITORS AND CONTRIBUTORS

Editors

Alberto D. Cimadamore is scientific director of the International Social Sciences Council's Comparative Research Programme on Poverty (CROP), located at the University of Bergen, Norway. He is a professor at the University of Buenos Aires and a researcher at the National Council of Scientific and Technological Research of Argentina (currently on leave). His research and publications are focused on the political economy of poverty, the international relations of poverty and development, and on regional integration in Latin America.

Gabriele Koehler is a development economist. She is a senior research associate at UNRISD, Geneva, and an Associate of the IDS, Sussex. Her research expertise is in the areas of human rights and social inclusion, economic and social policy, and trade and international investment. She co-edited *Development and Welfare Policy in South Asia* (Routledge, 2014). She serves on the boards of Women in Europe for a Common Future (WECF) and the UN Association Germany.

Having received his PhD in philosophy from Harvard, **Thomas Pogge** is Leitner professor of philosophy and international affairs and founding director of the Global Justice Program at Yale. He holds part-time positions at King's College London and the universities of Oslo and Central Lancashire. Pogge is the author of *World Poverty and Human Rights*, a member of the Norwegian Academy of Science, president of Academics Stand Against Poverty, and chair of the Comparative Research Programme on Poverty and of Incentives for Global Health.

Contributors

Bálint Balázs is managing director of the Environmental Social Science Research Group (ESSRG) R&D company, and lecturer in environmental sociology at the Institute of Nature Conservation and Landscape Management, St István University, Gödöllő, Hungary. He has international research experience in EU projects on transition to sustainability and local food systems, as well as science with and for society, transdisciplinary and cooperative research, and participatory action research. He is founder of the first Hungarian Science Shop in 2005.

Julio Boltvinik is researcher and professor at the Sociological Studies Centre (CES), El Colegio de México. His research topics are on poverty in Mexico, poverty measurement methods, foundational aspects of poverty and related concepts, and social policy in Mexico. He has taught courses on development topics, especially on basic needs and poverty, at several universities in Mexico, the UK, Norway and Italy. He has published widely on these topics.

Araceli Damián is a professor and researcher at El Colegio de México and Federal Deputy to the National Congress. She works on social policy, and from different perspectives on poverty: measurement methodologies, gender and employment. She is a leading researcher on time poverty and her most recent book, in Spanish, is *Time, the Forgotten Dimension in Poverty and Welfare Studies* (El Colegio de México, 2014).

Thana Campos is a postdoctoral research associate at the Von Hügel Institute, St Edmund's College, University of Cambridge. She holds a DPhil in law (jurisprudence) from the University of Oxford. Thana is also co-chair of ASAP Brazil and director of the Right to Health Research Group. She researches and publishes on global bioethics, legal theory and moral philosophy, with particular interests in global health governance and the right to health.

Paulo de Martino Jannuzzi is the national secretary of evaluation and information management of the Ministry of Social Development and Fight Against Hunger of Brazil, on secondment from the Brazilian Institute of Geography and Statistics. As a professor at the National School of Statistical Sciences (ENCE/IBGE) in Rio de Janeiro, and the National School of Public Administration, Brasilia, he teaches and researches in Public Statistics, Social Indicators and Monitoring and Evaluation of Programmes.

Bob Deacon is emeritus professor of international social policy at the University of Sheffield, UK, and a fellow of the Academy of Social Sciences. His most recent books are *Global Social Policy in the Making* and

Global Social Policy and Governance. He is founding editor of the journals *Critical Social Policy* and *Global Social Policy*. He has acted as adviser to several UN agencies.

Clarice Duarte is a professor in the Graduate Program in Political and Economic Law at Mackenzie University, where she leads the research group 'Social Rights and Public Policies'. She holds a PhD in philosophy and general theory of law from the University of São Paulo. Her research focuses on public policies, with particular emphasis on the implementation of social rights and the role of education policy in ending poverty and reducing social inequalities. She is also co-chair of ASAP Brazil and director of the ASAP Brazil Right to Education Research Group.

Natalia Escobar-Pemberthy is a doctoral candidate in global governance and human security at the University of Massachusetts Boston, where she also works as research associate at the Center for Governance and Sustainability. Her research focuses on environmental governance, the implementation of environmental conventions and the operationalization of the sustainable development agenda. She worked for several public administrations and at the Ministry of Foreign Affairs in Colombia. Since 2009, she has worked for Universidad EAFIT.

Maria Ivanova is director of the Global Environmental Governance Project, co-director for the Center for Governance and Sustainability, and associate professor of global governance at the McCormack Graduate School of Policy and Global Studies at the University of Massachusetts Boston. She served as a coordinating lead author of the Global Environmental Outlook (GEO-5), the flagship global environmental assessment published by UNEP. In 2013, she was appointed to the newly created UN Secretary-General's Scientific Advisory Board.

Manuel F. Montes is senior adviser on finance and development at the South Centre in Geneva. He was previously chief of development strategies, United Nations Department of Economic and Social Affairs (UNDESA), where he led the team that produced the World Economic and Social Survey (WESS). His recent publications have been in the areas of macroeconomic policy, development strategy, income inequality, climate change financing and industrial policy.

Rômulo Paes-Sousa, MD, PhD, has studied social protection policies, social inequality indicators, and monitoring and evaluation health and social protection policies. He is director of the UNDP World Centre for Sustainable Development. He was deputy minister of social development of Brazil, and National Secretary of Evaluation in the same institution. He has also worked in international academic institutions, such as the Institute of Development Studies, the London School of Hygiene and Tropical Medicine and the Oswaldo Cruz Foundation.

Deborah S. Rogers, PhD, has degrees in both the natural and social sciences. Current positions include affiliated scholar, Institute for Research in the Social Sciences, Stanford University, and president, Initiative for Equality. Her doctoral research at Stanford University focused on the development and impacts of socio-economic inequality. Past positions include director, Technical Information Project; project manager, Native American health disparities project, National Institutes of Health; and academic officer, International Human Dimensions Programme, United Nations.

Inês Virginia Soares holds a DPhil in law from the Catholic University of São Paulo (PUC-SP) and is a postdoctoral researcher at the Centre for the Study of Violence, University of São Paulo. Inês is also co-chair of ASAP Brazil. She researches and publishes on human rights, transitional justice, cultural rights, archaeology and law, with particular interests in the archaeology of repression and resistance, and the right to memory. Soares has been a federal prosecutor since 1997.

Jomo Kwame Sundaram has been assistant director general and coordinator for economic and social development at the Food and Agriculture Organization since 2012. He was assistant secretary-general for economic development in the UN Department of Economic and Social Affairs from 2005 to 2012, and research coordinator for the G24 Intergovernmental Group on International Monetary Affairs and Development. He has published extensively and was awarded the 2007 Wassily Leontief Prize for Advancing the Frontiers of Economic Thought.

INDEX

Note: Page numbers in *italic* refer to figures, those in **bold** to tables and *n* following a page number denotes an endnote.